Redefining Families
Implications for Children's Development

Redefining Families
Implications for
Children's Development

Edited by

Adele Eskeles Gottfried

California State University, Northridge
Northridge, California

and

Allen W. Gottfried

California State University, Fullerton
Fullerton, California

PLENUM PRESS • NEW YORK AND LONDON

Library of Congress Cataloging-in-Publication Data

Redefining families : implications for children's development / edited
 by Adele Eskeles Gottfried, Allen W. Gottfried.
     p.   cm.
 Includes bibliographical references and index.
 ISBN 0-306-44559-X
 1. Family--United States. 2. Social change--United States.
 3. Child development--United States.   I. Gottfried, Adele Eskeles.
 II. Gottfried, Allen W.
 HQ536.R4335 1994
 306.85'0973--dc20   93-47032
                                                               CIP

ISBN 0-306-44559-X

© 1994 Plenum Press, New York
A Division of Plenum Publishing Corporation
233 Spring Street, New York, N.Y. 10013

Printed in the United States of America

To Jeff and Michael
and to
Claire and Sylvia

Contributors

Robert L. Barret, Human Services Department, University of North Carolina at Charlotte, Charlotte, North Carolina 28223

Kay Bathurst, Department of Psychology, California State University, Fullerton, California 92634

Charlene E. Depner, Statewide Office of Family Court Services, San Francisco, California 94107

Patricia J. Falk, Cleveland-Marshall College of Law, Cleveland, Ohio 44115

Adele Eskeles Gottfried, Department of Educational Psychology and Counseling, California State University, Northridge, California 91330

Allen W. Gottfried, Department of Psychology, California State University, Fullerton, California 92634

Bert Hayslip, Jr., Department of Psychology, University of North Texas, Denton, Texas 76203

Norma Radin, School of Social Work, University of Michigan, Ann Arbor, Michigan 48109-1285

Bryan E. Robinson, Human Services Department, University of North Carolina at Charlotte, Charlotte, North Carolina 28223

R. Jerald Shore, Department of Rehabilitation Science, University of Texas Southwestern Medical School, Dallas, Texas 75235

Preface

Families are undergoing dramatic changes in our society. Our traditional views are being challenged by new family arrangements. These new family arrangements are forcing redefinitions of what constitutes a family and raising significant issues regarding the potential developmental consequences for children in these families, if such exist. Moreover, the ramifications of redefined families and their bearing on children's development extend into the legal, political, and societal arenas. This book focuses on the relationships between diverse family arrangements and children's development, as well as on legal and social implications.

Our interest in this area emanates from our experience in directing the Fullerton Longitudinal Study. In the course of this investigation, we observed families undergoing transformation, most commonly in maternal employment and marital status. Our initial research on the role of maternal employment in children's development provided the scientific foundation for our interest. Just as we feel that maternal employment and dual-earner families should be comprehensively researched regarding their relationships to children's development, we also believe that other contemporary family arrangements should receive extensive attention in the developmental literature. Hence, the idea for this book emerged.

Additionally, we have spoken with professionals in other fields, such as attorneys and judges, who have consulted with us about how diverse family arrangements may affect children's development. We have been interviewed frequently by reporters who have asked interesting questions pertaining to family environment, changes in family structure, and children's development. As a result of all of these experiences, we have developed a long-term interest in scientifically pursuing the role of contemporary family arrangements in children's development.

Our special gratitude is extended to Eliot Werner, Executive Editor of Plenum Publishing Corporation, for his friendship, support, and encouragement in giving us the opportunity to explore these contemporary family issues with regard to this book, as well as to our previous and forthcoming books. We sincerely thank the chapter authors for their enthusiasm and willingness to contribute their scholarly efforts to this book.

We especially wish to acknowledge our children, Jeff and Michael, who have contributed to our personal meaning of family.

Contents

Role of Maternal and Dual-Earner Employment Status in
Children's Development: A Longitudinal Study from Infancy
through Early Adolescence

Adele Eskeles Gottfried, Kay Bathurst, and Allen W. Gottfried

Revolution and Reassessment: Child Custody in Context

Charlene E. Depner

PART III. OVERVIEW

I
INTRODUCTION

1

Demography and Changing Families

Introduction to the Issues

Adele Eskeles Gottfried and Allen W. Gottfried

Family change is pervasive. We need only read our daily newspapers—or watch television news—to be exposed to the vast diversity of family forms in existence. Moreover, demographic data on the U.S. population has tracked family structure over a 75-year period and provides documentation of family changes (Wetzel, 1990). The traditional family (i.e., a two-parent family in which the father is the sole economic provider and the mother is the primary caretaker; Macklin, 1987), is now the minority family among those with children. In 1988, of families with children under 18 years old, only 32.7% consisted of married couples in which the father was the sole provider. Some of the most prominent trends concerning family change (Wetzel, 1990) include the entry of women into the work force, delayed childbearing, family dissolution, single-parenting, and the growth of nonfam-

Adele Eskeles Gottfried • Department of Educational Psychology and Counseling, California State University, Northridge, California 91330.   **Allen W. Gottfried** • Department of Psychology, California State University, Fullerton, California 92634.

Redefining Families: Implications for Children's Development, edited by Adele Eskeles Gottfried and Allen W. Gottfried. Plenum Press, New York, 1994.

ily households (individuals living together but unrelated biologically or legally).

Although there is detailed demographic data concerning family structure changes, little is known about the impact of such changes on children's development. The child development literature has amassed a body of research for which the predominant model, and the standard with which children in other families are compared, has been children growing up in traditional families. However, there is a growing body of data focusing on families other than those falling into the traditional category. The purpose of this book is to examine the contemporary literature and research across different nontraditional families, specifically with regard to children and their development.

Another impetus for this book emerged from our research on maternal employment, the home environment, and children's development (A. E. Gottfried, A. W. Gottfried, & Bathurst, 1988), and our earlier volume in the Plenum Studies Work and Industry Series, *Maternal Employment and Children's Development: Longitudinal Research* (1988). In our own research, and in the other studies presented in that book (Galambos, Petersen, & Lenerz, 1988; Goldberg & Easterbrooks, 1988; Hock, DeMeis, & McBride, 1988; Lerner & Galambos, 1988; Owen & Cox, 1988), it became apparent not only that did maternal employment have no detrimental outcomes for children across infancy, childhood, adolescence, and early adulthood, or across developmental domain, but that there were also no sleeper effects of maternal employment across time. The current research findings support the view that maternal employment itself is not detrimental to children's development (A. E. Gottfried & A. W. Gottfried, 1988; Hoffman, 1989). Rather, across studies, aspects of the environment, the mothers' work experiences, and role satisfaction as a worker or a parent were important variables that were related to children's development (A. E. Gottfried & A. W. Gottfried, 1988). These findings made us want to determine if this was also true of other types of nontraditional families. Hence, the concept for this book emerged. Our desire was to present a book in which it would be possible to examine results across family types in a single volume and to suggest trends and implications for children's development, research methodology, social policy, and the legal arena.

The choice of the specific types of families to be included in this book was based partly on demographic and partly on popular trends. Current demographic data based on the March 1991 Current Population Survey of children under 18 combined across ethnicity indicate a number of specific trends (Saluter, 1992). First, the proportion of married persons declined from 72% to 61% from 1970 to 1991, and the proportion of unmarried persons rose from 28% to 39% over the same period. Second, the proportion of children living with two parents declined from 85% to 72%, and the proportion of children living with one parent increased from 12% to 26% from 1970 to 1991. In 1970, 3.2% of children lived in the home of their grandparents; in 1991, this percentage was 5%. Of this 5%, 28% of the children lived in their grandparents' home with neither of their parents.

Of children living with one parent, the majority live with their mother (88%). However, there was an increasing—although small—trend toward children's living with their fathers. From 1970 to 1991, the percentage living with their fathers increased from 9.1% to 12.2%.

Of all children living with one parent, 37% (the largest proportion) was doing so because of divorce, whereas 24% lived with a married parent whose spouse was absent (Saluter, 1992).

Another very prominent trend was for mothers to be employed, and there was an increase in the proportion of dual-earner families (Hayghe, 1990). The percentage of dual-earner families with children increased from 43.4% to 63% from 1975 to 1988. Hence, the majority family with children under 18 years old was the family in which both the mother and the father were employed. There seems to be a paradox in that the majority family was also a nontraditional family. Various social and economic circumstances have combined to create this phenomenon (A. E. Gottfried & A. W. Gottfried, 1988; Hayghe, 1990).

Hayghe (1990) took the position that there is such a diversity of family situations that there is no longer a typical family. In addition to traditional and dual-worker families, Hayghe developed a category he called "other." This is a heterogeneous category in which the person who maintains the household is not in the labor force. According to Hayghe (1990), included are retired couples, families maintained by unmarried householders, and—most pertinent to this book—families in which the wife, but not the husband, is in the labor force. Of married couples, 2% with children under 18 were of this latter type, in which the wife—but not the husband—was employed (Hayghe, 1990). Hayghe's conclusion, in examining the percentages of all families with or without children, was that, whereas families have diverged from the traditional model of a married couple with only the husband in the labor force, no one type of family has replaced this model. Rather, diversity of families is more typical, with movement away from a modal type.

This conclusion is astounding when we consider its potential implications for children. Basically, children who are raised in a traditional family are now in the minority, and the child development literature must revamp itself to consider children's development within alternative models. Further, what is "normal" development, "typical" development, "optimal" development, or "modal" development will need redefinition, particularly with regard to the socialization of children.

Demographic data guided our selection, in part, of the chapters for this book. First, the dramatic increase in maternal employment and dual-earner families was the foundation for the Gottfried, Bathurst, and Gottfried chapter (Chapter 3). The increase in single parenting due, to a large extent, to divorce is the foundation for the chapter on custody arrangements by Depner (Chapter 4). The potential for role reversals, in which fathers assume the role of primary caretaker, is the foundation for the Radin chapter on primary-caretaking fathers (Chapter 2). The increase in the number of children living with their grandparents was our reason for including the Shore and Hayslip chapter on grandparenting (Chapter 7).

Demographic data are not surveyed with regard to sexual orientation (e.g., Saluter, 1992). However, the emergence and visibility of the gay and lesbian rights movements, as well as the recent attention paid to the complex issues of gay and lesbian parenting (Barret & Robinson, 1990; Falk, 1989), provided an important reason for including Falk's chapter on lesbian mothering (Chapter 5) and Barret and Robinson's chapter on gay fathering (Chapter 6). It is our view that parenting in lesbian and gay families will increase, particularly because of high divorce rates and the resultant custody issues, as well as the increase in the number of gay men and lesbian women who are open about their sexual orientation and their generativity desires (Clay, 1990). Indeed, this issue was poignantly and personally brought to our attention when gay and lesbian students in our child development classes were open not only about their sexual orientation, but also about their parenting or their desires to have family lives including children. A burgeoning literature is developing, and we wanted to have this issue represented in this book.

It is not possible to include all of the nontraditional family forms in one book. There are just too many, and we wanted to include those for which there is a literature on child development. We also wanted to include those with important social and legal policy implications. For example, based on the Gottfried *et al.* research, in which there was no detrimental effect of maternal employment on children's development, it was decided in a California Supreme Court case, *Burchard v. Garay* (1986), that maternal employment could not be used to discriminate against women in the determination of custody. All of the family types presented in this book have important social-policy as well as legal implications that are discussed.

The chapters in this book both review the pertinent literature and present the results of studies. The chapters represent contemporary knowledge in the field, and each set of authors has taken the opportunity to present its unique interpretations. The final chapter (Chapter 8) is an integration of the foregoing chapters, the purpose of which is to provide an overview of the current knowledge about children's development in nontraditional families. The views presented in that chapter represent our integration of the literature, issues, and findings of the other chapters, as well as our interpretations with regard to the current child development literature and theory, research methodology, and social policy and legal implications.

REFERENCES

Barret, R. L. & Robinson, B. E. (1990). *Gay fathers.* Lexington, MA: Lexington Books.

Burchard v. Garay, 42 Cal. 3d 531; *Cal. Rptr.*, P.2d (Sept. 1986).

Clay, J. W. (1990). Working with lesbian and gay parents and their children. *Young Children, 45,* 31–35.

Falk, P. J. (1989). Lesbian mothers: Psychosocial assumptions in family law. *American Psychologist, 44,* 941–947

Galambos, N. L., Petersen, A. C. & Lenerz, K. (1988). Maternal employment and sex typing in early adolescence: Contemporaneous and longitudinal relations. In A. E. Gottfried & A. W. Gottfried (Eds.), *Maternal employment and children's development: Longitudinal research* (pp. 155–189). New York: Plenum Press.

Goldberg, W. A., & Easterbrooks, M. A. (1988). Maternal employment when children are toddlers and kindergartners. In A. E. Gottfried & A. W. Gottfried (Eds.), *Maternal employment and children's development: Longitudinal research* (pp. 121–154). New York: Plenum Press.

Gottfried, A. E., & Gottfried, A. W. (Eds.). (1988). *Maternal employment and children's development: Longitudinal research.* New York: Plenum Press.

Gottfried, A. E., Gottfried, A. W., & Bathurst, K. (1988). Maternal employment, family environment, and children's development: Infancy through the school years. In A.

E. Gottfried & A. W. Gottfried (Eds.), *Maternal employment and children's development: Longitudinal research* (pp. 11–58). New York: Plenum Press.

Hayghe, H. V. (1990). Family members in the work force. *Monthly Labor Review, 113,* 14–19.

Hock, E., DeMeis, D., & McBride, S. (1988). Maternal separation anxiety: Its role in the balance of employment and motherhood in mothers of infants. In A. E. Gottfried & A. W. Gottfried (Eds.), *Maternal employment and children's development: Longitudinal research* (pp. 191–229). New York: Plenum Press.

Hoffman, L. (1989). Effects of maternal employment in the two-parent family. *American Psychologist, 44,* 283–292.

Lerner, J. V., & Galambos, N. L. (1988). The influences of maternal employment across life: The New York Longitudinal Study. In A. E. Gottfried & A. W. Gottfried (Eds.), *Maternal employment and children's development: Longitudinal research* (pp. 59–83). New York: Plenum Press.

Macklin, E. D. (1987). Nontraditional family forms. In M. B. Sussman & S. K. Steinmetz (Ed.), *Handbook of marriage and the family* (pp. 317–353). New York: Plenum Press.

Owen, M. T., & Cox, M. J. (1988). Maternal employment and transition to parenthood. In A. E. Gottfried & A. W. Gottfried (Eds.), *Maternal employment and children's development: Longitudinal research* (pp. 85–119). New York: Plenum Press.

Saluter, A. F. (1992). *Marital status and living arrangements: March 1991.* U.S. Bureau of the Census, Current Population Reports, Series P-20, No. 461, U.S. Government Printing Office, Washington, DC.

Wetzel, J. R. (1990). American families: 75 years of change. *Monthly Labor Review, 113,* 4–13.

II
ALTERNATIVE FAMILIES AND CHILDREN'S DEVELOPMENT

The chapters in this part address the role of nontraditional alternative family patterns in children's development. The changing demographics and social trends discussed in Part I have resulted in families that differ not only with regard to the traditional form, but also from each other. All chapters in Part II address these contemporary parental roles with regard to their actual and/or potential relationships to children's development. In Chapter 2, Radin presents her work and reviews the work of others regarding primary-caretaking fathers in intact families, who represent a reversal in the traditionally conceived maternal and paternal roles. In Chapter 3, Gottfried, Bathurst, and Gottfried present their extensive longitudinal study, from infancy through early adolescence, of maternal employment and dual-earner families. In Chapter 4, Depner puts forth a major new conceptualization and model of child custody and the family. Falk presents, in Chapter 5, a thorough analysis of the psychological and legal issues regarding lesbian parenting. In Chapter 6, Barret and Robinson present results from their own research, and that of others, regarding gay parenting issues and the children's perspectives when their father is gay. In Chapter 7, Shore and Hayslip test a model regarding custodial grandparents' well-being with data from their own study on grandparents.

Taken together, these six studies provide both original data and comprehensive reviews of the literature regarding alternative families and children's development. Across the chapters, (1) the children's ages are infancy through adolescence; (2) a broad array of developmental domains have been included (e.g., academic achievement, the affective domain, the behavioral domain, intelligence, and social and sex-role development); and (3) alternative families are considered in the context of family and environmental processes, socioeconomic status factors, and societal values. Conclusions and an overview are presented in Part III.

2

Primary-Caregiving Fathers in Intact Families

Norma Radin

INTRODUCTION

In the past two decades fathers have been "discovered" by both child development researchers and the mass media. There is now a voluminous literature in professional journals on various aspects of fathering. In magazines, newspapers, and television programs, stories abound about the "new father" and his role in the home. In contrast to a focus on father-absent families as in earlier decades, the emphasis today is on father-present families. This change implies not that studies and stories of single-parent homes have disappeared, but that there has been a major augmentation of interest in the two-parent family and, particularly, in the father's role beyond that of "breadwinner" and source of support for the mother.

Despite this burgeoning of information, there is scant evidence of an increase in data about men who have spouses and play a major role in child rearing. The report that follows focuses on this small but

Norma Radin • School of Social Work, University of Michigan, Ann Arbor, Michigan 48109-1285.

Redefining Families: Implications for Children's Development, edited by Adele Eskeles Gottfried and Allen W. Gottfried. Plenum Press, New York, 1994.

significant segment of the population, for it is in these families that one can obtain a clearer understanding of paternal influence, its outcomes, and the factors that facilitate and hinder men's making fathering a major activity in their lives. Five studies, rarely examined together, of primary caregiving or highly involved fathers in intact families are described, and some general conclusions about this pattern of child rearing are drawn. One investigation was conducted in Australia, one in Sweden, one in Israel, and two in the United States.

To provide a framework for the discussion of these investigations, most of which were initiated in the late 1970s and early 1980s, the chapter starts with an overview of various conceptualizations of the paternal role. The five studies are then reviewed, and the work of my colleagues and myself is described in some detail. The findings that emerged from the above studies concerning the determinants of high father involvement and the consequences for children are then discussed. The chapter concludes with directions for future research on partially role-reversed families.

CONCEPTUALIZATIONS OF THE FATHER ROLE

A review of the literature since the late 1970s indicates that there is no generally accepted view of the critical dimensions of fathering. One concept that appears to be emerging was developed by Michael Lamb and his colleagues (Lamb, 1986; Lamb, Pleck, Charnov, & Levine, 1985). According to this perspective, father involvement has three major components: (1) the extent of the father's actual interaction with his children; (2) the extent of the father's accessibility to his children; and (3) the degree of responsibility that the father assumes for his children. *Interaction* refers to direct face-to-face contact with the child through caretaking and other activities. *Accessibility* refers to the father's potential availability for interaction regardless of whether any direct interaction is taking place. *Responsibility* concerns the father's role in making sure that the child is taken care of, particularly when neither parent is available. This last aspect has been the least investigated (Lamb *et al.*, 1985).

Unfortunately, Lamb's framework is insensitive to several important dimensions that have emerged in studies of paternal behavior. One such factor is a differentiation of a father's involvement in child-care activities from his involvement in play, leisure, or affiliative activities with the child (Bailey, 1987; Crouter, Perry-Jenkins, Huston, & McHale, 1987; Easterbrooks & Goldberg, 1984; Grossman, Pollack, & Golding, 1988; Levy-Shiff & Israelashvili, 1988; Riley, 1991). This omission is serious because it has been found that the determinants of these two types of paternal participation are different (Grossman *et al.*, 1988; Levy-Shiff & Israelashvili, 1988; Riley, 1991).

Another important issue omitted from the Lamb framework is the question of absolute versus relative involvement in paternal activities. *Relative involvement* refers to the participation of fathers compared to the participation of mothers (e.g., the percentage of time each performs a particular child-care function). *Absolute involvement* assesses paternal participation without reference to any other family member (e.g., in terms of the hours the father spends alone with the child). It has been found that very different pictures of men in the home arise depending on which perspective is taken. For example, in relative, but not in absolute, terms, husbands participate in more housework when wives are employed than when the women are not working (Pleck, 1981). Working women do less housework than women who are not employed, and as a result, the constant amount that their husbands engage in assumes a larger percentage of the entire amount of housework in dual-earner families. The larger proportion may affect the children's perception of the paternal role and the parents' sense of equity in their work loads. Among the investigators who have examined the relative amount of paternal participation, usually in addition to the absolute amount, are Barnett and Baruch (1987), Baruch and Barnett (1986), De Frain (1979), Easterbrooks and Goldberg (1984), Radin (1982), Sagi (1982), and Volling and Belsky (1991). Among those who have written extensively about the absolute amount of father participation are Kotelchuck (1976), McBride (1990), Pleck (1983), Robinson (1977), and Russell (1982b).

Another issue not addressed in Lamb's framework is the level of detail in the data that must be collected to yield a valid portrait of the father's role. Some investigators have collected global information. For example, one large-scale study asked respondents, "On the average, on days when you're working (and not working) about how much time do you spend taking care of or doing things with your children?" (Pleck, 1986). Another relied on the investigator's judgment of who had primary responsibility for the child (Pruett, 1983). An alternate approach is seen in a study of Irish fathers in which their participation in 10 caretaking activities was assessed including such activities as singing to the baby and changing the babies' diapers (Nugent, 1991). A total score for the 10 activities was used in some analyses, and the scores for participation in 2 of the activities were used for other analyses.

Still other studies have obtained detailed information about the type of activities in which the fathers engaged with their children and then clustered the information into larger categories, which were used in the data analysis (Harold-Goldsmith, Radin, & Eccles, 1988; Jump & Haas, 1984). For example, my colleagues and I also collected relatively detailed data about paternal activities. Based on the theoretical literature on family roles, the activities were then placed in five categories: availability to the child; amount of involvement in physical child-care activities, in the socialization of the child, and in decision making about the child; and an overall estimate of the father's involvement in child rearing. A total score for the five components was then computed and used in most of the data analyses. (This involvement measure is discussed in greater detail at a later point in the chapter.)

When we analyzed our measure of paternal participation in terms of Lamb's framework, the total score encompassed all three dimensions of accessibility, responsibility, and dyadic interaction. The component of availability provided a measure of accessibility; the segment on physical care of the child assessed dyadic interaction; and responsibility was tapped by several parts, such as, the question about the percentage of time each parent was the child's primary caregiver (a portion of the overall estimate of father participation).

It would be beneficial to the entire field if a true consensus were to develop about the critical aspects of father involvement and how to assess them. It appears that not much progress has been made since the early 1980s, for a 1982 review of the literature (Cronenwett, 1982) indicates that 15 studies of paternal participation during the previous 10 years had assessed different dimensions. The author grouped the various activities into categories that are still being used, for example, availability to the child and participation in play and affective activities, in caretaking activities, and in decision making about the child.

The resolution of the consensus problem may lie in an integration of the Lamb framework with some of the omitted differentiations delineated above. This integration is beginning to develop. For example, a report on a recent investigation of fathering (Crouter &

Crowley, 1990) referred to the Lamb conceptualization and then stated that the focus would be on dyadic father–child activities and the father's accessibility. Dyadic interactions were subdivided into those that were required (e.g., child care) and those that were voluntary (e.g., leisure activities). Another pair of investigators (Volling & Belsky, 1991) similarly introduced their recent study by discussing the Lamb framework and indicating that responsibility and dyadic affective interaction, but not accessibility, would be assessed; obviously missing from the data collected was also information about dyadic interaction focused on caretaking. Remaining to be integrated into the Lamb framework in some way are the issues of relative versus absolute amount of paternal participation, as well as global versus specific involvement data.

STUDIES OF INTACT FAMILIES IN WHICH FATHERS PLAY THE ROLE OF PRIMARY CAREGIVER

The Pruett Investigation in the United States

Overview

Kyle Pruett, at the Child Study Center of Yale University, conceived his study as a pilot investigation of a phenomenon—fathers rearing babies in intact families—so unstudied that some clinical observations were needed before research questions could be framed (Pruett, 1989). The study addressed four areas: the development of infants 2 to 24 months old and the psychodynamic characteristics of the child-rearing fathers, their nurturing patterns, and their relationships with the infants' mothers (Pruett, 1983, 1985, 1989; Pruett & Litzenberger, 1992). A group of 17 families was recruited in two cohorts from the general pediatric practices in the greater New Haven, Connecticut, area. Nine two-parent families were recruited the first year, and eight the next year (Pruett, 1983).

The criterion for inclusion in the study was that, in the clinician's judgment, the father bore the major responsibility for parenting. Though not a criterion required by the study, all of the infants were firstborn. The families ranged across the socioeconomic spectrum from welfare receivers through professional workers; most were in the middle class. The children ranged in age from 2 to 22 months at the time of entry into the study; the mean was 8 months for the nine females and 12 months for the eight males. The mean age for the fathers was 24 years, and 25 years was the mean for the mothers. In most of the families, the mother was the primary or at least the coequal caretaker of the infant for the first four to six weeks after birth, at which time she typically returned to work.

By means of retrospective, analytically oriented interviewing techniques, the fathers were interviewed at home while caring for their infants. Extensive histories were taken, and naturalistic observations were recorded of the father–infant dyad engaged in typical child care. It was noted that the father's style of caretaking was not that of a mother substitute. Rather, it was a distillate of selected identifications and disidentifications with important individuals in his own life. Within two weeks of this interview, the babies were examined in a laboratory setting at the Yale Child Study Center; the Yale Developmental Schedules were used to assess their gross- and fine-motor performance, adaptive problem solving, language skills, and social functioning. A second extensive interview was conducted, usually in the home, with both mother and father, that yielded a marital history and recorded naturalistic observations of the family triad.

Two years after entering the study, all the original families except one, which had moved out of the area, were reinterviewed, and the children were reassessed by means of the original, somewhat expanded, investigation methods (Pruett, 1985). One couple was divorced, and the father had retained custody. Among the families remaining intact, the father continued as the primary caregiver in approximately 60% of the homes. However, even among the fathers who had returned to work or school, the strong attachment between father and child typically remained, with evidence of some reluctance to leave the child in the wife's care. For example, one father called home daily just to make sure everything was fine.

Eight years after the initial study, another follow-up was conducted with the 15 families still available (Pruett, 1992). The 7 female and 8 male children now ranged in age from 8 to 10 years. Of the 15 fathers, 11 were still playing a major role in child rearing, either sharing equally or providing the majority of the child care. A second divorce was now pending. The eight-year follow-up focused on the children in the context of the family primarily because there was no longer any question of their developmental competence, and family adaptation is the hallmark of functioning in youngsters of this age.

A two-hour interview was conducted in the home with all family members present. The questions posed were semistructured; for example, the family members were asked to go through their day from who got up in the morning first to who went to bed last at night and were then requested to comment on what the others had said. This approach provided many opportunities to observe dyadic and triadic relationships, problem-solving behaviors, displays of affect, limit setting, and nonverbal communication.

Antecedents of Fathers' Taking on the Primary-Caregiver Role in the Pruett Study

All 17 of the men reported themselves as having been parented traditionally; 13 came from intact families and the other 4 had lived predominantly with their mothers. None of the 17 felt that as teenagers they had had any idea of rearing their children. All seemed headed toward the expected roles of worker and father. One third of the sample had decided on the caretaking system the family would adopt before the pregnancy; the second third had decided during the pregnancy; and the last third had decided during the neonatal period. The third group had usually been pressed into the father–primary-caregiver arrangement for economic reasons; that is, the father had lost his job but the mother had not lost hers.

Of the 6 men who had chosen to serve as the primary caregiver before conception, 5 described their fathers as having been distant and uninvolved in their lives. They seemed to be paired in marriage with independent women who did not seek fulfillment in their lives through nurturing. Pruett speculated that the women less disposed toward a lifetime of nurturing may have triggered the nurturant role in men predisposed to it. Of the 11 men who had chosen to be the major caregiver after the birth of the child, 8 spoke of their families of origin in positive terms regardless of how physically available their father had been. There was no middle group; the men in this study had been either quite close to or quite distant from their fathers. It appeared to Pruett that the men wished either to repeat or remake their past.

In general, these caregiving men had had relatively little previous experience with young children. Thus, expertise in child care was not a determinant of the fathers' assuming the major child-rearing role. Similarly, social class variables appeared to play virtually no role in propelling the 17 men toward becoming the nurturing member of the family.

Consequences for the Children of Fathers' Taking on the Primary-Caregiver Role in the Pruett Study

In the first assessment of the children (Pruett, 1985; Pruett & Litzenberger, 1992) it was found that the majority of the infants functioned above the expected norms on standardized tests of development. The infants who were 2–12 months old often performed problem-solving tasks on the level of children 4–8 months their senior; personal and social skills were 2–6 months ahead of schedule. The older babies, 12–22 months old, also performed well. The time at which the parents decided on the child-care arrangement had little bearing on how well the children developed. Pruett concluded that children raised primarily by men can be active, robust, and thriving infants. These infants may also be especially attracted to stimulation from the external environment.

In the second assessment two years later (Pruett, 1989; Pruett & Litzenberger, 1992), the children's performance on the Yale Development Schedules were especially strong in the areas of adaptive problem solving and social functioning. There was no evidence that the gender identity of these children was in any way in jeopardy. There were no significant differences between the boys and the girls in reaching developmental milestones or in the overall levels of their activity. None of them was described by their parents as being afraid of strangers—interested, curious, or cautious, but never fearful. In addition, the majority of the children seemed to have mastered the integration of their attachments to their mothers and fathers in a way that enhanced their overall competence. Most of the babies seemed to have a heightened appetite for novel experience and stimuli. One explanation offered by Pruett for their advanced development was the robust and stimulating style of interaction common in father–child dyads. Another possibility was that the fathers chose to take responsibility for their baby. However, it should be noted that approximately one third of the sample had selected this lifestyle only after the father lost his job; thus, the choice was not completely voluntary.

A four-year follow-up of the children was described briefly (Pruett, 1985). There were no gross personality markers that reliably distinguished these children from their peers. There seemed to be no significant lack of flexibility in any of these children. If anything, there were rudimentary signs that these children were secure in their gender identities and perhaps were even more characterologically flexible than peers raised in traditional families, particularly in the ease with which they moved back and forth between identifications with maternal and paternal activities and attributes. Some of the precocious development reported during the second year of life seemed to have slackened somewhat in these children, although the data were still not fully analyzed. The apparent slowing down of their rapid development may have been an artifact of the earlier assessment procedures, which in general were more heavily loaded on "father-released functioning and behavior" (Pruett, 1985, p. 454). The investigator observed, overall, that there were no signs of overt pathology either cognitively or emotionally, and no evidence of psychological distress. These findings led Pruett to conclude that men as primary nurturing caregivers can do a creditable, adequate job of parenting.

The eight-year follow-up study (Pruett & Litzenberger, 1992) revealed that the children's gender identities remained stable and that the flexible gender-role performance reported previously continued to manifest itself. The preliminary conclusion reached was that the increased flexibility in gender roles expressed by the parents may have found its way into the expression of gender role in these children. Despite the flexibility, the girls were all comfortably feminine, and the boys, masculine.

In addition, there was something "scrappy" abut the social skills of the children, more notable in the girls, possibly because it was less expected. Pruett and Litzenberger (1992) speculated that this personal style might be some form of identification with the fathers' power and strength that was palpably present and integrated with their nurturing behavior. The children appeared to feel a sense of competence in making demands on the social environment in much the same way that their fathers did while playing the role of nurturer.

The Lamb Investigation in Sweden

Overview

The study by Michael Lamb and his colleagues (Lamb, Frodi, Hwang, & Frodi, 1982; Lamb, Frodi, Hwang, Frodi, & Steinberg,

1982a,b) was designed to take advantage of a unique national family policy adopted by the Swedish government during the 1970s. The government leaders recognized that equal employment opportunities for men and women could not be ensured until fathers relieved mothers of some traditional responsibilities for child care. Among the reforms designed to promote that goal was the establishment of a parental leave program available to men and women. Beginning in 1974, the government guaranteed 90% of the individual's regular salary for nine months to any parent who stayed home in order to care for a newborn child. The nine-month period could be divided between the two parents in any way they chose. By 1979, less than 15% of the new fathers in Sweden had taken paid parental leave and most of these had taken one month or less.

The study of Lamb and his colleagues was of the small number of men who had taken parental leave for more than one month, during which time they had had the primary responsibility for their infants' care. Among the goals of the investigation were to determine whether there were quantitative and qualitative differences in the behavior of these nontraditional parents compared to traditional husbands and wives during the infants' first months. The sample consisted of 52 couples, all of which lived in the same Swedish city and were expecting their first child. The participants were recruited through childbirth preparation classes and had middle-class to upper-class backgrounds, occupations, and education. One half of the sample (26 couples) consisted of families in which the fathers planned to stay home as primary caregiver for one or more months. The other half consisted of couples in which the father planned to take little more than the two weeks' leave assured to all new mothers and fathers through the national health insurance program. The two groups were similar in demographic variables, except that the nontraditional spouses were slightly better educated than the traditional parents.

The parents were interviewed during the third trimester of pregnancy concerning a number of issues, including how the parents planned to divide the parental leave. The Bem Sex-Role Inventory (Bem, 1974), a measure of the respondent's orientation to traditional sex roles, was also administered. When the infants were 5 months old, the parents were again interviewed separately in their homes to disclose, among other things, the degree of paternal involvement in caretaking and in interaction with the child. Just before the infants' first birthday, the parents were recontacted and asked how the parental leave had actually been divided. If the father had taken parental leave, the couple was asked when and for how long. The families were then reclassified according to this information. Despite the initial plan of 26 fathers to take parental leave for at least one month, only 17 of them had taken more than one month. The mean was 2.8 months, and 34 fathers of the original 52 had taken only 2 weeks or less, for a mean of 0.24 months. One family was no longer available for the study.

At 3 months of age, the infants were observed for an hour twice in their own homes: once when interacting with their father, and once when interacting with their mother. During these observations, one of the investigators recorded a detailed account of the infant's and the parent's behavior by using a keyboard device. From the observational records, a summary measure of parental behavior was created that included the categories of vocalizations, contact behavior (e.g., touching and kissing), functional behavior (e.g., changing the baby), and play.

When the children were 8 months and 16 months old they were again observed at home interacting with both of their parents for about 110 minutes. The parents were asked to behave as naturally as possible and were encouraged to remain in the room. During these sessions, an observer again used a keyboard-recorder device to code the parental and infant behavior. Among the categories of parental behavior used were play, physical contact, affectionate behavior, and caretaking behavior. Four of the infant's behaviors were placed in the category of attachment behaviors (e.g., approaching the parent or touching the parent). Five infant behaviors were classed as affiliative (e.g., smiling at the parent or vocalizing to the parent). Analysis of these observational data was based on the revised family classifications.

One of the major findings from the observational data collected when the infants were 3 months and 8 months old was the gender difference in the style of parental behavior, regardless of the parents' relative responsibility for child rearing. The maternal and paternal interactional styles found in previous studies (Belsky, 1979; Lamb, 1976, 1980; Yogman, Dixon, Tronick, Als, & Brazelton, 1979) of fathers emitting more physically stimulating and idiosyncratic behaviors while mothers engage in more caretaking activities and more conventional forms of play emerged to some extent, but not entirely, in this study.

Regardless of family type, the mothers were more likely than the fathers to engage in contact behaviors, such as touching and tickling, and in vocalizing, soothing, and caretaking, but there were no significant gender differences in the occurrence of play. The conclusion reached was that parental gender appeared to be a more important influence on the style of parental behavior than on the family child-rearing pattern.

Antecedents of Fathers' Taking on the Primary-Caregiver Role in the Lamb Study

At the time of the 1982 report (Lamb, Frodi, Hwang, & Frodi, 1983), the investigators had not yet determined whether any of the attitudinal data collected in the prenatal interview was predictive of the family's adopting a nontraditional pattern of child rearing. There were, however, substantial differences between the nontraditional families, in which the fathers planned to care for the infants for at least one month, and the traditional families in which they did not, despite a similarity in background variables such as age and occupation. Fathers-to-be in nontraditional families valued parenthood more and their work less than their wives did. The reverse was true in the traditional families, in which the men valued work more and parenthood less than did their wives. In addition, the nontraditional families were less sex-typed than their traditional peers on the Bem Sex-Role Inventory. The investigators concluded that the value of parenthood and work were important influences on the anticipated division of parental responsibilities.

It was clear from the five-month interview data that, although the value placed on work and parenthood remained stable, the anticipated child-care plans had not been fully enacted. The nontraditional fathers did report more caretaking and involvement than the traditional fathers, but there were no differences in the mothers' reports of their spouse's caretaking and involvement. Neither parent's scores on the Bem Sex-Role Inventory were related to their observed behaviors. Further, only 17 of the 26 fathers who had planned to had actually assumed primary caretaking activities. By 16 months old, all of the infants were again receiving primary care from their mother.

Consequences for the Children of Fathers' Taking on the Primary-Caregiver Role in the Lamb Study

The investigators reported that few differences were found in the father–child relationships observed at 3, 8, and 16 months of age between the traditional families and those in which the fathers had served as primary caregivers for an average of 2.8 months. There were also no differences between the two groups in the children's attachment or affiliative behaviors assessed when they were 16 months old. Further, children in both groups revealed a preference for their mothers in the display of attachment behaviors; increased paternal involvement had no effect on the patterns of preference. Lamb and his colleagues (Lamb, Frodi, Hwang, & Frodi, 1983) speculated that the absence of differences in the children may have been due to the absence of difference in the playfulness of Swedish mothers and fathers. When they are highly involved in child care, therefore, fathers may not become as "affectively salient" as they are in the United States. This finding suggests that the characteristic involvement of fathers in play may be much more important than was previously believed. Large amounts of time spent with stimulating, playful fathers may affect children's development, but the time factor may be irrelevant if the father's playfulness is the same as the mother's (Russell, 1986). It is also possible that three months is too short a time for primary-caregiving fathers to have an impact on their children's development, although the investigators did not discuss this point.

The Russell Investigation in Australia

Overview

The goals of Graeme Russell's study (Radin & Russell, 1983; Russell, 1982a,b, 1986, 1987; Russell & Radin, 1983) conducted in and near Sydney, Australia, included (1) comparing the lifestyles and child-care patterns of shared-caregiving families and traditional families, particularly in the divisions of labor for child care and the time spent in parent–child interaction; (2) determining the antecedents of the shared-family caregiving pattern, including employment factors, personal characteristics, and sex-role self-concepts; and (3) determining the consequences of a shared-caregiving lifestyle in family relationships.

The criterion for inclusion as a shared-caregiving family (Russell, 1982b) was that the parents lived together and shared the caregiving of the child, or that the father had the major responsibility. In addition, the father had to have sole responsibility for his children for at least 15 of their waking hours each week. The families also had to have at least one child under 10. The sample consisted of 50 families (1) recruited by random sampling in shopping centers; (2) known to people who were recruited; or (3) responding to advertisements placed on university, community, and preschool bulletin boards. The data were obtained from interviews conducted in the parents' homes. For the first part of the interview, both the mother and the father were present and replied to questions concerning family lifestyle and division of labor. For the second part, the mother and the father were interviewed separately on topics such as beliefs about parental roles, reasons for adopting their lifestyle, and problems of adjustment. The parents in 33 of the families also completed the Bem Sex-Role Inventory.

The mean age of the fathers was 31 and of the mothers was 29. In comparison to a similar group of traditional families that the investigator had studied, these families had fewer children (1.7 versus 2.3) and older children. In an enlarged sample of 71 nontraditional families described in a later report, Russell (1986) indicated that 52% had only one child, all had a preschool-aged child, and only 10 had a child under 6 months old. The average age of the youngest child in the enlarged sample was 3.5 years and that of the oldest was 5.8 years. In the comparable traditional sample, the average ages were, respectively, 2.3 years and 5.7 years.

Shared-caregiving parents were more highly educated and had higher occupational ratings. However, there was a wide diversity in the fathers' occupations, which ranged from unskilled to professional. In all families, at least one parent had flexibility in work hours. The mothers worked outside the home an average of 40 hours per week, and the fathers worked 28 hours per week. In 22% of the families, the fathers were unemployed; in 30%, the men worked part time; and in 48%, they worked full time. Of the mothers, 86% worked full time and 14% part time.

The fathers were found to have sole responsibility for the children 26 hours per week and the mothers 15 hours per week. The normative pattern in traditional families in Australia is for the mother to have sole responsibility for approximately 40 hours per week and fathers only 2 hours per week. In shared-caregiving families, the fathers reported being available for an average of 54 hours per week and the mothers 49; the corresponding figures in traditional families were 33 hours for fathers and 76 hours for mothers.

Based on the joint family interviews, estimates were made of two types of activities: caregiving, such as feeding and dressing, and play, plus other significant interactions, such as regularly helping with homework. The nontraditional fathers spent 9 hours in caregiving per day; their spouses spent 11 hours. In traditional families, these figures were 2 hours and 20 hours, respectively. A similar pattern emerged in play activities. In nontraditional families, the figure was 18 hours for the fathers and 16 hours for the mothers. In traditional families, the comparable figures were 10 hours and 23 hours.

In relative terms, the shared-caregiving families split their child-oriented activities 50-50, and the absolute amount of time spent by both parents combined was very similar in nontraditional and traditional families: 53 hours per week for the former group and 56 hours for the latter. According to Russell (1982b), it is difficult to compare these nontraditional fathers with those in studies reporting the relative amount of involvement of mothers and fathers (De Frain, 1979; Radin, 1981a), but he felt that the men in the Australian study clearly had a heavy commitment to daily caregiving regardless of their wives' involvement.

Antecedents of Fathers' Taking on the Primary-Caregiver Role in the Russell Study

The parents were asked their main reason for adopting their nontraditional lifestyle; four types of explanations were offered: (1) the inability of the father to gain employment; (2) the parents' needing or wanting the extra income from having both parents work; (3) the desire of the mother to pursue a career; and (4) beliefs that both parents should be involved in child care. Prior knowledge and experience were also predisposing factors: Significantly more fathers had attended the birth of their children and had read books on child rearing in the shared-caregiving group than in the comparable traditional sample. Related to beliefs as determinants of parental caregiving were the differences between traditional and nontraditional fathers in their views about men's ability to care for children. For example, the fathers who were more highly involved than their traditional peers believed that fathers are as capable of performing the caregiving role as mothers. However, as Russell acknowledged, it is impossible to say if the lifestyle was the antecedent or the consequence of those beliefs.

The Bem Sex-Role Inventory scores revealed that the fathers in the shared-child-rearing group had higher femininity scores and that the mothers in those families had higher masculinity scores, than the parents in the traditional families. Once again, the investigator indicated that the direction of influence was uncertain, and it is possible that the lifestyle may have affected the parents' sex-role self-concepts. These Bem findings differed from those of De Frain (1979) and Radin (1981a), as Russell pointed out. For example, De Frain found no differences in the sex-role scores of shared-role fathers in a random sample of fathers, and Radin found no differences between primary caregivers and traditional fathers. However, differences in interpreting the Bem scores, which have several components, and in approaches to measuring father involvement may have accounted for the discrepancies. The different sociocultural contexts of the families may also have been relevant.

The age and number of the children in the family appeared to play a role as antecedent conditions in the Russell study. Fewer and older children were found in homes with highly involved fathers, although only the former factor showed a significant difference between traditional and nontraditional families in the full sample of 71 father-caregiving families.

Russell concluded that there were many paths to the adoption of a shared-caregiving arrangement. Among the factors he found to be important were the family financial situation; the employment potential of the parents, especially of the mothers; flexibility in the hours of employment; demographic factors; prior experience in and knowledge about child care; beliefs about the roles of parents; and the sex-role self-concepts of the parents. These various factors may also interact in different ways in different families.

Consequences for Children of Fathers' Taking on the Primary-Caregiver Role in the Russell Study

No instruments were administered to the children, but Russell (1982b) reported that 76% of the fathers and 64% of the mothers felt that their children had not experienced any major problems with the change in the child-care arrangement. Over 60% of both parents felt that their children now had a closer relationship with their father, and that there was now a very strong bond between the fathers and their children. All of the men were very enthusiastic about this change. Approximately one third of both parents felt that their children had an improved relationship with their mothers and fathers, but over one quarter of both parents believed that the mother–child relationship was not as close as it had been.

In the two-year follow-up (Russell, 1982b) of the families who were interviewed as part of the first cohort of shared-caregiving families (data were collected in several time periods), 18 of the 23 families were located and reinterviewed. In only four of the families (22%) was the child-care pattern the same as it had been in the initial interview. The overwhelming majority (93%) of the families still saw the major benefit of the shared-child-rearing arrangement as the improved father–child relationship.

In a later report (Russell, 1986), Russell discussed his two-year follow-up of the full sample of 71 shared-child-rearing families. He reinterviewed 27 of these families and found 10 of the 27 (37%) were still in the same nontraditional pattern. In the larger follow-up sample, approximately two thirds of both parents said that the improved relationship between father and child was the major advantage of the nontraditional lifestyle. However, there was also some increased tension and conflict in the father–child relationship, probably as a consequence of the frustrations and demands of being a full-time caregiver. Russell did not perceive this as an entirely negative outcome, as many mothers welcomed what they saw as a more realistic father–child relationship.

The Radin Investigation in the United States

Overview

Radin's study (Radin, 1981a, 1982, 1988; Radin & Goldsmith, 1985; Radin & Russell, 1983; Radin & Sagi, 1982; Russell & Radin, 1983; Williams & Radin, 1993; Williams, Radin, & Allegro, 1992) was initiated in 1978 to shed light on the outcomes for family members when the fathers took on the major responsibility for their young children while their wives worked or attended school. This family form emerged in the late 1970s in many college communities such as the Ann Arbor, Michigan, area, where the study was conducted. At that time, published studies of such families were as rare as the men themselves (Levine, 1976). The nontraditional child-care arrangement provided an opportunity to test whether it was the male gender or the male role that accounted for the observed unique effects that fathers have on children and for the men's sharply different behavior with boys and girls (Radin, 1981b, 1986). Further, a study of primary-caregiving fathers in intact families would permit an examination of two possible antecedents (personal characteristics and socialization experiences) of this child-care pattern. At the time the investigation was planned, there had been much speculation (Hoffman, 1977; Lamb & Bronson, 1980) on what would occur to the children in such homes, but there were few hard data.

Two follow-up studies of the still-intact families were conducted, one after 4 years (Radin & Goldsmith, 1985) and one after 11 years (Williams et al., 1992; Williams & Radin, 1993). The former focused on the stability of the father primary-caregiver arrangement and the latter on long-term child outcomes.

HYPOTHESES. Various theories and a large body of research data (e.g., De Frain, 1979; Eiduson & Weisner, 1978; Gersick, 1979; Hoffman, 1977; Kagan, 1958; Payne & Mussen, 1965; Radin, 1972, 1981b; Reuter & Biller, 1973; Sears, 1953) provided the foundation for generating predictions about possible antecedents and consequences of fathers' playing a major role in rearing children. Based on social learning theory and theories of identification, it was posited that men who chose to reject their traditional fathers as models would have fathers who were less available, less loving, and less powerful in decision asking in the family than the fathers of men playing the traditional paternal role.

Findings concerning the attitudes of the children, particularly the daughters, of working mothers led to the second hypothesis that more nontraditional than traditional wives would have had mothers who worked while their children were young. The issue of the parents' sex-role orientations was explored, but no hypothesis was generated, as it was unclear whether these self-concepts were antecedents or consequences of adopting a nontraditional lifestyle.

Concerning consequences for the children, role theory, primarily concepts related to role makers as autonomous individuals (Aldous,

1974; Brown, Perry, & Harberg, 1977; Tangri, 1972), and modeling theory (Bandura, 1967, 1977) led to the hypothesis that children reared in partially role-reversed families would manifest more internality, or a more internal locus of control, than their peers in traditional homes. It was also hypothesized that the offspring, particularly the sons, of role-reversed parents would be more empathetic than their peers in traditional families because caregiving fathers would be likely to be more sensitive to the child's needs and more empathetic, and this behavior would be modeled by the children, especially by boys (Bandura, 1967, 1977; Barnett, King, Howard, & Dino, 1980; Gewirtz & Stingle, 1968; Kagan, 1958; Mischel, 1970).

No hypothesis was posited about the effect on the children's sex-role development when they were reared by primary-caregiving fathers, as the relevant theories and research findings were contradictory (e.g., Biller & Borstelman, 1967; Bronfenbranner, 1958; Kagan, 1958; Kohlberg, 1966; Maccoby & Jacklin, 1974; Money & Ehrhardt, 1972; Mussen & Distler, 1960). Similarly, conflicting evidence and concepts precluded a hypothesis about the impact on the children's cognitive development (Hoffman, 1977) or on the children's perceptions of parental roles (Kohlberg, 1966; Meyer, 1980; Pleck, 1975). These child behaviors were explored, however.

THE SAMPLE. To control for extraneous variables, potential participants were restricted with respect to social class and age of child. The sample (Radin, 1982) consisted of 59 intact middle-class families, the vast majority of which were white, with a child 3–6 years old. There were 32 boys and 27 girls in the study, and the average child's age was 54 months. The children spent a mean of 17 hours per week in a day-care center or kindergarten. The average age of the fathers was 34; the average length of time the family had had the current child-care arrangement was 35 months; and the average Hollingshead (1975) Index of Social Status for the father and for the family put both within the middle and upper classes. (Only occupation and education are incorporated into this scale; a score can be computed for either parent or for the family by combining data concerning both parents.)

Participants were sought through newspaper articles, radio announcements, flyers left at day-care centers, and notices posted at student housing centers asking for two-parent families with fathers involved in child care. The traditional families were recruited through contacts of project staff and friends of contacts. Most of the subjects lived within 50 miles of Ann Arbor, a university town, and were clearly self-selected. Families in which the mothers were the primary caregivers and also worked more than 10 hours per week were excluded, as that population was to be investigated in a doctoral dissertation of a staff member.

THE PROCEDURE. Three appointments were made with the family. In the first, the father was interviewed at home for approximately one hour. In the second interview, the mother was asked the same questions, either at home or at her place of employment. In the third session, again in the home, a series of tasks was administered to the child. The most important instruments used with the children were (1) the Stanford Preschool Internal-External Scale (SPIES), a measure of the child's locus of control (Mischel, Zeiss, & Zeiss, 1974); (2) the revised It-Scale (Biller, 1969; Brown, 1956), which assesses the child's sex-role orientation; (3) a shortened version of the Kagan Parent Role Test (Kagan & Lemkin, 1960), which taps the child's view of the qualities associated with each parent by asking questions such as "Who spanks the most, mothers or fathers?"; (4) the Borke Empathy Scale (Borke, 1971); and (5) the Peabody Picture Vocabulary Test (PPVT), a test of verbal intelligence.

The parent interview included questions about the father's child-rearing role and his nurturance with his preschooler. Very similar questions were asked about each parent's own father's involvement in his or her family of origin and also how he or she felt about it. To create the items pertaining to child rearing, modifications were made in instruments developed and validated by other investigators. In addition, the parents completed the Bem Sex-Role Inventory and a shortened version of the Cognitive Home Environment Scale (Radin & Sonquist, 1968), which assesses the educational materials in the home, the direct teaching of the child, and each parent's future expectation for her or his sons and daughters. A total score was also obtained reflecting the overall cognitive stimulation in the home.

In a pilot study (Radin, 1982), an effort was made to use the parent's own views to classify the families into three groups: high, medium, and low paternal involvement in child rearing. It soon became clear that the mothers and the fathers did not classify themselves in that way. As one mother said, "I will show you our weekly schedule on the refrigerator, and you tell me in which group I belong." It was therefore decided to develop a scale of paternal involvement for the investigation and to embed it in the interview protocol. Based on the total scale score, the 59 families were divided into three groups. Those with the top third of the scores (20 families) were labeled the father-primary-caregiver group; those with the lowest third of the scores (20 families) were labeled the mother-primary-caregiver group. Families with the middle scores (19 families) were called the intermediate group. (The original plan was to have 60 families in the study, but one of the children developed the measles and was not available for testing when the data analysis had to start.)

The scale that was developed, called the Paternal Involvement in Child Care Index (PICCI), included items that the literature indicated would portray a broad spectrum of parental caregiving behavior with children. The PICCI contained five components: (1) the father's overall involvement in child care; (2) the father's responsibility for child care (e.g., feeding and bathing the child); (3) the father's responsibility for the socialization of the child (e.g., setting limits on the child's behavior); (4) the father's involvement in decision making regarding the child (e.g., regarding when to discipline the child); and (5) availability to the child (e.g., the frequency with which the father was home during the week for lunch). The child-care and socialization components were adapted from those used by Gecas (1976); the decision-making items were taken from instruments developed by Price-Bonham (1976) and Blood and Wolfe (1960); the availability items were taken from a scale developed by Reuter and Biller (1973).

The components pertaining to child care and socialization measured the relative amount of father participation in each activity by asking the percentage of time each family member had primary responsibility for each task and then weighting the father's percentage by the frequency with which the respondent said the task was performed. Decision making was also a relative assessment; the component inquired about the father's power in decision making about the child relative to the wife's power. The availability component obtained information about the frequency of the father's presence in the home at different times of the day, an absolute measure of involvement. The overall statement of paternal participation had two subparts: one about relative participation (the percentage of time each family member was the primary caregiver) and one about absolute participation (how involved the father was, using a 5-point scale to reply). Thus, the PICCI's assessment of paternal involvement was approximately one half a relative measure and one half an absolute measure of his participation. All of the components were significantly intercorrelated with one another in the responses of both mothers and fathers except for decision making. It was kept in the scale, however, because of its conceptual importance to paternal involvement in child care.

The father's total PICCI score was added to the mother's total score to yield a grand total score. It was this figure that was divided into thirds to form the three groups. The means for the total father score and the total mother score (40.3 and 40.6, respectively) were remarkably close, considering neither parent knew how the other had responded or how we were scoring their replies. There were 10 boys and 10 girls in the father-primary-caregiver and mother-primary-caregiver groups; in the intermediate group, there were 12 boys and 7 girls. The groups' labels appeared to be valid, for they were closely associated with both the mothers' and the fathers' global estimates of the percentage of time the father had primary responsibility for the children. For the father-primary-caregiver group, the mean percentage cited by the fathers was 58%, and by mothers, 56%. (These figures may not appear to be different from a 50-50 arrangement, but we have found that, once the figure for father's participation exceeds 50%, the families are qualitatively different and very scarce.) For the intermediate group, the figures were 40% and 41% for fathers and mothers, respectively. For the mother-primary-caregiver group the respective figures for fathers and mothers were 22% and 23%.

In the father-primary-caregiver group, all the mothers worked or attended school full time, and all the fathers but one had some type of part-time job or attended school. Of the fathers who were working (2 were full-time students), 3 were university faculty members, 2 were sales representatives working out of their own homes, and 2 were writers, and 1 individual held each of the following positions: schoolteacher, part-time research assistant, part-time computer programmer, rabbi, doctor, self-employed businessman, engineer, toolmaker's apprentice, and child-care worker in a psychiatric hospital.

The wives were employed in occupations such as university faculty member, nurse, and social worker. Two wives were full-time students. In the mother-primary-caregiver group, all of the men were working full time except one, who was a student. The husbands held such positions as engineer, university faculty member, and accountant. By the study's design, none of the mothers worked over 10 hours per week. In the intermediate group, all of the fathers were employed or attending school full time; 13 of the mothers worked full time and 3 half time, and 3 were unemployed.

There were no significant differences between the father-prime and mother-prime groups in child's age, father's age, Hollingshead family index or social status, Hollingshead father index of social status, the number of hours per week the child was in day care or school, or in the PPVT score.

Antecedents of Fathers' Taking on the Primary-Caregiver Role in the Radin Study

A fairly clear pattern emerged concerning the antecedents of partial role reversal. The mothers who perceived their own fathers as having been less involved in child care when they were growing up and who also had very positive feelings about their fathers had husbands who were heavily involved in child rearing. It appeared that the women wished to create a less frustrating experience for their children. There was little evidence of a link between the husband's view of his own father and his current participation in child rearing. Further, concordant with the hypothesis, in significantly more families in the father-prime group than in either of the two other groups, the mothers of both parents had worked outside the home before they were 10 years of age. Overall, it appeared that early socialization experiences were a major influence on a family's decision to adopt a nontraditional child-care pattern.

In contrast, the parents' sex-role orientation was insignificant as a determinant of partial role reversal. The mothers' masculine and feminine Bem scores were unrelated to any of the measures of paternal child rearing, and the fathers' masculinity scores were related to two components of the PICCI in obverse ways: They were negatively associated with physical care of the child and positively related to power in decision making. Further, when primary caregivers and traditional fathers were compared, there was no significant difference in the fathers' Bem masculinity or femininity scores.

As to the role of economic necessity, in only 2 of the 20 families did the mother and father agree that the mother was working because she had to do so, and in these 2 cases, the mothers indicated that, if given a choice, they would work part time rather than full time. The general conclusion was that the women were working primarily because it was their choice. In contrast, only 1 of the primary-caregiving mothers expressed a desire for employment. It had not been predicted, but it appeared that the mother's desire for a career was an important factor propelling the family into a paternal child-rearing arrangement.

In the four-year follow-up (Radin & Goldsmith, 1985), it was found that only 5 fathers (25% of the original group) were still primary caregivers. The data also indicated that, for families with sons, the antecedents of maintaining a partially role-reversed child-care pattern were somewhat different from those of adopting the arrangement initially. Only in families with daughters was the mother's perception of her father's nonavailability still a predictor of her husband's involvement. In homes with sons, it was the father's negative view of his own father's involvement that was the important determinant of his stability in the father-primary-caregiver role. This factor had not been important in 1977.

The explanation offered for the change in antecedents was that, at the age of the children in the four-year follow-up (7–9), boys form a close relationship with their fathers, turning to them for guidance and instruction (Ross, 1982). In addition, there is a spurt in the growth of rationality in children in the postpreschool years, referred to as the "5-to-7 shift" (Konner, 1978). Both factors may result in the father's becoming more invested in his son at this time, so that his relationship with his own father is more salient. Some support for this hypothesis was found in the stability of paternal involvement with sons between 1977 and 1981, while fathers' participation in their daughters' care declined.

Consequences for Children of Fathers' Taking on the Primary-Caregiver Role in the Radin Study

As predicted, the amount of paternal involvement was positively related to the child's internality; that is, children of fathers with greater participation were more likely to have an internal locus of control, especially with regard to responsibility for negative outcomes, as revealed by their scores on the SPIES. Children of primary-caregiving fathers were also significantly more internal than their peers from mother-primary-caregiver families.

In addition, there were strong indications on the Kagan Parent Role Test that the mothers were perceived as less punitive and the fathers as more punitive when paternal involvement was higher.

There was again a significant difference between children in the father-prime and mother-prime groups on perceived maternal punitiveness: Children in the nontraditional group had lower scores than their peers in traditional families.

It was surprising to find an accentuation of gender stereotypes in perceptions of parental traits by children reared in partially role-reversed families. The reason may have been that the fathers who spent a good deal of time with their children had as masculine a sex-role orientation on the Bem Sex-Role Inventory as men whose wives were the primary caregivers. The net effect may have been that a vivid example of a "manly," powerful father was ever-present, and that the children's stereotyped perception of fathers as punitive and mothers as nonpunitive was thereby enhanced. Russell's study of shared caregiving fathers (Russell, 1980, 1986) provided some support for this explanation. He found that both parents perceived the fathers as stricter than the mothers, and that more conflict arose between the fathers and their children when the men became heavily involved in child care.

The data from the Cognitive Home Environment Scale revealed that the highly involved fathers spent more time in efforts to stimulate their children's cognitive growth, but the direct teaching efforts were focused on their sons and not their daughters. The involved fathers may have violated many role expectations, but they still appeared to demonstrate the preference for sons exhibited by traditional fathers. The mothers in the father-prime families spent less time in direct teaching activities than the traditional mothers. Perhaps parents who are at work or at school during the day have trouble finding time for such activities.

As important as the significant findings were the nonsignificant results. There was no difference in the children's sex-role orientation when the fathers were the primary caregivers, an outcome consonant with the lack of differences in the sex-role orientation of the traditional and the nontraditional mothers and fathers. The rigidity of preschoolers' categorizations may also have been responsible (Kamii & Radin, 1970); their perceptions of what a mother is and what a father is did not accept ambiguous boundaries. There was evidence of a positive correlation between the amount of father participation on some PICCI components and the children's scores on the PPVT, but for the most part, the associations were nonsignificant.

Like Russell, we found that the fathers described the advantages of the high involvement pattern in terms of being closer to their children. However, 40% of the primary-caregiving fathers believed that the arrangement interfered with their jobs. Their spouses described the advantages in terms of a reduction in the stress and guilt they experienced working or studying full time while their child was still a preschooler. Nevertheless, 60% of the mothers expressed regret at not having enough time to be with their children and at missing a lot of their growing up.

THE 11-YEAR FOLLOW-UP. Thirty-two families were located who were still intact and willing to participate in the follow-up, in which both parents and their now-teenaged child were interviewed on the phone. Unless all three participated, the family was not included in the study. Two reports described the findings pertaining to the long-term consequences for children stemming from the childrearing pattern when they were preschoolers and when they were 7–9 years old (Williams & Radin, 1992; Williams *et al.*, 1992). In the Williams *et al.* paper, the teenagers' expectations regarding their future employment and future child-rearing arrangements were the dependent variables investigated. The father-involvement group of the family during the initial study and in the four-year follow-up were the independent variables. As generally predicted, a greater amount of paternal involvement in the teens' preschool years was predictive of adolescent support of a nontraditional employment arrangement. For example, there was greater approval of both spouses' working full time and sharing child care, and less approval of the husband's working full time and the wife's not working and caring for the children full time.

Also as hypothesized, more paternal involvement when the child was 7–9 years old was predictive of support of more nontraditional child-rearing arrangements. For example, teens who had experienced more father participation were more likely to approve an arrangement in which the parents shared child care equally or in which there was higher father involvement. They were less likely to approve of a child-care arrangement in which the mother's involvement was high and father's was low.

The difference in consequences of high father participation when the children were 3–5 and 7–9 was explained in terms of the developmental level of the children and the differences in parental behavior as children mature. The preschoolers may have been strongly influenced by the concrete examples of a male not tied to a 9 to 5 job and woman going off to work each day; the school-aged children may have had the mental capacity to conceptualize various aspects of the maternal and paternal roles they experienced. It is also possible that direct and indirect parental instruction in behavior relevant to future family roles was more prevalent and powerful in families when children were old enough to take on family tasks than when they were preschoolers.

In no case was the traditional parental arrangement predictive of more nontraditional values on the part of the adolescents, and in no case was a nontraditional parental arrangement predictive of more traditional values. Norm-violating parental socialization practices therefore do appear to have an impact on children's gender-related attitudes, although this impact may take a decade to become evident.

The second report, by Williams and Radin, describes an exploration of whether the amount of father involvement in the preschool or early school years, and/or the amount of maternal employment during those periods, was predictive of the adolescents' academic behavior (i.e., self-reported grades and plans for graduate education). It was found that past maternal employment had a more powerful impact than the amount of father involvement. Part-time maternal employment appeared to be optimal, especially when accompanied by high father participation. There was no evidence that increased father involvement in child rearing by itself, influenced grades or expectations for higher education. Perhaps father involvement was a poor determinant of academic endeavors because the men who were very involved in child rearing almost invariably paid a price in terms of their career. Although the primary-caregiving men were well educated, their own life tended not to be an exemplar of an achieving professional. For example, one primary-caregiving father, formerly a teacher, was a self-employed baker; another taught part time and was heavily involved in volunteer work. These positions permitted extensive hours of child care. Thus, a mixed message regarding education and occupational advancement may have been conveyed by the caregiving fathers. The message to get good grades and an advanced degree (assuming this message was conveyed by these middle-class men) may have been counterbalanced by the fact that the father had put his own career on the back burner to become a more involved caregiver.

It was also notable that, both in the preschool years and in the 11-year follow-up, there was almost no relationship between the amount of father involvement and the children's cognitive performance. The absence of a link between the quantity and the quality of paternal participation may help to explain these findings, for paternal nurturance has been found to have a strong influence on a son's mental development (Radin, 1981b), but these primary-caregiving fathers were no more nurturant than their traditional peers.

The Sagi Investigation in Israel

Overview

Sagi (Radin & Sagi, 1982; Sagi, 1982; Sagi, Koren, & Weinberg, 1987) conducted a partial replication of the Radin study near Haifa, Israel, making some major procedural changes to accommodate the cultural context, to adjust to financial constraints, and to eliminate the self-selected nature of the sample. The hypotheses generated were the same, and in both countries, the sample was limited to intact families with a preschool-aged child. For the most part, the instruments were also the same, although not all of the child assessments were used. In Israel, Hebrew versions of the SPIES, Kagan's Parent Role Perception Test, the revised *It* scale, and Borke's Empathy Test were administered to the children in the nursery school or kindergarten. When a test's pictures were inappropriate for Israel, an equivalent substitute was used.

A Hebrew version of the parent interview schedule was administered to the fathers in their homes, and scores on the Paternal Involvement in Child Care Index (PICCI) were computed in the same way as in the United States. All five of the PICCI components were found to be highly intercorrelated. The interview schedule also included the same questions concerning paternal involvement in the respondent's family of origin. Major differences between the Israeli and the U.S. studies included the omission of the Bem Sex-Role Inventory and the PPVT from the list of administered instruments in Israel, the omission of the mothers from the respondents interviewed, and the absence of follow-up investigations.

Families were also recruited differently. The investigators approached the entire child population of the age range desired (3–6 years) in a middle-class town near Haifa. The child's teacher provided all parents with a short questionnaire requesting them to rank independently the amount of time they were involved with their child in comparison with the spouse. Only families in which both parents agreed on the level of paternal involvement with the child were considered potential participants. To be included in the study, families had to meet the following additional criteria: They had to be intact, with no more than two children; the age of the parents could not exceed 40 years; they had to belong to the middle class as assessed by the older version of the Hollingshead scale (Hollingshead, 1957); and the child had to have no intellectual or behavioral problems as assessed by the teacher.

These criteria were met by 150 families. The final sample of 60 was selected by including 15 families in which there was agreement that the father was more involved than the mother, 20 families in which the mothers and the fathers agreed that both parents took equal responsibility for child rearing, and 25 families randomly selected from the remaining 115 families in which there was agreement that the mothers were the primary caregivers. The final level of involvement and membership in the three groups reflecting high, intermediate, and low amounts of paternal involvement was determined by the replies to the questionnaire administered to the 60 fathers selected for the study. All of the families were Jewish Israelis; none were Arabic.

The sample consisted of 30 boys and 30 girls with an average age of 51 months; the fathers averaged 34 years of age. Because the Israeli preschool educational system provides regular nurseries for children as young as 2 years old, the current child-care arrangement had been in effect for an average of 20 months, and the children spent an average of 30 hours per week in a nursery or kindergarten. In families where the father was the primary caregiver, 11 mothers were employed full time and 9 were not working. In the intermediate group, 10 of the 20 mothers worked full time, and in the traditional families, 2 of the 20 mothers were full-time employees.

Antecedents of Fathers' Taking on the
Primary-Caregiving Role in the Sagi Study

When the PICCI five component scores of the fathers' involvement with his child were intercorrelated with the same five component scores of the father's father's involvement, all but 1 of the 25 correlations were significant. The fathers' modeling of their own fathers' child rearing was the likely explanation. It was notable that, in the Radin study, only 2 of the 25 same correlations were significant. The investigators speculated that there may have been stability in child-rearing patterns across the generations in Israel to counteract the many threats to stability in other areas of Israeli life.

Consequences for the Children of Fathers' Taking on the Primary-Caregiving Role in the Sagi Study

In agreement with the U.S. study, Sagi found that children in the father-primary-caregiver group demonstrated significantly more internality on the SPIES than did the groups with less father involvement. However, there were also conflicts in the findings. In Israel, greater father involvement was negatively related to the children's perceptions of their fathers as punitive on the Kagan Parent Perception Test, rather than positively related as in the U.S. study. Because the children's perception of their fathers' nurturance on the Kagan test and the fathers' self-perceptions of their nurturance were significantly correlated in both countries, there appeared to be validity in the children's views.

Overall, high paternal participation had a more powerful impact on the children in Israel. In the replication (Radin & Sagi, 1982), but not in the original study (Radin, 1981a, 1982), the children of more involved fathers were more empathetic and had scores on the *It* Scale significantly different from those of their peers in traditional families. Both the sons and the daughters of more involved fathers had higher masculinity scores on the *It* Scale, and a significant interaction effect between the father involvement group and the gender of the child emerged. Girls in the father-prime and intermediate groups obtained significantly higher scores than girls in the mother-prime group. An examination of the means indicated that the scores of the daughters in the nontraditional homes had moved toward the middle of the scale. This shift reflected a more androgynous orientation because the scale is bipolar: The high end indicates a masculine orientation, and the low end a feminine orientation. Radin and Sagi (1982) believed that the change in the daughters' scores was probably the result of their being reared by more nurturant, involved fathers who were not sex-stereotyped themselves and who did not respond to girls in a sex-stereotyped fashion; as a consequence, the daughters were less sex-stereotyped, in accordance with a major theory of sex-role learning in girls (Johnson, 1975).

The discrepancies in outcomes in the two countries were attributed primarily to the Israeli fathers' heavy involvement in all aspects of the child's life, as evidenced by the high intercorrelations of the PICCI components. The average intercorrelation was .67 for the Israeli fathers in contrast to .25 for the American fathers. Further, the highly participant Israeli fathers appeared to be more nurturant than their traditional peers, as demonstrated by the close association of the men's self-perceptions of their nurturance and the amount of their involvement, as well as by the children's perceptions of them as more nurturant. In addition, almost half of these men had taken on the role although their wives were not working or active in volunteer activities (personal communication from Sagi, 1981). Thus, the men appeared to be unusually child-oriented. In the United States, only one PICCI component was related to fathers' self-perceived nurturance, and the children reared in the role-reversed families perceived their fathers as more punitive, rather than more nurturant, than did the children reared in traditional homes. The Bem scores of the primary-caregiving American fathers were also no different than those of peers playing a minimal role in child rearing.

In general, the findings in Israel and the United States provided strong support for social learning as a major factor in the socialization process. All men taking on a large role in rearing a preschooler in intact families can be considered role creators and, as such, are likely to be autonomous and have an internal locus of control. Their internality is likely to be modeled by their children, and they are likely to reinforce differentially such behavior in their sons and their daughters. Thus, the children in both countries demonstrated greater internality than the children in traditional families. But for children to be more empathetic, involved fathers had to demonstrate greater empathy themselves, as was the case in Israel, because empathy, or interpersonal sensitivity, is an aspect of nurturance. There was no indication of greater sensitivity or nurturance among the highly involved American men when they were compared with their traditional peers. Hence, their children's empathy did not differ from that of their peers reared in mother-primary-caregiver homes.

CONCLUSIONS CONCERNING DETERMINANTS
OF FATHERS' TAKING ON THE ROLE OF
PRIMARY CAREGIVER IN INTACT FAMILIES

All five studies shed light on conditions leading to a father-primary-caregiver pattern of child rearing. Pruett described the men in his investigation as desiring to repeat or remake their past. Sagi and Radin described the same phenomenon as modeling one's own father or trying to compensate for his failures. In the Israeli study, the findings for the modeling explanation were strong; in the U.S. study, the compensatory pattern emerged initially in regard to mothers' feelings and four years later with regard to fathers of sons when the predictors of stability in the partially role-reversed arrangement were examined. However, the modeling phenomenon was also operative in the U.S. investigation because more parents in the father-primary-caregiver group had experienced a mother who was employed and all of the role-reversed wives were working or going to school full time. Neither Lamb nor Russell discussed the child-rearing arrangement in the parents' families of origin.

Russell, Pruett, and Radin indicated that parent employment and financial considerations were among the determinants of the nontraditional child-care arrangement. Pruett found that approximately one third of his families had been forced into the pattern as a result of the father's unemployment while the mother still had a job. In all of Russell's shared-caregiving families, either the mother or the father had some flexibility in hours of employment or one of them was working part time. In addition, approximately 10% of his 50 caregiving fathers were unable to find employment, and in almost one fourth of his sample, maternal career factors played a role. Very few of the wives of caregiving fathers in the Radin investigation indicated that they had been forced to work against their wishes, but over half of both parents agreed that the mothers worked because they had to and also because they wished to.

There were two potential antecedents about which conflicts emerged; one was the importance of a belief system about sharing child rearing, and the second pertained to the parents' sex-role orientation. As for the former, about one fourth of the parents in Russell's sample of nontraditional families had chosen that pattern because they were ideologically committed to sharing child care and felt very strongly that both parents should be involved. Lamb and his colleagues found that men who planned to spend over one month as primary caregivers valued parenthood over work, but there was no indication that these values were predictive of subsequent paternal behavior.

The belief issue was not discussed in the other studies, but there was an implication that ideology was not relevant in the Pruett study. Most of the men who had decided before the pregnancy on a father-child-care arrangement had wives who did not seek their fulfillment in life through maternal activities, and the men described their own fathers as distant. These factors appeared to be the important antecedents, not a belief system.

Sex-role orientation was one of the determinants in Russell's Australian investigation of shared child rearing. However, neither Lamb's Swedish study nor Radin's American investigation found sex-role orientation on the same instrument to be associated with partial role reversal. Whether this discrepancy in findings is attributable to cultural differences or to the wider socioeconomic stratum embraced in Russell's sample remains to be investigated.

Finally, the Lamb study highlighted the importance of institutional factors as a determinant of fathers' playing a major role in child rearing. If it had not been for the government's policy of paying most of the salary of either parent when he or she stayed home with a newborn for up to nine months, it is doubtful if many of the nontraditional fathers would have assumed the role of primary caregiver. Even with the policy in place, their term as primary caregivers averaged less than three months.

The demographic factors of age and number of children arose in the Australian investigation as determinants of a shared-child-rearing arrangement. The child's age was controlled in all of the other studies, and as the children were quite young and often the firstborn, family size was not an important antecedent of partial role reversal. It is notable, however, that none of the five families that maintained the father-primary-caregiver pattern over a four-year period in the Radin study increased their family size during this span of years; the two contrast families, which were in the same group initially but reverted to a mother-primary-caregiver arrangement, both had additional children in the intervening four years. These findings suggest that family size may, at minimum, be a factor facilitating the maintenance of the father-primary-caregiver pattern.

In sum, two determinants of fathers' functioning as the major caregiver in intact families emerged across cultures: (1) the parents' perceptions of the fathering they had experienced as children and (2) financial-employment factors, particularly problems in the fathers' obtaining jobs, the mothers worked, and maternal career aspirations.

Support for these conclusions can be seen in a number of investigations on the paternal role *per se*. A Massachusetts study (Barnett & Baruch, 1987) of middle-class families with 5- or 9 year-old children found that the mothers' employment status predicted how involved the fathers were with the children. In families where the mother was employed, the number of hours she worked was one of the strongest predictors of the father's participation. When the mother was not employed, the major determinant was the father's perception of the quality of fathering he had received as a youngster, with the lowest quality being predictive of the most participation. Similarly, in a California study of the parents of infants (Feldman, Nash, & Aschenbrenner, 1983), it was found that the wives of husbands involved in caregiving were often women who had had positive relationships with their own fathers.

The role of the working wife as the gatekeeper of the amount of paternal participation was highlighted by Cowan and Cowan (1987), whose longitudinal study indicated that women who "left space" for their spouses to become involved with the baby through their own involvement in work outside the family had husbands who took responsibility for the care of the children. In contrast, in another investigation (McKenry, Price, Gordon, & Rudd, 1986), the fathers asserted that they participated more in child rearing because they desired to do so when their wives enjoyed work and were working for economic reasons. Both factors may well be involved. Mothers may leave the gate open, but fathers have to wish to walk through it for shared caregiving to ensue.

Finally, several studies of nontraditional families of various types supported the compensatory hypothesis that fathers become more involved with their children when their own fathers were uninvolved in their upbringing (De Frain, 1979; Eiduson & Alexander, 1978; Kimball, 1984).

CONCLUSIONS CONCERNING THE CONSEQUENCES FOR THE CHILDREN OF FATHERS' TAKING ON THE ROLE OF PRIMARY CAREGIVER IN INTACT FAMILIES

It appears from all five studies that children are not damaged by having a primary-caregiving father. The Lamb and Russell studies had the least information on the issue, but Russell's shared-caregiving parents reported that their children had not experienced any major problems from their pattern of child care and that the father–child relationship had improved. The latter result may well have foreshadowed future benefits for the children (Lamb & Oppenheim, 1989). In the Lamb investigation, the men were primary caregivers for a very short period of time, but there was no ill effect on their children's behavior associated with security of attachment.

Three of the studies reported evidence of positive outcomes for the children. The most robust findings were found in the Israeli study. The preschool-aged children of highly involved fathers were found to be more empathetic, and to have a more internal locus of control than their peers in traditional families. There was also evidence of a more androgynous orientation on the part of the girls. The Radin study also found greater internality in the children of primary-caregiving fathers than in peers in mother-primary-caregiving homes when concurrent measures were used. Eleven years later, the children reared in nontraditional homes had a more flexible, less sex-role-stereotyped attitude toward their future roles as parents and employees, which had a high likelihood of being more adaptive to life circumstances in the coming decades.

The Pruett investigation of children under 4 years old reared primarily by their fathers in intact homes reported signs of advanced development at 1–2 years of age. For the most part, the children performed above the expected norms on standardized tests of development. In general, they were described as robust, thriving infants. In a follow-up when the children were approximately 4 years old, there were still no signs of psychological distress or mental illness. Rather, these children showed signs of being secure in their gender identities and being more flexible, particularly in their movement back and forth between identification with maternal and paternal activities and attributes. Gender flexibility was even more apparent in the 8-year follow-up. This finding concerning flexibility in gender-relevant behavior is in keeping with the data collected in Radin's 11-year follow-up. Pruett reported that some of the precocious development observed during the second year of life seemed to have slackened somewhat 2 years later, possibly as an artifact of the infant assessment instruments. However, at ages 8–10 years, there appeared to be no question of these children's overall competence, along with a "scrappy" self-confidence.

In sum, there is no reason to believe that children's development is impaired as a result of being reared primarily by their fathers in two-parent homes, and there is some evidence that their growth is enhanced in desirable directions. The reason for these effects is not known, however. At least part of the reason may be attributable not to greater contact with fathers, or to greater contact with certain types of fathers, but to the fact that this arrangement permits the child to benefit from having two highly involved parents with different behavioral styles; the children are thereby assured a diversity of stimulation (Lamb & Oppenheim, 1989). The father-primary-caregiver pattern may also permit both parents to do what is important to them, at least when there is a voluntary component. Both parents are thereby more fulfilled, and the result, in all probability, is warmer, more satisfying family relationships, which benefit the children (Lamb & Oppenheim, 1989). Thus, the indirect effects of high father participation, particularly through its effect on the mother and her behavior with the child, may be as important as the direct paternal effects on the sons and daughters (Lamb, Pleck, & Levine, 1985).

DIRECTIONS FOR FUTURE RESEARCH
ON INTACT FAMILIES IN WHICH FATHERS
TAKE ON THE ROLE OF PRIMARY CAREGIVER

Need for Further Research

In the light of recent research and conceptualizations about the paternal role, more sophisticated investigations can now be conducted of fathers who function as primary caregivers in two-parent families. The questions elicited by this arrangement are still important because some seminal theories on the development of males and females are based on the gender of the child's primary socializer and attachment figure (Chodorow, 1974; Lynn, 1974; Pruett, 1985). Further, as women's roles in society change, it has been postulated that men's roles must change as well if working mothers are to avoid being overburdened, for they also serve as the children's major caregivers (Hoffman, 1983). The impact of changes in both parental roles on children needs to be investigated in depth if there is to be widespread support of an atypical family arrangement when mothers work, that is, shared caregiving.

In couples in which the mothers are more invested in their occupational role than the fathers, the men's taking on the role of major child rearer could benefit both the parents and the children, as the studies discussed above suggest. The 11-year follow-up by Radin indicated that there were some families in which a comfortable accommodation through partial role reversal had been made between mothers with fast-track careers and fathers for whom the occupational role was secondary to other life interests. It is likely that the number of families considering such an arrangement will increase in future years as more women gain access to high-level positions and more men learn the gratifications of putting family relations and community-religious-fraternal activities above competition in the occupational world. For pragmatic as well as theoretical reasons, it is therefore important for researchers to collect data from diverse samples on the long-term consequences of fathers' functioning as the primary caregivers. Such information needs to be disseminated widely so that mothers and fathers can make informed, rational decisions about the child-rearing pattern they will adopt.

New Research Designs

A significant advance in research design would be made if future investigators of primary caregiving fathers were to identify the domain of their research in terms of the Lamb conceptualization, that is, to specify if they were focusing on the father's role in dyadic interactions, on his availability, and/or on his responsibilities. This classification should be further refined into categories, such as caretaking activities and play activities, if not into more fine-grained distinctions. Future investigators should also identify whether their data reflected the father's relative or absolute amount of participation in child care, or whether both domains have been explored. Ideally, the data should be analyzed separately for each perspective so that the correlates of each measurement approach can be determined.

To optimize the outcomes of research on partially role-reversed families, investigators should have expertise in child development as well as in family dynamics. If one researcher's expertise does not span both areas, then a collaboration between two or more individuals is called for. Studying merely the parents' perspectives without assessing the children is as incomplete as assessing the children without obtaining data on the mothers and fathers. It is also critical that both parents' perspectives be investigated, as well as the children's. Obtaining data on the parents' family of origin directly from the grandparents would yield very valuable supplementary information concerning the transmission of socialization patterns across the generations.

Cross-cultural and cross-ethnic studies are needed that use the same core instruments and research design with different populations to determine which findings reflect pervasive, inherent antecedents and outcomes of partial role reversal, and which are largely a reflection of the norms or laws of a particular group. The Radin and Sagi studies, although limited in many ways, provide revealing data about divergent responses to fathering in the family of origin, as well as different consequences for children who experienced qualitatively different types of paternal caregiving. What a rich body of data would have been collected if Russell, Lamb, Pruett, Sagi, and Radin had known about one another's planned studies and had been able to agree on some common assessments to be made of the parents and the children.

Finally, longitudinal studies are essential. The Radin investigation showed that partial role reversal had no impact on the children's gender-relevant attitudes when they were preschoolers, a period of rigid categorizations; yet the early experience of living with a primary-caregiving father and a working mother reduced their sex-role stereotyping during adolescence. A unique 26-year longitudinal study (Koestner, Franz, & Weinberger, 1990) revealed that empathy in 31-year-old adults was strongly predicted by paternal involvement in child care when they were 5 years old. Not many investigations can be continued for two and a half decades, but it is to be hoped that any contemporary researcher studying men who are caregivers of young children will build in strategies for keeping in touch with the families for at least five years to permit an assessment of the children when they reach new developmental levels.

Not included as part of the Radin follow-up studies, but needed in future studies, are data about outcomes for families that have separated or divorced. There was anecdotal evidence in the four-year follow-up (Radin & Goldsmith, 1985) that child custody battles were very bitter when the men had played a major role in child rearing. Pruett found that 2 of his original 17 families were currently or about to be divorced, and both mothers believed that the child-care decision had had a role in the marital dissolution. Not to pursue this information may result in the loss of important knowledge about possible negative outcomes of partial role reversal for both children and parents. Custody conflicts and strains caused by paternal child rearing in intact families may be preventable with sufficient research data about the phenomenon.

In conclusion, our society is changing rapidly, and family forms are changing equally, if not more, rapidly. It is hoped that investigators will try to keep abreast of these changes and gain some understanding of what is currently occurring rather than be forced to catch up on events years later. If nothing else, such an approach would inform us about a group of pioneers who may be at the forefront of a large wave soon to follow.

REFERENCES

Aldous, J. (1974). The making of family roles and family change. *The Family Coordinator, 23*, 231–235.

Bailey, W. T. (1987, April). *Infancy to age five: Predicting fathers involvement.* Paper presented at the meeting of the Society for Research in Child Development, Baltimore.

Bandura, A. (1967). The role of modeling processes in personality development. In W. W. Hartup & N. L. Smothergell (Eds.), *The young child: Review or research* (pp. 42–58). Washington, DC: National Association for the Education of Young Children.

Bandura, A. (1977). *Social learning theory.* Englewood Cliffs, NJ: Prentice-Hall.

Barnett, M.A., King, L. M., Howard, J. A., & Dino, G. A. (1980). Empathy in young children. *Developmental Psychology, 16*, 243–244.

Barnett, R. C., & Baruch, G. K. (1987). Determinants of fathers participation in family work. *Journal of Marriage and the Family, 49*, 29–40.

Baruch, G. K., & Barnett, R. C. (1986). Fathers' participation in family work and children's sex-role attitudes. *Child Development, 57*, 1210–1223.

Belsky, J. (1979). Mother-father-infant interaction: A naturalistic observational study. *Developmental Psychology, 15*, 601–607.

Bem, S. L. (1974). The measurement of psychological androgyny. *Journal of Consulting and Clinical Psychology, 42*, 155–162.

Biller, H. B. (1969). Father dominance and sex-role development in kindergarten-age boys. *Developmental Psychology, 1*, 87–94.

Biller, H. B., & Bornstelmann, L. (1967). Masculine development: An integrative review. *Merrill-Palmer Quarterly, 13,* 253–294.

Blood, R., & Wolfe, D. (1960). *Husbands and wives: The dynamics of married living.* New York: Macmillan.

Borke, H. (1971). Interpersonal perception of young children: Egocentrism or empathy? *Developmental Psychology, 5,* 263–269.

Bronfenbrenner, U. (1958). The study of identification through interpersonal perception. In R. Tagiuri & L. Petrillo (Eds.), *Personal-perception and interpersonal behavior.* Stanford, CA: Stanford University Press.

Brown, D. G. (1956). Sex-role preference in children. *Psychological Monographs, 70* (14, Serial No. 287).

Brown, P., Perry, L., & Harberg, E. (1977). Sex-role attitudes and psychological outcomes for black and white women experiencing marital dissolution. *Journal of Marriage and the Family, 39,* 519–561.

Chodorow, N. (1974). Family structure and feminine personality. In M. Z. Rosaldo & L. Lamphere (Eds.), *Women, culture, and society.* Stanford, CA: Stanford University Press.

Cowan, C. P., & Cowan, P. A. (1987). Men's involvement in parenthood. In P. W. Berman & F. A. Pedersen (Eds.), *Men's transition to parenthood* (pp. 145–174). Hillsdale, NJ: Erlbaum.

Cronenwett, L. R. (1982). Father participation in child care: A critical review. *Research in Nursing and Health, 5,* 63–72.

Crouter, A. C., & Crowley, M. S. (1990). School-aged children's time along with fathers in single- and dual-earner families. *Journal of Early Adolescence, 10,* 296–312.

Crouter, A. C., Perry-Jenkins, M., Huston, T. L., & McHale, S. M. (1987). Processes underlying father involvement in dual-earner and single-earner families. *Developmental Psychology, 23,* 431–440.

De Frain, J. (1979). Androgynous parents tell who they are and what they need. *The Family Coordinator, 28,* 237–243.

Easterbrooks, M. A., & Goldberg, W. A. (1984). Toddler development in the family: Impact of father involvement and parenting characteristics. *Child Development, 55,* 740–752.

Eiduson, B. T., & Alexander, J. W. (1978). The role of children in alternative family styles. *Journal of Social Issues, 34,* 149–167.

Eiduson, B. T., & Weisner, T. S. (1978). Alternative family styles: Effects on young children. In J. Stevens & M. Mathews (Eds.), *Mother/child, father/child relationships.* Washington, DC: National Association for the Education of Young Children.

Feldman, S. S., Nash, S. C., & Aschenbrenner, B. G. (1983). Antecedents of fathering. *Child Development, 54,* 1628–1636.

Gecas, S. (1976). The socialization and child care roles. In F. I. Nye (Ed.), *Role structure and analysis of the family* (pp. 33–59). Beverly Hills, CA: Sage.

Gersick, K. E. (1979). Fathers by choice: Divorced men who receive custody of their children. In G. Levinger & O. C. Moles (Eds.), *Divorce and separation* pp. 307–323). New York: Basic Books.

Gewirtz, J. L., & Stingle, K. G. (1968). Learning of generalized imitation as the basis of identification. *Psychological review, 75,* 374–397.

Grossman, F. K., Pollack, W. S., & Golding, E. (1988). Fathers and children: Predicting the quality and quantity of fathering. *Developmental Psychology, 24,* 82–91.

Harold-Goldsmith, R., Radin, N., & Eccles, J. S. (1988). Objective and subjective reality: The effects of job loss and financial stress on fathering behaviors. *Family Perspective, 22,* 309–325.

Hoffman, L. W. (1977). Changes in family roles, socialization, and sex differences. *American Psychologist, 32,* 644–657.

Hoffman, L. W. (1983). Increased fathering: Effects on the mother. In M. E. Lamb & A. Sage (Eds.), *Fatherhood and family policy* (pp. 167–190). Hillsdale, NJ: Erlbaum.

Hollingshead, A. B. (1957). *Two-Factor Index of Social Position.* Available from the Department of Sociology, Yale University, New Haven, CT 06502.

Hollingshead, A. B. (1975). *Four-Factor Index of Social Status.* Available from the Department of Sociology, Yale University, New Haven, CT 06502.

Johnson, M. M. (1975). Fathers, mothers, and sex-typing. *Sociological Inquiry, 45,* 15–26.

Jump, T. L., & Haas, L. G. (1984, October). *Fathers in transition.* Paper presented at the meeting of the National Council on Family Relations, San Francisco.

Kagan, J. (1958). The concept of identification. *Psychological Review, 65,* 296–305.

Kagan, J., & Lemkin, J. (1960). The child's differential perception of parental attributes. *Journal of Abnormal and Social Psychology, 61,* 440–447.

Kamii, C., & Radin, N. (1970). A framework for a preschool curriculum based on Piaget's theory. In I. J. Athey & D. O. Rubadeau (Eds.), *Educational implications of Piaget's theory* (pp. 89–100). Waltham, MA: Blaisdell.

Kimball, G. C. (1984). *Why do couples role share?* Unpublished manuscript. University of California, Chico, CA.

Koestner, R., Franz, C., & Weinberger, J. (1990). The family origins of empathetic concern: A 26-year longitudinal study. *Journal of Personality and Social Psychology, 58,* 709–717.

Kohlberg, L. (1966). A cognitive developmental analysis of children's sex-role concepts and attitudes. In E. E. Maccoby (Ed.), *The development of sex differences.* Stanford, CA: Stanford University press.

Konner, M. (1978). Social and personality development: An anthropological perspective. In M. E. Lamb (Ed.), *Social and personality development* (pp. 227–251). New York: Holt, Rinehart, & Winston.

Kotelchuck, M. (1976). The infant's relationship to the father: Experimental evidence. In M. E. Lamb (Ed.), *The role of the father in child development* (pp. 329–344). New York: Wiley.

Lamb, M. E. (1976). Interactions between eight-month-old children and their fathers and mothers. In M. E. Lamb (Ed.), *The role of the father in child development* (pp. 307–327). New York: Wiley.

Lamb, M. E. (1980). What can "research experts" tell parents about effective socialization? In M. D. Fantini & R. Ardenas (Eds.), *Parenting in a multicultural society.* New York: Longman.

Lamb, M. E. (1986). The changing roles of fathers. In M. E. Lamb (Ed.), *The father's role: Applied perspectives* (pp. 3–27). New York: Wiley-Interscience.

Lamb, M. E., & Bronson, S. K. (1980). Fathers in the context of family influences: Past, present, and future. *Social Psychology Digest, 9,* 336–353.

Lamb, M. E., Frodi, A. M., Hwang, C.-P., & Frodi, M. (1982). Varying degrees of paternal involvement in infant care: Attitudinal and behavioral correlates. In M. E. Lamb (Ed.), *Nontraditional families: Parenting and child development* (pp. 549–590). Hillsdale, NJ: Erlbaum.

Lamb, M. E., Frodi, A. M., Hwang, C.-P., Frodi, M., & Steinberg, J. (1982a). Mother- and father-infant interaction involving play and holding in traditional and nontraditional Swedish families. *Developmental Psychology, 18,* 215–221.

Lamb, M. E., Frodi, M. A., Hwang, C.-P., Frodi, M., & Steinberg, J. (1982b). Effects of gender and caretaking role in parent-infant interaction. In R. N. Emde & R. Harmen (Eds.), *Development of attachment and affiliative systems.* New York: Plenum Press.

Lamb, M. E., Frodi, M. A., Hwang, C.-P., & Frodi, A. M. (1983). Effects of paternal involvement on infant preferences for mother and fathers. *Child Development, 54,* 450–458.

Lamb, M. E., & Oppenheim, D. (1989). Fatherhood and father-child relationships. In S. H. Cath, A. Gurwitt, & L. Gunsberg (Eds.), *Fathers and their families* (pp. 11–26). Hillsdale, NJ: Analytic Press.

Lamb, M. E., Pleck, J. H., Charnov, E. L., & Levine, J. A. (1985). Paternal behavior in humans. *American Zoology, 25,* 883–894.

Lamb, M. E., Pleck, J. H., & Levine, J. A. (1985). The role of the father in child development: The effects of increased paternal involvement. In B. S. Lahey & A. E. Kazdin (Eds.), *Advances in clinical child psychology* (Vol. 8, pp. 229–266). New York: Plenum Press.

Levine, J. A. (1976). *Who will raise the children: New options for fathers (and mothers).* New York: Lippincott.

Levy-Shiff, R., & Israelashvili, R. (1988). Antecedents of fathering: Some further exploration. *Developmental Psychology, 24,* 434–440.

Lynn, D. B. (1974). *The father: His role in child development.* Belmont, CA: Brooks/Cole.

Maccoby, E. E., & Jacklin, E. N. (1974). *The psychology of sex differences.* Stanford, CA: Stanford University Press.

McBride, B. A. (1990). The effects of a parent education play group program on father involvement in childrearing. *Family Relations, 39,* 250–256.

McKenry, P. C., Price, S. J., Gordon, P. B., & Rudd, N. M (1986). Characteristics of husbands' family work and wives' labor force involvement. In R. A. Lewis & R. E. Salt (Eds.), *Men in families* (pp. 73–83). Beverly Hills, CA: Sage.

Meyer, B. (1980). The development of girls' sex-role attitudes. *Child Development, 51,* 508–514.

Mischel, W. (1970). Sex-typing and socialization. In P. H. Mussen (Ed.), *Carmichael's manual of child psychology* (Vol. 2, 3rd ed.), New York: Wiley.

Mischel, W., Zeiss, R., & Zeiss, A. (1974). Internal-external control and persistence: Validation and implications of the Stanford Preschool Internal-External Scale. *Journal of Personality and Social Psychology, 29,* 265–278.

Money, J., & Ehrhardt, H. A. (1972). *Man and woman, boy and girl.* Baltimore: Johns Hopkins University Press.

Mussen, P., & Distler, L. (1960). Childrearing antecedents of masculine identification in kindergarten boys. *Child Development, 31,* 89–100.

Nugent, J. K. (1991). Cultural and psychological influences on the father's role in infant development. *Journal of Marriage and the Family, 53,* 475–485.

Payne, D. E., & Mussen, P. H. (1965). Parent-child relations and father identification among adolescent boys. *Journal of Abnormal and Social Psychology, 52,* 358–362.

Pleck, J. H. (1975). Masculinity-femininity: Current and alternative paradigms. *Sex Roles, 1,* 161–178.

Pleck, J. H. (1981). *Changing patterns of work and family roles*. Paper presented at the meeting of the American Psychological Association, Los Angeles.

Pleck, J. H. (1983). Husbands' paid work and family roles. In H. Z. Lopata & J. H. Pleck (Eds.), *Research in the interweave of social roles: Families and jobs* (Vol. 3, pp. 251–333). Greenwich, CT: JAI Press.

Pleck, J. H. (1986). Employment and fatherhood: Issues and innovative policies. In M. E. Lamb (Ed.), *The father's role: Applied perspectives* (pp. 384–412). New York: Wiley-Interscience.

Price-Bonham, S. (1976). A comparison of weighted and unweighted decision-making scores. *Journal of Marriage and the Family, 38*, 629–640.

Pruett, K. D. (1983). Infants of primary nurturing fathers. *Psychoanalytic Study of the Child, 38*, 257–277.

Pruett, K. D. (1985). Oedipal configurations in young father-raised children. *The Psychoanalytic Study of the Child, 40*, 435–460.

Pruett, K. D. (1989). The nurturing male. In S. H. Cath, A. Gurwitt, & L. Gunsberg (Eds.), *Fathers and their families* (pp. 389–405). Hillsdale, NJ: Analytic Press.

Pruett, K. D. (1992). Latency development in children of primary nurturing fathers: Eight-year follow-up. *The Psychoanalytic Study of the Child, 47*, 85–101.

Pruett, K. D., & Litzenberger, B. (1992). Latency development in children of primary nurturing fathers: Eight-year follow-up. *The Psychoanalytic Study of the Child, 47*, 85–101.

Radin, N. (1972). Father-child interaction and the intellectual functioning of four-year-old boys. *Developmental Psychology, 6*, 353–361.

Radin, N. (1981a). Childrearing fathers in intact families: 1. Some antecedents and consequences. *Merrill-Palmer Quarterly, 27*, 489–514.

Radin, N. (1981b). The role of the father in cognitive/academic and intellectual development. In M. E. Lamb (Ed.), *The role of the father in child development* (2nd ed., pp. 379–427). New York: Wiley.

Radin, N. (1982). Primary caregiving and role-sharing fathers. In M. E. Lamb (Ed.), *Nontraditional families: Parenting and child development* (pp. 173–204). Hillsdale, NJ: Erlbaum.

Radin, N. (1986). The influence of fathers upon sons and daughters and implications for school social work. *Social Work in Education, 8*, 77–91.

Radin, N. (1988). Primary caregiving fathers of long duration. In P. Bronstein & C. P. Cowan (Eds.), *Fatherhood today* (pp. 127–143). New York: Wiley.

Radin, N., & Goldsmith, R. (1985). Caregiving father of preschoolers: Four years later. *Merrill-Palmer Quarterly, 31*, 375–383.

Radin, N., & Russell, G. (1983). The effect of fathers on child development: A consideration of traditional families and those with highly involved fathers. In M. E. Lamb & A. Sagi (Eds.), *Fatherhood and social policy* (pp. 191–218). Hillsdale, NJ: Erlbaum.

Radin, N., & Sagi, A. (1982). Childrearing fathers in intact families in Israel and the U.S.A. *Merrill-Palmer Quarterly, 28*, 111–136.

Radin, N., & Sonquist, H. (1968). *The Gale preschool program: Final report*. Ypsilanti, MI: Ypsilanti Public Schools.

Reuter, M. W., & Biller, H. B. (1973). Perceived paternal nurturance-availability and personality adjustment among college sales. *Journal of Consulting and Clinical Psychology, 40*, 339–342.

Riley, D. (1991, April). *Social network correlates of fathers' involvement in childrearing in the*

U.S. Paper presented at the meeting of the Society for Research in Child Development, Seattle.

Robinson, J. (1977). *Changes in America's use of time, 1965–1975.* Cleveland: Cleveland State University, Communications Research Center.

Ross, J. M. (1982). Mentorship in middle childhood. In S. H. Cath, A. R. Gurwitt, & J. M. Ross (Eds.), *Developmental and clinical perspectives* (pp. 243–252). Boston: Little, Brown.

Russell, G. (1980, July 15–17). Fathers as caregivers: Possible antecedents and consequences. Paper presented to the study group on: *The role of the father in child development: Theory, social policy, and the law.* University of Haifa, Haifa, Israel.

Russell, G. (1982a). *The changing role of fathers.* St. Lucia, Australia: Queensland University Press.

Russell, G. (1982b). Shared-caregiving families: An Australian study. In M. E. Lamb (Ed.), *Nontraditional families: Parenting and child development* (pp. 139–171). Hillsdale, NJ: Erlbaum.

Russell, G. (1986). Primary caretaking and role-sharing fathers. In M. E. Lamb (Ed.), *The father's role: Applied perspectives* (pp. 29–57). New York: Wiley.

Russell, G. (1987). Fatherhood in Australia. In M. E. Lamb (Ed.), *The father's role: Cross-cultural perspectives* (pp. 333–358). Hillsdale, NJ: Erlbaum.

Russell, G., & Radin, N. (1983). Increased paternal participation: The father's perspective. In M. E. Lamb & A. Sagi (Eds.), *Fatherhood and family policy* (pp. 139–165). Hillsdale, NJ: Erlbaum.

Sagi, A. (1982). Antecedents and consequences of various degrees of paternal involvement in childrearing: The Israeli project. In M. E. Lamb (Ed.), *Nontraditional families: Parenting and child development* (pp. 205–232). Hillsdale, NJ: Erlbaum.

Sagi, A., Koren, N., & Weinberg, M. (1987). Fathers in Israel. In M. E. Lamb (Ed.), *The father's role: Cross-cultural perspectives* (pp. 197–226). Hillsdale, NJ: Erlbaum.

Sears, P. S. (1953). Childrearing factors related to the playing of sex-types roles. *American Psychologist, 8,* 432 (Abstract).

Tangri, S. S. (1972). Determinants of occupational role innovation among college women. *Journal of Social Issues, 28,* 177–199.

Volling, B. L., & Belsky, J. (1991). Multiple determinants of father involvement during infancy in dual-earner and single-earner families. *Journal of Marriage and the Family, 53,* 461–474.

Williams, E., & Radin, N. (1993). Paternal involvement, maternal employment, and adolescent academic achievement. *American Journal of Orthopsychiatry, 63,* 306–312.

Williams, E., Radin, N., & Allegro, T. (1992). Sex-role attitudes of adolescents raised primarily by their fathers. *Merrill-Palmer Quarterly, 38,* 457–476.

Yogman, M. W., Dixon, S., Tronick, E., Als, H., & Brazelton, T. B. (1979, March). *The goals and structure of face-to-face interaction between infants and fathers.* Paper presented at the meeting of the Society for Research in Child Development, New Orleans.

3

Role of Maternal and Dual-Earner Employment Status in Children's Development

A Longitudinal Study from Infancy through Early Adolescence

Adele Eskeles Gottfried,
Kay Bathurst, and Allen W. Gottfried

INTRODUCTION

The research reported in this chapter is concerned with investigating the role of maternal employment in children's development in our longitudinal study from infancy through early adolescence. In our prior research (A. E. Gottfried, A. W. Gottfried, & Bathurst, 1988), we studied maternal employment and children's development from

Adele Eskeles Gottfried • Department of Educational Psychology and Counseling, California State University, Northridge, California 91330.   Kay Bathurst and Allen W. Gottfried • Department of Psychology, California State University, Fullerton, California 92634.

Redefining Families: Implications for Children's Development, edited by Adele Eskeles Gottfried and Allen W. Gottfried. Plenum Press, New York, 1994.

infancy (1 year) through early childhood (7 years) and found no differences between the children of employed and nonemployed mothers. Further, we examined the environmental contexts of the children and found that, although there were few differences, the employed mothers held consistently higher educational attitudes for their children from the preschool years onward. Interestingly, the fathers of children with employed mothers were significantly more involved with their children.

One of the conclusions of our research was that, if there is any impact of maternal employment on children's development, it is mediated through the children's environment. This conclusion was based on the significant relationships found in our research between home environment and children's development from infancy through childhood (A. E. Gottfried *et al.*, 1988; A. W. Gottfried & A. E. Gottfried, 1984). Moreover, we proposed that maternal employment or nonemployment involves a network of factors that balance each other out and produce no net differences between the children of employed and nonemployed mothers. One of the balancing factors is the fathers' role, and we suggested that future research examine the dimensions of this role in more detail so that some of the influential factors may be discerned. Hence, we are following this up in our current research.

This chapter has two purposes. The first concerns extending our research findings from middle childhood through early adolescence. The second is to examine aspects of mothers' and fathers' child involvement and work roles.

PRIOR RESEARCH AND CURRENT ISSUES REGARDING MATERNAL EMPLOYMENT AND CHILDREN'S DEVELOPMENT

Over the past 40 years, the role of maternal employment in children's development has been investigated. The proliferation of research generally corresponds to the increasing phenomenon of maternal employment. In the 1950s, maternal employment was a minority phenomenon (Nye & Hoffman, 1963). Research in the 1950s reflected the negative biases of society as well as those of professional and popular opinion. Much of the research in the 1950s and 1960s was oriented to determining if maternal employment had a detrimental effect on children's development. Maternal absence through employment was believed to be deprivational, and research was designed to test the maternal deprivation perspective (Burchinal, 1963; Nye, Perry, & Ogles, 1963).

The incidence of maternal employment changed dramatically in the decades following the 1950s. Rather than being a minority phenomenon, maternal employment continued to increase across the school-age years and even did so among the mothers of children under 6. In the 1980s, approximately 50% of mothers were employed, and this number continues to rise today. In our own research, the percentage of employed mothers rose from 36% when the children were 1 year of age in 1979 to 80% when the children were age 12 in 1991, and only one mother was consistently not employed throughout the course of the study. This finding reflects the changes that are occurring in society. Changing economic conditions, the women's movement, and the search for women's personal meaning and identity through employment are often identified as factors responsible for this increase (A. E. Gottfried et al., 1988; Hoffman, 1989).

Early research concerning the impact of maternal employment on children's development compared the development of the children of employed and nonemployed mothers without recognition of the heterogeneity of these employment groups. If differences between these children were obtained, they were attributed to maternal employment, and not to the other confounded factors, such as socioeconomic status, which pervade the categories (A. E. Gottfried, 1988).

The earlier literature on maternal employment and children's development produced widely conflicting results (as reviewed in A. E. Gottfried et al., 1988). As we pointed out, numerous differences between studies in the methodology and samples employed, the measures used, and the developmental domains studied contributed to the discrepant findings.

Along with the increase in the incidence of maternal employment, the methods used to study maternal employment have become more sophisticated, and the conceptualization of the issues has become more differentiated. There is a growing convergence of research evidence that, overall, there is little difference in the development of children of employed and nonemployed mothers that can be attributed to maternal employment per se (A. E. Gottfried et al., 1988; Hoffman, 1989). The role of maternal employment in children's development is now viewed as being embedded in very complex psychological, social, and work contexts (A. E. Gottfried & A. W. Gottfried, 1988; Hoffman, 1989).

There is continuing research to identify the specific conditions and contexts that modify the impact of employment on children (A. E. Gottfried & A. W. Gottfried, 1988; Zedeck, 1992). Factors that are currently of interest include the work attitudes of the family, occupations, work and family schedules, parental and sex-role attitudes of the parents, role strain, work–family spillover, work conditions, the anxiety states of the family members, the age and sex of the child, family ethnicity, marital and/or partner status, socioeconomic status, home environment, child-care conditions, and the specific type of developmental outcome (Goldsmith, 1989; A. E. Gottfried, 1988; Zedeck, 1992).

In our last book (A. E. Gottfried & A. W. Gottfried, 1988), we concluded that maternal employment is not a detriment to children. This is an important conclusion that represents a major conceptual step forward in the field. Parents and children seem to be resilient in meeting the demands of child rearing in the context of parental employment. Maternal employment is a *family* issue, not just a *women's* issue (A. E. Gottfried & A. W. Gottfried, 1988). Based on the literature reviews and the longitudinal evidence presented by us and by all of the contributing authors in our prior book (A. E. Gottfried & A. W. Gottfried, 1988), we concluded that the most favorable family setting is one in which the mothers are satisfied with their roles (whether they are employed or nonemployed); in which the home environment is intellectually stimulating and emotionally responsive to the children; in which stress is reduced and father involvement is increased; and in which the parents in employed-mother families experience little work–family interference and stable child care arrangements (A. E. Gottfried & A. W. Gottfried, 1988).

In our prior work, we also called for further research concerning the balance of factors regarding the families of employed and nonemployed mothers. It is our view that, in two-parent families, both maternal and paternal employment need to be examined in the family setting with regard to the children's development. Hence, in this chapter, we not only report on our longitudinal research regarding maternal employment, family environment, and children's development through age 12 but also examine dimensions of both the mothers' and the fathers' involvement with their children, as well as aspects of their employment in relation to their children's development.

DUAL-EARNER FAMILIES

There has been an increasing interest in dual-earner families (Gilbert & Dancer, 1992; Hoffman, 1989; Mortimer & London, 1984; Silberstein, 1992). This phenomenon creates new challenges for the family with children. Whereas the economic resources of the family are increased, so are the demands of combining work and family roles engaged in by the parents.

Of particular interest with regard to the current research is the degree of participation of the fathers in dual-earner families. A. E. Gottfried et al. (1988) found that, when the mothers were employed, the fathers were more involved with their young children than when the mothers were not employed. Greater father involvement was also positively related to an increased maturity in children's adaptive and social behaviors. These findings were obtained when the children were ages 6 and 7. A pertinent issue concerns fathers' involvement as children get older. Do fathers in dual-earner families continue to remain more involved? This question is addressed in the present research, as we have continuously measured fathers' involvement across the study. Fathers' participation in interaction with their children and child-care responsibilities is higher when the mother is employed and increases as the mothers' employment hours increase (Baruch & Barnett, 1983; Biernat & Wortman, 1991; Darling-Fisher & Tiedje, 1990; Gilbert, 1985; Hoffman, 1989; Russell, 1982; Staines & Pleck, 1983). Hoffman (1989) suggested that the increased father involvement with children in dual-earner families may be beneficial in the children's development and may offset the effects of their mothers' employment. The present research provides an opportunity to examine fathers' involvement with their children in dual-earner families through childhood and early adolescence.

Another important issue with regard to dual-earner families concerns dimensions of the parents' work and their relationship to the children's development. Employment status is a heterogeneous category, and employment differs with respect to such factors as occupation, work hours, and flexibility of work hours. Although maternal employment status itself may have no relationship to children's development, more differentiated aspects of the employment role may have important implications for children's development.

The issues of particular developmental interest in the current research concern the number of work hours, work flexibility, and the parental occupation. These dimensions of the work role have developmental importance as they potentially affect the amount of time the parents have available to spend with the child and may also affect the provision of cognitive stimulation and social-emotional responsiveness. Our interest in the developmental impact of work hours and scheduling is highlighted by Kanter's assertion (1977) that the amount of time and the timing of occupational commitments are "among the most obvious and important ways occupational life affects family life" (p. 31). We examine both mothers' and fathers' work roles with regard to these dimensions.

Our previous research findings with regard to work hours and mothers' occupations (A. E. Gottfried *et al.*, 1988) also indicated the developmental importance of these factors. In our earlier work, the number of mothers' work hours was negatively related to children's achievement at ages 5 and 6, and to the environmental variable of educational stimulation at age 7 (A. E. Gottfried *et al.* 1988). However, none of the other child-outcome or environmental measures were related to maternal work hours. There have been other suggestions in the literature that longer work hours are negatively related to family processes. Owen and Cox (1988) found that mothers of infants reported more anxiety when they worked more than 40 hours a week. Staines and Pleck (1983) found that individuals who reported a high number of work hours also reported higher work/family conflict.

However, other factors may provide a balance for long work hours. A. E. Gottfried *et al.* (1988) found that mothers who had longer work hours also had higher occupational status. Occupational status was *positively* related to children's intelligence, achievement, and maturity of social behavior. Mothers with higher occupational status had higher educational attitude scores with regard to their children. Therefore, mothers' occupational status and work hours appeared to balance each other with regard to their impact on the child's development and home environment.

So far, there have been no research reports linking parental work flexibility to children's developmental outcomes; only family stress or time spent with children has been examined. As there is an opportunity for flexibility in work hours, such as in the increase in the availability of flexible work hours in some work settings (Hughes & Galinsky, 1988; Kanter, 1977; Zedeck & Mosier, 1990), we reasoned that work flexibility would allow parents to be more available to their children, and that this availability would be favorable for the children and the home environment. Staines and Pleck (1983) reported that there was significantly less work/family conflict when individuals had more autonomy and greater control over their work schedules. Time spent with their children was facilitated when the parents had greater control over their schedules, and this was particularly true of those with nontraditional shifts (Staines & Pleck, 1983). Bohen and Viveros-Long (1981) reported contradictory findings, in that parents who had the option of choosing a flexible schedule did not report spending more time with their children. However, the absence of direct measures of parents' perceptions of autonomy may have contributed to the negative findings. Nevertheless, those who used flextime were more satisfied with their work schedules, and spending more time with family members was the most important reason offered by flextime participants. In the present research, both mothers' and fathers' work flexibility were examined in relation to their children's development and environment, through childhood and early adolescence.

Our earlier work focused predominantly on maternal employment and children's development. The present research expanded this focus to include data regarding fathers' work roles as well. For both mothers and fathers, our longitudinal data permit us to study the relationships between parental work roles, children's development, and home environment through early adolescence. By including both mothers and fathers, this research provides an important developmental contribution that prior research on dual-earner families has not addressed.

ISSUES OF THE PRESENT RESEARCH

Longitudinal Research

Longitudinal research provides an opportunity to examine prospective long-term relationships and the impact of maternal employment on children's development, home environment, and family processes (Galambos, Petersen, & Lenerz, 1988; Goldberg & Easterbrooks, 1988; A. E. Gottfried et al., 1988; Hock, DeMeis, & McBride, 1988; Lerner & Galambos, 1988; Owen & Cox, 1988). This opportunity is particularly important in this field of study because it allows an examination of the significance of maternal employment with respect to the child's development over a period of time, rather than at a single point in time. The replicability of effects over time is necessary to determine if the effects are transient or stable. Another important aspect of conducting maternal employment research longitudinally has been the attempt to discern if there are any "sleeper effects"; that is, if there are no significant effects of maternal employment at an earlier point in time, there may be an association between maternal employment and subsequent children's development.

This chapter addresses longitudinal relationships between maternal employment and children's development from infancy (age 1 year) through early adolescence (age 12 years). These relationships are examined across a broad array of developmental domains, including intelligence, academic achievement, social and emotional functioning, motivation and self-concept, and behavioral adjustment. Our study is unique in providing long-term data across such a wide array of developmental functioning in children. In addition to longitudinal data, the contemporaneous relationships between maternal employment and children's development at ages 8–12 are reported. The major issues with regard to the longitudinal study of maternal employment and children's development concerns whether any differences, if obtained, are due to maternal employment *per se* and not to other confounded factors, and whether any effects obtained are stable or transient.

Home Environment

In our prior work, we examined the impact of maternal employment on the children's home environment (A. E. Gottfried *et al.*, 1988). There were few differences between the employed and nonemployed mothers with regard to the stimulation and social-emotional responsiveness of the home from infancy through early childhood. However, employed mothers held higher educational attitudes (higher aspirations, less TV viewing, and more out-of-school lessons) for their children from the preschool years on, and the fathers were more involved during early childhood. Children's academic achievement, social maturity, and behavioral adjustment were favorably related to their mothers' educational attitudes in contemporaneous and longitudinal analyses. Fathers' involvement was favorably related to the children's social maturity.

In our present research, we continue the study of maternal employment and children's home environment. The issues that are addressed with regard to home environment are: (1) Over the elementary and preadolescent years, are there any differences in children's home environment as related to maternal employment *per se?* (2) Does earlier maternal employment have any relationship to subsequent home environment from infancy through early adolescence?

Dual-Earner Families

A substantial proportion of our sample consisted of dual-earner families. Though dual-career and dual-worker families have been distinguished along the dimension of long-term commitment for the former (Gilbert & Dancer, 1992), in the present study all such families are generically called *dual-earner* because we have a continuum of occupations represented on the Hollingshead Four-Factor Scale, rather than a categorized variable. Consistent with our purpose as stated above, we address the relationships between specific aspects of the mothers' and fathers' work roles and the children's development and home environment. Specifically, parental occupation, number of weekly work hours, and flexibility of scheduling are addressed.

Fathers' and mothers' involvement with their children is also examined with regard to dual-earner families. Based on our own data (A. E. Gottfried *et al.*, 1988) and prior research reported above, fathers were expected to be more involved in dual-earner families. We have a unique opportunity to study father and mother involvement and its relationship to children's development across the childhood years, as we have repeatedly measured this variable throughout the course of the study.

METHOD

Background of the Fullerton Longitudinal Study

In the fall of 1979, a longitudinal investigation of children's development was initiated. One hundred and thirty 1-year-olds and their families were selected from birth notifications of hospitals surrounding California State University, Fullerton. The only selection criteria were that the infants have no neurological or visual abnormalities. (A. W. Gottfried & Gilman, 1983). All infants were full term and of normal birth weight. Additionally, all the families spoke English. The return rate of the subjects never fell below 80% over the course of the study. However, in specific analyses, *N*'s vary because of completeness of data. Overall, we maintained a high continuation rate in the study. Every attempt was made to obtain complete data for all children and families.

Of the 130 infants recruited at 1 year, 52% were male and 48% were female; 117 were white and 13 were from other racial groups. The sample represented a wide range of middle-class families as measured by the Hollingshead Four Factor Index of Social Status (A. W. Gottfried, 1985; Hollingshead, 1975). Other major contemporary socioeconomic indicators corroborated this appraisal. However, the Hollingshead index was used in our analyses because it incorporates the occupation of employed mothers into its computation of family social status (A. W. Gottfried, 1985). On the average, the parents were in their late 20s when the study children were born. Of the 130 infants, 53% were firstborns, and 47% were second- through fifth-borns.

Overall the composition of the sample with regard to gender and birth order was similar across the study. At ages 8 and 12, the percentages of boys and girls were 58% and 42%, respectively, and 55% and 45%, respectively. Birth order percentages were similar across the study.

Employment Status and Demographic Characteristics

The number of mother–child participants with respect to maternal employment data was 106, 106, 104, 103, and 100 at the 8-, 9-, 10-, 11-, and 12-year assessments, respectively. The percentage of employed mothers was 71%, 68%, 75%, 84%, and 80% at ages 8, 9, 10, 11, and 12, respectively. As reported in A. E. Gottfried *et al.* (1988), the percentage of employed mothers ranged from 36.2% to 64.2% between 1 through 7 years of age. Our sample was consistent with national trends (see Chapter 1), indicating the prevalence of maternal employment. Further, as the children became older, the percentage of maternal employment increased. Part-time and full-time employment status were merged in all analyses, as our previous research and the research of others presented in our previous book (A. E. Gottfried & A. W. Gottfried, 1988) revealed no significant differences in child or environmental measures in relation to employment schedule.

In order to determine if the mothers' employment status (employed vs. nonemployed) was significantly associated with their marital status (married vs. not married), the child's sex, and the number of children in the home, chi-square analyses were conducted. In order to minimize Type I errors, the alpha level was adjusted with a sequential Bonferroni correction for the three sets of analyses. Therefore, for analyses with marital status, child's sex, and number of children in the home, .05 was divided by 5, and the p value indicating the largest difference was tested. Subsequent p values were tested by dividing .05 by the number of remaining tests until nonsignificance was reached. There were no significant associations between maternal employment status and marital status, the child's sex, and the number of children in the home. The percentage of mothers in this study who were married was 88% at age 8 and 81% at age 12.

Demographic data regarding the sample from ages 8–12 are presented in Table 1, including socioeconomic status, fathers' occupational status, mothers' and fathers' educational level, and mothers' occupations. Differences between the employed and nonemployed groups were tested with t-tests, with attainment of significance adjusted with the Bonferroni procedure described above. Significance is noted only if the critical value of t was equal to or less than that obtained by means of the Bonferroni procedure. A consistent difference emerged in that the socioeconomic status of families with nonemployed mothers was significantly higher than that of families with employed mothers at all ages except 9 and 12 (which approached significance but missed the level when the Bonferroni correction was used). There were no significant differences between the samples with regard to fathers' occupation and mothers' and fathers' education (except at age 10, when fathers in nonworking-mother families had a higher education). Further, the difference between mothers' and fathers' occupations were not significantly different as assessed by matched-group t tests. Information about the sample through age 7 is presented in A. E. Gottfried et al. (1988).

Procedure

From ages 8–12, the children received a comprehensive battery of psychological tests once each year in the university laboratory. The battery included major standardized instruments with high reliability and validity. Each battery was individually administered. The breadth

Table 1. Comparison of Demographic
Variables by Maternal Employment Status[a]

Age of child and demographic factors	Maternal employment status			
	Nonemployed	Employed	t	df
8 years				
SES	53.2 (9.7)	48.2 (8.7)	2.6**	104
Mothers' occupation		5.9 (1.6)		
Fathers' occupation	7.2 (1.4)	6.7 (1.9)	1.4	97
Mothers' education	14.2 (1.8)	14.6 (2.1)	–1.1	104
Fathers' education	15.2 (2.6)	15.2 (2.3)	.1	101
9 years				
SES	52.6 (11.6)	48.9 (8.8)	1.8	104
Mothers' occupation		6.2 (1.5)		
Fathers' occupation	7.2 (1.3)	6.7 (1.8)	1.3	94
Mothers' education	14.3 (1.8)	14.6 (2.2)	–.7	104
10 years				
SES	55.5 (8.9)	48.4 (8.4)	3.6***	101
Mothers' occupation		6.2 (1.4)		
Fathers' occupation	7.3 (1.5)	6.4 (1.9)	2.1[b]	93
Mothers' education	14.4 (1.7)	14.7 (2.2)	–.7	102
Fathers' education	16.4 (2.6)	15.0 (2.2)	2.5*	96
11 years				
SES	54.3 (8.9)	48.0 (8.1)	2.9**	101
Mothers' occupation		6.1 (1.4)		
Fathers' occupation	7.5 (1.5)	6.4 (2.0)	2.0[b]	91
Mothers' education	14.6 (2.1)	14.6 (2.1)	–.1	101
Fathers' education	16.1 (3.0)	15.1 (2.2)	1.5	97
12 years				
SES	54.2 (10.2)	49.1 (7.9)	2.4[b]	95
Mothers' occupation		6.3 (1.4)		
Fathers' occupation	7.3 (1.8)	6.4 (2.2)	1.5	90
Mothers' education	14.5 (2.1)	14.9 (2.2)	–.7	95
Fathers' education	15.7 (3.2)	15.2 (2.3)	.9	92

[a]Standard deviations are presented in parentheses. All t tests are two-tailed.
[b]Nonsignificant after Bonferroni correction was applied.
*$p < .05$ **$p < .01$ ***$p < .001$

of developmental domains included cognitive, achievement, behavioral, social and emotional, and academic motivation.

During the laboratory assessment, the mothers completed surveys, questionnaires, and standardized inventories regarding maternal employment, family demographics, the quality of family relationships, home environment, and children's behavioral functioning. Teachers also completed standardized scales pertaining to classroom behavioral functioning. At age 8, a direct observation of the home was conducted to assess the home environment.

Before age 8, the children were assessed in the laboratory once every 6 months from 1 to 3.5 years, and yearly from age 5 onward. The mothers completed surveys, questionnaires, and inventories at the time of the laboratory assessment. Home visits occurred at 15 and 39 months, at which time the home environment was directly assessed. Complete details can be found in A. E. Gottfried *et al.* (1988) and A. W. Gottfried & A. E. Gottfried (1984).

Although the mothers were the primary respondents across the years of investigation, the fathers who were living in the home were asked to participate in the eight-year assessment. We anticipated that the fathers would add effectively to the wealth of data that were being collected on the families involved in the project. A packet of forms was sent to the fathers, and in it were the same surveys and questionnaires that the mothers had completed in the lab. The fathers completed these forms and returned them to the lab. Of the 106 families participating in the eight-year assessment, 10 had no father figure in the home. Of the remaining 96, 7 had a father figure who was either a stepfather or a live-in partner, and these dads were included in the analyses of father data unless otherwise noted. Of the available fathers, 69% completed the Family Functioning Inventory and the Home Environment Survey, 93% completed the Parent/Child Activities scale, and 65% completed the Family Environment Scale. These measures are described below.

Measures

Across all measures, higher scores corresponded to a greater amount of the quality being assessed. The descriptions below present the major features of the measures.

Parental Employment

At each age, the mothers completed a survey regarding their employment status, their occupation, the flexibility of their employment, and the number of hours they were employed weekly during the weekday and the weekend (rounded to the nearest hour). They also completed the same information regarding the child's father (father living in the home). Employment status was coded as nonworking or working (part- and full-time employment were combined). Occupation was coded by use of the Hollingshead Four Factor Index. Flexibility was rated on a 6-point scale ranging from not flexible (1) to very flexible (6). The number of hours was scored as the total number of hours reported. There were very few parents who reported weekend work hours at each age. Hence, weekend work was not analyzed further, as it did not provide enough variability.

Intellectual Performance

The Wechsler Intelligence Scale for Children—Revised (WISC-R; Wechsler, 1974) was administered at ages 8 and 12. Results for the Full Scale IQ score are presented.

Academic Achievement and Motivation

The Woodcock-Johnson Psycho-Educational Battery (Woodcock & Johnson, 1977) was administered at ages 8, 9, and 10; the Woodcock-Johnson Psycho-Educational Battery—Revised (Woodcock & Johnson, 1989) was administered at ages 11 and 12. Grade-corrected percentile scores in reading, math, and knowledge (science, social studies, and humanities) were available at ages 8 and 9; at ages 10–12, grade-corrected percentile scores in reading and math were available.

Teachers completed the Teacher Version of the Child Behavior Checklist (CBCL; Achenbach, 1991b). Teachers rated the children's academic competency in reading and math on a 5-point scale ranging from far below grade level (1) to far above grade level (5). The teachers also rated the children on their classroom functioning using a 7-point scale, including how hard working the child was, how appropriately the child was behaving, how much the child was learning, and how happy the child was.

At ages 9 and 10, the children's academic intrinsic motivation was assessed through the administration of the Children's Academic Intrinsic Motivation Inventory (CAIMI; A. E. Gottfried, 1986). A downward extension of this instrument, the Young Children's Academic Intrinsic Motivation Inventory (Y-CAIMI; A. E. Gottfried, 1990) was administered at age 8. Both instruments measure children's enjoyment of learning and mastery orientation across subject areas, and school in general. The children rated their own academic intrinsic motivation in both inventories. The CAIMI is a reliable and valid instrument comprising five subscales; reading, math, social studies, science, and school in general. The Y-CAIMI is a reliable and valid instrument comprising four subscales; reading, math, school in general, and enjoyment of difficult schoolwork. A total Y-CAIMI score is also computed by summing subscales.

The children's academic anxiety was measured through the children's own ratings of items from the Children's Academic Anxiety Inventory (A. E. Gottfried, 1985) which assessed their worry about taking tests and doing well in school. Areas measured at age 8 were reading, math, school in general, and total score; and reading, math, social studies, science, and school in general were measured at ages 9 and 10.

Social-Emotional

Children's social maturity was assessed with the Vineland Adaptive Behavior Scales (Sparrow, Balla, & Cicchetti, 1984) at ages 8 and 9. Presented here is the total adaptive standard score on the Vineland, which measures the social sufficiency of children in communication, daily living skills, and socialization.

Children's self-concept was measured with the Baltimore Self-Esteem Questionnaire (BSEQ; Simmons, Rosenberg, & Rosenberg, 1973) at ages 9–12. The BSEQ produces a global index of self-esteem. The children rated themselves on six statements, and the scale score is the sum across the ratings. At ages 9 and 10 the nonacademic scales of the Self-Description Questionnaire (SDQ; Marsh, 1988; Marsh, Parker, & Smith, 1983) were administered. There are four nonacademic subscales: Physical Ability, Physical Appearance, Peer Relationships, and Parent Relationships. These four subscales and their sum, which formed a General scale, were analyzed. The children rated themselves as to how true each statement was about themselves. Each scale score is the sum of eight items.

Behavioral Adjustment

From ages 8 through 12, the parent version of the Child Behavior Checklist (Achenbach, 1991a) was administered to the mothers. Teachers also completed the Teacher Version of the Child Behavior Checklist (Achenbach, 1991b). (The N for analyses regarding the teachers' data varied depending on the completeness of their inventories across items and ages on the behavioral adjustment and academic achievement sections of the Child Behavior Checklist. The maximum N was 92, and the minimum N was 60.) Both inventories required the respondent to rate the child on a variety of behaviors that are included in different scales and two broad-band scores: internalizing and externalizing. Analyses were conducted on the internal, external, and total behavior-problem scores. The results were the same for the subscales and the total score, and only the total score is presented.

Home and Family Environment

Because the study of environment-development relationships has been a major focus of our research (A. W. Gottfried & A. E. Gottfried, 1984; A. E. Gottfried *et al.*, 1988), a variety of environmental assessments were conducted. Children's homes were visited at 15 months, 39 months, and 8 years, at which times the infancy, preschool, and elementary versions of the Home Observation for Measurement of the Environment (HOME; Bradley, Caldwell, Rock, Hamrick, & Harris, 1988; Caldwell & Bradley, 1984) were administered. The HOME scales provide reliable and valid measurement of social-emotional and physical stimulation in the home, as well as stimulation of child competencies (Elardo & Bradley, 1981; A. W. Gottfried & A. E. Gottfried, 1984) through direct observation and interview with the caretaker. The use of the HOME scales at three ages allowed an investigation of longitudinal and contemporaneous relationships between maternal employment status and the children's development. The use of the infancy and preschool versions of the HOME is extensively described in A. E. Gottfried *et al.* (1988). The total score from these two earlier versions was used in prospective longitudinal analyses in the present study to be described below.

The elementary version of the HOME consists of 59 items forming 8 subscales and a total score: Emotional and Verbal Responsivity; Encouragement of Maturity; Emotional Climate; Growth Fostering Materials and Experiences; Provision for Active Stimulation; Family Participation in Developmentally Stimulating Experiences; Paternal Involvement; and Aspects of Physical Environment.

Home Environment Survey

In order to have a continuous measurement of the environment over the course of this research, and to tap environmental features not measured by the HOME and focusing more specifically on educational stimulation and parental involvement, we developed our own Home Environment Survey (HES; Bathurst, 1988; A. E. Gottfried et al., 1988). This survey is based on theories and our own conceptualization of the role of the proximal environment in children's development (A. E. Gottfried et al., 1988; A. W. Gottfried & A. E. Gottfried, 1984; A. W. Gottfried, A. E. Gottfried, Bathurst, & Guerin, 1994). The mothers completed the Home Environment Survey when the children were ages 5, 7, 8, 9, 10, and 12. The data on ages 5 and 7 were reported earlier (A. E. Gottfried et al., 1988).

At each age, items on the HES were factor-analyzed with varimax rotations for data reduction purposes to produce the most simple and meaningful structure from the data. Items were retained if they loaded at .30 or higher. Items were slightly different at each age to accommodate the changing environments of children with their advancement in age. At age 8, 20 items formed six factors: Learning Opportunities; Reading Involvement with Child; TV Time; Mothers' Time Involvement with Child; Fathers' Time Involvement with Child; and Academic Assistance. We decided to eliminate this last factor because it included only two items, so that internal-consistency estimates were low, and also because one of the items, in hindsight, was ambiguous in meaning. At age 9, 21 items formed five factors: Learning Opportunities; Cultural Enhancement; Reading Involvement with Child; Mothers' Time Involvement with Child; and Fathers' Time Involvement with Child. At age 10, 16 items made up 4 factors: Learning Opportunities; Reading Involvement with Child; Mothers' Time Involvement with Child; and Fathers' Time Involvement with Child. At age 12, 21 items formed four factors: Learning Opportunities; Cultural Enhancement; Mothers' Time Involvement with Child; and Fathers' Time Involvement with Child. Additional items analyzed separately were educational aspirations for the child (ages 8–12) and amount of TV viewing by the child, the mother, and the father (age 12).

In order to distinguish between time spent with the child during the school week and on weekends, the mothers were asked to report the amount of time (hours and minutes) they spent taking care of and doing things with their child on an average school day and on an average weekend day. These data were collected at all ages. The mothers also reported on the amount of time the fathers spent with the child for these variables. The fathers also reported about themselves and the mothers when the child was age 8.

Reliability and validity for the HES were investigated throughout the course of the study (e.g., Bathurst, 1988) and showed predominantly moderate to moderately strong stability and internal consistency. The HES showed strong construct, concurrent, and predictive validity with other environmental scales, and many measures of achievement, intelligence, and social maturity indicated that the HES scales related to independent measures in a theoretically meaningful and predictable fashion (Bathurst, 1988; A. E. Gottfried *et al.*, 1988).

In addition to the HES scales, we developed items to measure the mothers' and the fathers' involvement in sharing specific activities with their child on a regular weekly basis. This Parent/Child Activities Scale was administered to the mothers when the children were ages 8, 9, and 12 and to the fathers when the children were 8. Each parent responded about himself or herself and about the other parent in the home (if one was present). Examples of items are playing games, sports, reading with the child, and teaching academic skills to assess the amount of involvement in a variety of activities. The scale consists of 17 items, which are summed. At each age, there was a mothers' and fathers' total as reported by the mother; at age 8, there was a mothers' and fathers' total as reported by the father.

Family Functioning

The Family Functioning Inventory (Bathurst, 1988) was developed for use at the eight-year assessment so that we could obtain an overall global measure of the quality of family life. Two independent factors were developed. The first scale, Positive Family Functioning, measures familial openness, supportiveness, and cohesiveness. An example item is "Members of our family get along well together." The second scale, Family Regulation, measures familial organization and regulation. An example item is "Rules and regulations are part of our family's routine." We modified the inventory at the 9- and 10-year assessments in order to increase internal consistency estimates; the items have remained consistent since the 10-year assessment. For the period from ages 8 through 12, the median alpha coefficients were .84 for Positive Family Functioning and .65 for Family Regulation. The parents rated the degree to which each statement in the inventory described their family on a scale from 1 (not true) to 6 (very true). The scale scores were computed by averaging the ratings across the items loading on each scale. The mothers completed the inventory at each age; the fathers completed the inventory at the eight-year assessment only.

Family social climate was assessed with the Family Environment Scale (FES; Moos & Moos, 1981), a reliable and valid instrument administered to the mothers at the 8-, 10-, and 12-year assessments, and to the fathers at the 8-year assessment. The FES evaluates 10 family dimensions: cohesion, intellectual-cultural, active-recreational, expressiveness, conflict, moral-religious, control, organization, independence, and achievement orientation.

RESULTS AND DISCUSSION

Contemporaneous Analyses

The primary question investigated was whether maternal employment was significantly related to children's development and home environment at contemporaneous ages (e.g., eight-year maternal employment as related to eight-year developmental and environmental outcomes). Because of the enormity of the data set from ages 8–12, data analyses occurred in two phases consistent with our previous analytic strategy (A. E. Gottfried et al., 1988). The first was a screening phase, in which sets of related outcome variables were subjected to 2 × 2 (Maternal employment status × Sex of child) MANOVA's (individual variables were subjected to 2 × 2 ANOVA's) in order to ascertain if there were any significant differences between employed and nonemployed mothers, and if there was an interaction between maternal employment and child's sex. The sex main effect was of no particular interest in this study and is not reported here. If either the main effect for maternal employment or the interaction between maternal employment and the child's sex were nonsignificant, no further analyses were conducted. If either the main effect or the interaction was significant, the second phase of analysis was conducted, called the follow-up phase. In this phase, significant effects from MANOVA were followed up by regressions to determine if maternal employment status continued to be significant after controlling for socioeconomic status, marital status (married vs. not married), the number of children in the home, and the home environment (the total score from the HOME inventory at age 8 was used). This latter variable was used only for regressions involving child development variables. In regressions designed to follow up the main effects of maternal employment status, the sexes remained combined, and sex was included in the regressions as a predictor in order to be consistent with our prior analyses (A. E. Gottfried *et al.* 1988). In all regressions, criteria variables were the pertinent developmental or environmental variable for which a significant main effect had been obtained. Predictor variables were maternal employment status (entered first, hierarchically) and the relevant control variables (entered stepwise).

In regressions designed to follow up interactions, parallel analyses were conducted separately for boys and girls, as we were interested in whether maternal employment status had different effects for boys and girls. In these regressions, the criterion variable was the developmental or environmental variable for which a significant interaction had been obtained; the predictor variables were maternal employment status, which was entered first hierarchically, and socioeconomic status, marital status, the number of children in the home, and the environmental measure (entered into in regressions only for child outcome variables). These latter four variables were entered stepwise.

For all regressions, if maternal employment was significant after the stepwise addition of the latter variables, it is reported below as significant. However, if maternal employment no longer remained significant after the addition of the remaining variables, it is not reported below because the significant main effect or interaction in MANOVA can be considered spurious, as it was confounded with other variables.

Child Development Outcomes

Overwhelmingly, there were no significant differences between the children of employed and nonemployed mothers across the ages and measures. This finding pertained to both boys and girls because interactions between maternal employment and the child's sex were, for the most part, nonsignificant. The findings are summarized in Table 2. Across age, developmental domain, and source of report (testing, parent report, teacher report, or child report), the contemporaneous analyses indicated pervasive nonsignificance of maternal employment status.

Table 2. Summary of Relationships between Maternal Employment Status and Developmental Outcomes in Contemporaneous Analyses

Developmental measure	Ages (years)
Nonsignificant findings	
Intelligence	
WISC-R IQ	8, 12
Achievement and school performance	
Woodcock-Johnson	
Reading	8, 9, 10, 11, 12
Math	8, 9 (boys), 10, 11, 12
Knowledge[a]	8, 9
CBCL teacher ratings[a]	
Reading	8, 9, 10, 11
Math	10, 11
Hard working	8, 9, 10, 11
Learning	8, 9, 10, 11
Behaving	8, 9, 10, 11
Happy	8, 9, 10, 11
Academic motivation	
CAIMI[a] and Y-CAIMI	
All subareas and totals	8, 9, 10
Academic anxiety[a]	
All subareas	8, 9, 10
Total score	8 (boys)
Social-emotional and behavioral	
Vineland Total Adaptive Score[a]	8, 9
Baltimore Self-Esteem[a]	9, 10, 11, 12
Self-Description Questionnaire[a]	9 (girls), 10
CBCL parent total	8, 9, 10, 11, 12
CBCL teacher total[a]	8, 9, 10, 11
Significant findings	
Achievement	
Woodcock-Johnson	
Math	9 (girls)
CBCL teacher ratings	
Math	8, 9
Academic motivation	
Academic Anxiety	
Total	8 (girls)
Social-emotional and behavioral	
Self-Description Questionnaire	9 (boys)

[a]Woodcock-Johnson Knowledge not administered after age 9; CBCL Teacher Ratings not administered after age 11; Y-CAIMI administered at age 8; CAIMI administered at ages 9 and 10; Academic Anxiety Inventory administered at ages 8, 9, and 10; Anxiety total available only at age 8; Baltimore Self-Esteem not administered at age 8; SDQ available for ages 9 and 10.

The few significant findings that were obtained were not generalizable across ages, across domain, or across sex. The significant findings were that, for children of employed mothers, there were: lower math achievement as reported by teachers only at ages 8 and 9; lower math achievement on the Woodcock-Johnson for girls only at age 9; higher academic anxiety on the total score for girls only at age 8; and higher self-concept for boys on the Total score of the SDQ only at age 9. These significant findings are weak, particularly in the context of the pervasive nonsignificant effects of maternal employment status on math achievement across age. Moreover, even within age, there was no consistency in the significant outcome, as math achievement was nonsignificant on the Woodcock-Johnson at age 8 whereas it was significant in teachers' reports on the Child Behavior Checklist. Regarding anxiety, there were no significant effects of maternal employment status at ages 9 and 10 for either sex. Regarding the boys' higher self-esteem at age 9, there were no significant differences at any other age for either sex. Because of the large number of statistical tests that were conducted, we consider these few significant effects to be overshadowed by the consistent pattern of nonsignificance.

Environment

The results for environment were similar to those obtained for developmental outcome. There was pervasive nonsignificance with regard to the effects of maternal employment status on aspects of the home environment across age, sex, and the environmental domain, including stimulation, family climate, cultural and learning opportunities, and family functioning. These results are summarized in Table 3. Hence, maternal employment was found not to be detrimental to children's home environment.

The significant findings were inconsistent and not replicated across age or sex. These included significantly more learning opportunities for boys at age 9, less reading involvement for children at age 10, and greater expressiveness for girls at age 10 when their mothers were employed. Again, one is struck by the lack of significance of these variables at other ages (learning opportunities at ages 8, 10, and 12; reading involvement at ages 8, 9, and 12; and expressiveness at ages 8, 10, and 12). Hence, we interpret these few significant findings as spurious or unreliable.

Table 3. Summary of Relationships between Maternal Employment
Status and Environmental Outcomes in Contemporaneous Analyses[a]

Environmental measure	Ages (years)
Nonsignificant findings	
HOME scales	
Subscales and total	8[b]
Home Environment Survey[b]	
Learning Opportunities	8, 9 (girls), 10
Reading Involvement	8, 9, 12
Cultural Enhancement	9, 12
TV Time	8, 12
Number of Activities	8
Educational Aspirations	8, 9, 11, 12
Family Environment Scale	
Mother's reports	8, 10, 12
Father's reports	8[b]
Family Functioning Inventory: General and regulation factors	
Mother's reports	8, 9, 10, 11, 12
Father's reports	8[b]
Significant findings	
Home Environment Survey	
Learning Opportunities	9 (boys)
Reading Involvement	10
Family Environment Scale	
Expressiveness scale	10 (girls)

[a]Unless otherwise specified, environmental measures were assessed via mothers.
[b]HOME scales administered only at age 8; Home Environment Survey administered at ages 8, 9, 10,
and 12. Reported results in the age column indicate ages at which subscales are available; Family
Environment Survey administered to mothers when children were ages 8, 10, and 12, and to
fathers when children were age 8; Inventory of Family Functioning administered to mothers when
children were ages 8–12, and to fathers when children were age 8.

Prospective Analyses

Prospective analyses were conducted to determine if maternal
employment status had any long-term relationship to the children's
development or home environment. Ages 8 and 12 were used as the
two ages at which developmental and environmental outcomes were
examined, as these were the beginning and end points of the period
examined in this study. Outcomes at age 8 were predicted from maternal employment status from infancy (1 year), preschool (3.5 years),
and the early school years (6 years). At age 12, outcomes were pre-

dicted from each of these three periods, and also from two periods in the middle childhood years (ages 8 and 10).

Analyses were conducted in two phases, as they were in the contemporaneous analyses. In order to determine if there were any significant relationships between maternal employment status and outcomes at ages 8 or 12, 2×2 (Maternal employment status × Child's sex) MANOVA's were conducted on related sets of outcome variables (ANOVA's were conducted on individual outcome variables) from each predictor age to outcomes at ages 8 and 12. For example, at age 8, the WISC-R IQ score was analyzed in three separate ANOVA's that used maternal employment status at 1 year, 3.5 years, and 6 years (the sex of the child was the same in each analysis). At age 12, the WISC-R IQ score was analyzed in five separate ANOVA's that used maternal employment status at 1 year, 3.5 years, 6 years, 8 years, and 10 years. It was not possible to use repeated measures MANOVA or ANOVA, as the individuals who were employed or not employed were not necessarily the same across the ages, and the n of the sample would have been greatly reduced. Because of the number of tests conducted on specific variables in the prospective analyses as opposed to the contemporaneous analyses, we considered using a *post hoc* adjustment, such as Bonferroni. However, the results show that Type I errors were not a problem in this research because of the pervasive absence of significance of maternal employment status from the earlier ages through the later ages, and it was not necessary to modify the p values with a Bonferroni adjustment.

Phase two consisted of the follow-up phase, in which any significant finding was further analyzed by means of multiple regressions in order to determine if maternal employment status would continue to remain significant after controlling for socioeconomic status, marital status, the number of children in the home, the home environment (this latter variable was used only in regressions with developmental measures), and the child's sex (used in regressions with sexes combined). These regressions were conducted prospectively. For example, if at age 8 there was a significant effect of maternal employment status from age 1, the regression was conducted with the 1-year predictors, in which maternal employment status was entered hierarchically on the first step, and the other predictors were entered stepwise in succeeding steps. The environmental measure used was the most contemporaneous Total HOME Inventory score (at 1 year, the infancy measure was used; at 3.5 and 6 years, the preschool measure was used; at 8 and 10 years the elementary measure was used). Using the HOME Total across the ages yielded consistency in the measurement and construct used.

Child Development Measures

As obtained for the contemporaneous analyses, there was a pervasive pattern of nonsignificant findings across measures, indicating no support for the view that there are "sleeper effects" of maternal employment at subsequent ages. A summary of these findings can be found in Table 4.

The few significant findings were inconsistent and were not replicated by other prospective analyses. The significant findings at age 8 were that, when the mothers were employed at age 6, the girls had higher math anxiety, the children had fewer behavior problems as reported by their mothers, and they had more behavior problems as reported by their teachers. These latter two effects for behavior problems are inconsistent with each other and were not replicated by the 1- and 3.5-year prospective analyses to age 8 data, nor in the 12-year prospective analyses for mothers' reports and contemporaneous analyses for both mothers' and teachers' reports. Higher math anxiety in girls of employed mothers at age 6 was not replicated by prospective analyses from maternal employment status at 1 and 3.5 years, nor by contemporaneous analyses at 8, 9, and 10 years. At age 12, there was a single significant finding: Boys had lower self-esteem on the BSEQ when the mother had been employed at age 1. This finding was not replicated at any other age. Hence, it is our conclusion these four significant findings were sporadic results attributable to the large number of analyses conducted.

Environment

The prospective analyses for home environment were virtually all nonsignificant. These results are summarized in Table 5. The significant findings were that, for girls whose mothers had been employed when they were age 3.5, there were higher regulation scores on the Family Functioning Inventory at age 8, and that when the mothers had been employed when the children were age 1, the number of activities engaged in at age 8 was higher, the educational aspiration for boys at age 12 were higher, and the regulation scores for girls on the Family Functioning Inventory at age 12 were higher.

Table 4. Summary of Relationships between Maternal Employment
Status and Developmental Outcomes in Prospective Analyses

Developmental outcome measures	Prospective analyses: Ages (years)
Nonsignificant findings	
Prospective analyses from ages 1, 3.5, and 6, to 8 years:	
Intelligence	
WISC-R IQ	1, 3.5, 6
Achievement and school performance	
Woodcock-Johnson	
Reading	1, 3.5, 6
Math	1, 3.5, 6
Knowledge	1, 3.5, 6
CBCL teacher ratings	
Reading	1, 3.5, 6
Math	1, 3.5, 6
Hard working	1, 3.5, 6
Learning	1, 3.5, 6
Behaving	1, 3.5, 6
Happy	1, 3.5, 6
Academic motivation	
Y-CAIMI subareas and total	1, 3.5, 6
Academic anxiety	
Reading, general, and total scores	1, 3.5, 6
Math	1, 3.5, 6 (boys)
Social-emotional and behavioral	
Vineland total adaptive score	1, 3.5, 6
CBCL parent total	1, 3.5
CBCL teacher total	1, 3.5
Significant findings	
Academic motivation	
Academic anxiety: Math	6 (girls)
Social-emotional and behavioral	
CBCL parent total	6
CBCL teacher total	6
Nonsignificant findings	
Prospective analyses from 1, 3.5, 6, 8, and 10, to 12 years	
Intelligence	
WISC-R IQ	1, 3.5, 6, 8, 10
Achievement and school performance	
Woodcock-Johnson	
Reading	1, 3.5, 6, 8, 10
Math	1, 3.5, 6, 8, 10

(*Continued*)

Table 4. (*Continued*)

Developmental outcome measures	Prospective analyses: Ages (years)
Social-emotional and behavioral	
Baltimore Self-Esteem	1 (girls), 3.5, 6, 8, 10
CBCL parent total	1, 3.5, 6, 8, 10

Significant findings	
Social-emotional and behavioral	
Baltimore Self-Esteem	1 (boys)

When viewed in the context of the vast amount of nonsignificance across ages, genders, and measures, these few individual findings do not alter our conclusion that maternal employment status is unrelated to children's environments longitudinally from infancy through early adolescence.

Consistency of Employment

In our prior work, the pattern of the mothers' employment consistency was examined with regard to whether consistent and inconsistent patterns of employment or nonemployment were associated with developmental or environmental outcomes. Consistency bore little relationship to either type of outcome. It was our intention to examine this issue in the present study as well. However, these analyses were not possible because, by the time the children were 12 years old, there was only one mother who had been consistently not employed, and only three mothers had been consistently employed. These findings appear largely attributable to the increase of maternal employment over the course of the study, which increased the number of women who were inconsistently employed, as mothers who had not previously been employed joined the work force. These findings support the views that women's work-force participation shows inconsistent patterns (Maret, 1983).

Parental Involvement with Child: Time and Activities

In our prior work, we found that the fathers' involvement with their children was greater in mother-employed families. In order to follow up this finding over the course of the study in a manner

Table 5. Summary of Relationships between Maternal Employment
Status and Environmental Outcomes in Prospective Analyses[a]

Environmental outcome measure	Prospective analyses: Age (years)
Nonsignificant findings	
Prospective analyses from 1, 3.5, and 6, to 8 years	
HOME scales	
Subscales and total	1, 3.5, 6
Home Environment Survey	
Learning Opportunities	1, 3.5, 6
Reading Involvement	1, 3.5, 6
TV Time	1, 3.5, 6
Number of Activities	3.5, 6
Educational Aspiration	1, 3.5, 6
Family Environment Scale	
Mothers' reports	1, 3.5, 6
Fathers' reports	1, 3.5, 6
Family Functioning Inventory	
General factor	
Mothers' reports	1, 3.5, 6
Fathers' reports	1, 3.5, 6
Regulation factor	
Mothers' reports	1, 3.5 (boys), 6
Fathers' reports	1, 3.5, 6
Significant findings	
Home Environment Survey: Number of activities	1
Family Functioning Inventory	
Mothers' reports: Regulation factor	3.5 (girls)
Nonsignificant findings	
Prospective analyses from 1, 3.5, 6, 8, and 10, to 12 years	
Home Environment Survey	
Cultural Enhancement	1, 3.5, 6, 8, 10
Reading Involvement	1, 3.5, 6, 8, 10
TV Time	
Child watches	1, 3.5, 6, 8, 10
Mother watches	1, 3.5, 6, 10
Father watches	1, 3.5, 6, 8, 10
Educational aspiration	1 (girls), 3.5, 6, 8, 10
Family Environment Scale	
All subscales	1, 3.5, 6, 8, 10
Family Functioning Inventory	
General factor	1, 3.5, 6, 8, 10
Regulation factor	1 (boys), 3.5, 6, 8, 10

(Continued)

Table 5. (*Continued*)

Environmental outcome measure	Prospective analyses: Age (years)
Significant findings	
Home Environment Survey	
Educational Aspiration	1 (boys)
Family Functioning Inventory	
Regulation factor	1 (girls)

[a]Unless otherwise specified, environment was assessed via mothers.

consistent with our emphasis on the balance of roles between mothers and fathers, data were collected from ages 8 through 12 concerning both fathers' and mothers' involvement, including both the time spent and the activities engaged in with the child.

The time spent with the child was differentiated into the amount of time spent on school days and on the weekends so that we could determine if there would be any differences in the role of maternal employment in the time spent with the child both during the week, when parents were working and children were in school, and on the weekends, when almost all the parents were not working and children were not in school. These data were rounded to the nearest .5 hour.

A total score of time involvement with the child based on the items described above was computed for mothers and fathers at each age. This total also included an item regarding the number of days the parent spent discussing schoolwork with the child. Additionally, in order to detect differences between the weekday and weekend hours, we conducted analyses of the items regarding time spent with the child on school days and weekends. On the composite total scores, individual items were converted to stanines in order to equate the scale of measurement across the items. For the individual items, the actual amount of time reported was used.

In addition to time involvement with the child, analyses were conducted on the Parent/Child Activities Scale. When the child was age 8, both mothers and fathers living in the home completed this scale. Further, the mothers reported about themselves and the fathers, and the fathers reported about themselves and the mothers. For ages 9–12, only the mothers completed the items, and they reported about themselves and the fathers.

For both the contemporaneous and prospective analyses of these data, for consistency with the analyses reported in this chapter and in our prior work (A. E. Gottfried *et al.*, 1988), we used the two-phase analytic strategy detailed above. MANOVA (of related items) or ANOVA (of individual items) was conducted, followed by regressions for significant main effects of maternal employment status or for the interaction between maternal employment status and the child's sex. Hence, significant effects are reported only if they were significant in the regression analyses. For clarity of presentation, the results of the univariate *F* are presented in the text.

Contemporaneous Analyses

Contemporaneous analyses were conducted on the parents' time involvement with their children at ages 8, 9, 10, and 12 years, and on parent–child-shared activities at ages 8, 9, and 12 years.

The results clearly indicated greater time involvement of the fathers with their children when the mothers were employed. At all ages, the fathers in mother-employed families spent more time with their children than the fathers in families in which the mother was not employed, although this effect attained statistical significance only at ages 8 and 12. Further, the fact that these significant results occurred above and beyond the control variables shows that the fathers' time involvement was uniquely related to maternal employment status. The total time the fathers spent with their children was significantly higher when the mothers were employed at age 8, F $(1,88) = 4.40$, $p = .04$, and at age 12, F $(1,78) = 5.26$, $p = .02$. The means for total time, reported in stanines for employed versus nonemployed mothers, were 5.02 and 4.30, respectively, at age 8, and 5.10 and 4.20, respectively, at age 12. (Stanines were computed only on the mothers' reports of the fathers' time involvement). The similarity of these scores at ages 8 and 12 is interesting and does not suggest a decrease in the fathers' time involvement as the children got older. At age 8, the time the fathers spent with their children on school days was significantly greater when the mothers were employed than when they were not employed. For mothers' reports, F $(1,88) = 6.45$, $p = .02$, and for fathers' reports, F $(1,63) = 9.29$, $p = .003$. The means (reported in hours) for employed- and nonemployed-mother families were 2.13 and 1.52, respectively (mothers' reports), and 2.28 and 1.20, respectively (fathers' reports). Whereas the findings for the time spent with the children on school days reached statistical significance only at age 8, the means were in the same direction across the ages. The similarity of the mothers' and the fathers' reports is noteworthy inasmuch as the parents completed the inventories separately. This finding supports the validity of reports from mothers and fathers with regard to these variables. The amount of weekend time the fathers spent with their children was not significantly different for employed- and nonemployed-mother families. There were no sex differences in the time variables.

Regarding the fathers' sharing of activities with their children, a significant interaction between maternal employment status and the child's sex for the fathers' reports was obtained at age 8, F (1,83) = 7.86, $p < .01$. The follow-up regressions revealed that the fathers shared significantly more activities with their sons in mother-employed than in mother-nonemployed families, but there were no significant differences with regard to maternal employment status for daughters. Means, reported as the total number of activities, for mother-employed and mother-nonemployed families were 12.22 and 9.44, respectively. There were no other significant differences regarding the fathers' activities.

Regarding the mothers' involvement with their children, there were no significant main effects for maternal employment status in any time or activity variable. At ages 8 and 12, maternal employment status interacted with the child's sex in the total amount of time spent with the children, F (1,98) = 4.55, $p = .04$, and F (1,89) = 6.64, $p = .01$, respectively. Follow-up regressions revealed that the employed mothers spent significantly more time with their sons than the nonemployed mothers, but there were no significant differences for daughters with regard to maternal employment status. Means, reported in stanines, for employed and nonemployed mothers when the children were age 8 were 5.17 and 4.24, respectively, and when the children were age 12, the means were 5.41 and 4.60, respectively. A similar, though nonsignificant, pattern was found at age 9.

Regarding the mothers' sharing of activities with their children at age 8, there was a significant interaction between maternal employment status and the child's sex as reported by the fathers, F (1,82) = 4.30, $p = .04$. Follow-up regressions indicated that the employed mothers shared significantly more activities with their sons than did the nonemployed mothers (but there were no significant differences for the daughters). The means were 11.81 and 9.81 for employed and nonemployed mothers, respectively.

In summary, regarding the fathers, the present findings support our previous findings of more paternal involvement with the children in families with employed mothers than in families with nonemployed mothers (A. E. Gottfried *et al.*, 1988) and extend them further, to age 12. These data also support an extensive body of literature indicating that fathers are more involved with their children when the mothers are employed, as reviewed earlier.

These data also support our view of the balance of roles in the homes of employed mothers; that is, fathers spend more time with their children when the mothers are employed. The fathers' time with their children (at age 8) on school days was significantly higher when the mothers were employed, again suggesting the balancing that occurs with regard to parental family roles.

The child gender differences obtained for both the mothers' and the fathers' sharing of activities, and for the mothers' time involvement, were all in the same direction. These findings, although suggesting a pattern, were nevertheless not pervasive across age, measure, or parent. As mothers and fathers responded similarly to sons and daughters, there is no evidence of same-sex preference. The gender difference obtained may have to do with the parents' perceived needs of their children, differential parental press created by boys and girls, or parental attitudes. Additional research will be needed to test both the replicability and generality of these findings and the potential processes explaining them.

Prospective Analyses

In order to determine if maternal employment at an earlier time was related to greater parental involvement at subsequent ages, prospective analyses were conducted. We used our two-phase analytic strategy (MANOVA or ANOVA first, followed by regressions where significance occurred), as described above. The parental involvement variables described in the immediately foregoing section for ages 8 and 12 were the dependent measures. Maternal employment status at ages 1, 3.5, and 6 years was used to predict parental involvement variables at age 8; maternal employment status at ages 1, 3.5, 6, 8, and 10 years was used to predict parental involvement variables at age 12. All results reported below were significant in both phases of the analyses. For clarity of presentation, univariate ANOVA results are presented.

These analyses further supported the increased involvement of fathers with their children when the mothers are employed. The fathers' total time with children at age 8 was significantly predicted by maternal employment status from 3.5 and 6 years. The fathers spent more time with their children at age 8 when the mothers had been employed in these earlier years: at 3.5 years, F $(1,89) = 5.65$, $p = .02$, with the means for working and nonworking mothers being 5.11 and 4.46, respectively (stanines); at 6 years, F $(1,83) = 3.99$, $p < .05$, with means for the working and nonworking mothers being 5.06 and 4.42, respectively (stanines). There were no significant interactions with sex. The father's weekday time involvement with their children at age 8 was significantly related to maternal employment. When the mother's had been employed when the children were aged 3.5 and 6, the fathers spent significantly more weekday time with their children: at 3.5 years, F $(1,89) = 11.98$, $p < .001$; at 6 years, F $(1,83) = 7.64$, $p < .01$. The means for working and nonworking mothers were 2.30 and 1.57 hours, respectively, for 3.5-year analyses, and 2.25 and 1.56 hours, respectively, for 6-year analyses.

Regarding the 12-year data, the fathers' time involvement with their children continued to be predicted by earlier maternal employment status. When the mothers had been employed when the children were aged 3.5 and 8, the fathers spent significantly more time with their children at 12 years: for the 3.5 year analyses, F $(1,79) = 4.17$, $p = .05$; for the 8-year analyses, F $(1,77) = 4.54$, $p = .04$. The means for working and nonworking mothers were 5.25 and 4.58, respectively, in the 3.5-year analyses, and they were 5.19 and 4.44, respectively, in the 8-year analyses (stanines). The fathers' weekday time with their children at age 12 was significantly greater when the mothers had been employed when the children were age 8, F $(1,78) = 8.25$, $p < .01$. The means for working and nonworking mothers were 1.94 and 1.15 hours, respectively. Interactions with sex were not significant. All significant results were obtained with regard to the mothers' reports of the fathers' involvement.

There were no significant prospective effects of maternal employment on parental activities with the children, or on the time mothers spent with their children.

These data are particularly important in showing that fathers' involvement with their children appears to be formed in the earlier years and is persistent over time. In this study, the fathers' increased time involvement when their children were ages 8 and 12 was predicted by maternal employment when the children were 3.5 years, as well as older. The absence of sex differences in the prospective analyses is consistent with our earlier data regarding fathers' involvement through age 7 (A. E. Gottfried *et al.*, 1988) and with the predominance of contemporaneous findings.

Dual-Earner Analyses

In order to determine the balance between the mothers' and the fathers' work roles in relationship to the children's outcomes and environmental factors, multiple regressions were conducted. Ages 8 and 12 were selected as the developmental points in these analyses because these were the beginning and end points of the period focused on in this research. The aspects of parental work role that were analyzed were the mothers' and the fathers' occupational status, the number of work hours during the week, and work flexibility.

The methodology used was designed to maximize N, to minimize multicollinearity between the predictors, and to minimize Type I errors. Hence, the following analytic strategy was used. For each outcome measure, three separate multiple regressions were conducted. The predictors were (1) mothers' and the fathers' occupational status; (2) the mothers' and the fathers' work hours; and (3) the mothers' and the fathers' flexibility. This strategy allowed each of these three aspects of work roles to be analyzed without being influenced by correlations with the other predictors. To minimize Type I error, we examined the significance of the overall R before examining the significance of individual predictors. Only if R was significant were the individual predictors examined for their contribution. Cohen and Cohen (1983) recommended this procedure for reducing spurious findings. Finally, in order to use as homogeneous a sample as possible to prevent confounding with marital status, we included only families in which both biological parents were living in the home with the child.

In order to determine if there were any relationships between the child's sex and parental occupation, work hours, and flexibility, MANOVA's were conducted at ages 8 and 12. No significant sex differences were obtained for mothers' or fathers' work variables at either age. In order to maximize N, the sexes were combined in all subsequent regression analyses.

The analyses showed that parental occupation had a pervasive relationship to both the children's developmental outcomes and the children's environment. Significant R's and the contributions of maternal and paternal occupation are presented in Tables 6 and 7. Regarding developmental outcomes, parental occupation substantially, significantly, and positively predicted intelligence, achievement and school performance, and academic motivation. Interestingly, social-

Table 6. Multiple Regressions for Parental Occupation
at Ages 8 and 12: Developmental Measures[a]

Developmental measure	Multiple R F (df)	Significant predictors
	Age 8	
WISC-R	.49***	Mother's occupation***
	8.88 (2, 55)	Father's occupation**
Woodcock-Johnson		
Reading	.33*	Father's occupation*
	3.28 (2, 55)	
Math	.43**	Father's occupation**
	6.32 (2, 55)	
Knowledge	.63***	Mother's occupation***
	18.42 (2, 55)	Father's occupation***
Child Behavior Checklist: Teachers		
Learning	.41*	Father's occupation*
	4.53 (2, 45)	
Y-CAIMI		
Math	37*	Mother's occupation*
	4.33 (2, 55)	
Difficult	.37*	Mother's occupation*
	4.31 (2, 55)	
	Age 12	
WISC-R	.43**	Father's occupation**
	6.10 (2, 54)	
Woodcock-Johnson		
Reading	.41**	Father's occupation**
	5.38 (2, 54)	
Math	.38*	Father's occupation**
	4.42 (2, 54)	

[a]Only significant findings are reported. N's ranged from 48 to 58 across analyses. Subjects included only employed mothers and fathers in homes with both biological parents present.
*p < .05 **p < .01 ***p < .001

Table 7. Multiple Regressions for Parental Occupation
at Ages 8 and 12: Environmental Measures[a]

Environmental measure	Multiple R F (df)	Significant predictors
Age 8		
HOME		
Provision for Active Stimulation	.51***	Mother's occupation***
	9.91 (2, 55)	Father's occupation***
Physical Environment	.33*	Mother's occupation*
	3.47 (2, 55)	
Total	.46**	Mother's occupation**
	7.40 (2, 55)	
Home Environment Survey		
Learning Opportunities	.67***	Mother's occupation***
	22.39 (2, 54)	Father's occupation***
TV Time	.54***	Mother's
	11.05 (2, 54)	occupation*** (—)
Number of Activities	.46**	Mother's occupation***
	7.32 (2, 54)	
Educational Aspiration	.44**	Mother's occupation**
	6.65 (2, 54)	Father's occupation**
Father involvement in activities	.37*	Mother's occupation*
Mothers' report	4.15 (2, 54)	
Family Environment Scale: Mothers' report		
Independence	.45**	Father's occupation***
	6.98 (2, 55)	
Intellectual/cultural	.56**	Mother's occupation***
	14.31 (2, 55)	Father's occupation***
Active/recreational	.45**	Mother's occupation***
	6.86 (2, 55)	
Family Environment Scale: Fathers' report		
Intellectual/cultural	.37*	Mother's occupation**
	5.50 (2, 39)	
Family Functioning Inventory		
General factor	.36*	Mother's occupation*
	4.11 (2, 54)	
Age 12		
Home Environment Survey		
Cultural Enhancement	.53***	Mother's occupation**
	9.36 (2, 58)	Father's occupation*
Educational Aspiration	.47***	Mother's occupation*
	7.21 (2, 52)	
Mothers' Time Involvement	.34*	Father's occupation*
	3.41 (2, 52)	

(*Continued*)

Table 7. (*Continued*)

Environmental measure	Multiple R F (df)	Significant predictors
Family Environment Scale: Mothers' report		
Intellectual/cultural	.39**	Father's occupation
	4.89 (2, 54)	

ᵃOnly significant findings are reported. N's ranged from 42 to 58 across analyses. Subjects included only employed mothers and fathers in homes with both biological parents present. Negative beta weights are indicated in parentheses.
*p < .05 **p < .01 ***p < .001

emotional and behavioral adjustment measures were not predicted by parental occupation. Regarding environment, parental occupation was substantially, significantly, and positively related to features of the environment dealing predominantly with the provision of stimulation, learning opportunities, cultural enhancement, intellectual focus, and educational aspirations for the child.

These findings were consistent at ages 8 and 12. These data are consistent with the child development data. These data may be interpreted as indicating that parental occupation is associated with an orientation toward academic and intellectual achievement and aspirations, and that parents of higher occupational status not only have children who are more able in these areas but also provide an environment conducive to these outcomes. Both the mothers' and the fathers' occupational status significantly contributed to the outcomes. There was no discernible pattern in either the mothers' or the fathers' occupations contributing more to any specific type of development or environmental feature. It should be noted that the fathers' involvement in activities with their children at age 8 was predicted by the mothers' occupational status, a finding that may indicate that, as mothers' jobs become more demanding, fathers share more activities with their children. In complementary fashion, mothers' time involvement with their child at age 12 was significantly predicted by the fathers' occupational status, a finding suggesting that, as fathers' occupation becomes more demanding, mothers spend more time with their children. These findings support our view that parents in dual-earner families balance each others' roles.

The results regarding the mothers' and the fathers' work hours were almost all nonsignificant. There were no significant multiple regressions for child developmental outcomes at either age. Hence, there were no detrimental effects of parental work hours with regard to child outcomes. There were a few significant relationships between parental work hours and parental involvement and environmental variables. At age 8, parental work hours significantly predicted the amount of time the mothers spent with their children, $R = .39$, F $(2,54)$ $= 4.97$, $p<.01$; the amount of time the fathers spent with their children, $R = .41$, F $(2,55) = 5.49$, $p<.01$; and emotional and verbal responsivity on the HOME scale, $R = .41$, F $(2,55) = 5.44$ $p<.01$.

These data indicate that both the mothers *and* the fathers spent less time with their children as their work hours increased. Consistent with our data supporting balance of roles, the fathers' time involvement with their children increased as the mothers' work hours increased, but it decreased as their own work hours increased. This finding indicates a dynamic interplay between maternal and paternal work hours. Regarding the verbal and emotional responsivity scale, scores were lower as the mothers' work hours increased. As this was the only HOME scale out of eight plus the Total score to be significantly related to parental work hours, it is not consistent with the remainder of the scales, and we felt that it was of limited significance and possibly a statistical artifact. At age 12 years, there were no significant relationships between parental employment hours and parental involvement with the child. Of all the regressions at age 12, only two were significant, indicating that, as the mothers worked more hours, they had a higher moral religious score on the FES, and that, as fathers worked more hours, the children watched more TV.

Regarding flexibility of parental employment, virtually all the analyses were nonsignificant. Parental flexibility played a negligible role in both the children's development and their home environment.

CONCLUSIONS

Our data continue to show that children with employed and nonemployed mothers develop equivalently well. Their home environments are also not significantly different. There continue to be no consistent gender differences with regard to developmental and environmental outcomes, and there are no sleeper effects from infancy through early adolescence (also see A. E. Gottfried *et al.*, 1988). There was an overwhelming pattern of nonsignificance across contemporaneous and prospective analyses, across developmental and environmental domains, across time, and for both sexes. The sporadic significant findings are inconsistent, not replicated over time, and pale in the enormity of the findings of nonsignificance. The present data provide longitudinal continuity from infancy through early adolescence and can be combined with the results reported previously (A. E. Gottfried *et al.*, 1988).

The present data provide evidence of the balance of roles that occurs in dual-earner families. This evidence was obtained with regard to parents' time involvement with their children. Fathers spent more time with their children when the mothers were employed, and they spent more time with their children at age 8 on school days. This latter finding on the patterning of fathers' involvement is supported by Crouter, Perry-Jenkins, Huston, and McHale (1987), who found that fathers in dual-earner families spent more time in child care than fathers in single-earner families, but that the leisure time of fathers in dual- and single-earner families was not different. It may be that when the mothers are employed, the fathers' increased time involvement concerns the necessities rather than the more optional activities.

There was a significant longitudinal trend for fathers to spend more time with their children at ages 8 and 12 when the mothers had been employed earlier. In particular, the mothers' employment when the children were 3.5 predicted the fathers' time spent with the children at ages 8 and 12. This early age seems to be important. It is our interpretation that patterns of father involvement begin early, and that age 3.5 is important in our data because it is the preschool period in which regular time patterns develop around preschool and family.

The dual-earner regression analyses indicate that parental occupation has a strong and pervasive relationship to the cognitive and academic achievement aspects of children's development and home environment. Both the mothers' and the fathers' occupational status were positively related to the children's intellectual and academic performance and motivation, to intellectually stimulating aspects of the home environment, and to parental aspirations for their children's achievement. It is very difficult to identify a single aspect of parental occupation that is responsible for these sizable relationships. The intellectual and educational attainments of the parents, the values and motivations of the parents, and the activities engaged in by the parents are all likely to be associated with parental occupation.

Work hours and flexibility were for the most part unrelated to the developmental and environmental variables. With regard to flexibility, our data are consistent with the findings of Bohen and Viveros-Long (1981). Our view of the balance of roles was further supported by a finding with regard to parental work hours. Although the amount of time spent with the children at age 8 was lower as the mothers and the fathers worked longer hours, the fathers also spent more time with their children as the mothers' work hours increased. This finding represents an adjustment in family life linked to maternal employment. These findings indicate that in dual-earner families, questions regarding the impact of work on the children must account for both parents.

We propose that, considering the current data, as well as those of our earlier study (A. E. Gottfried *et al.*, 1988), a more profitable view of the issue of the impact of maternal employment on children's developing concerns the concept of family adaptation. Many factors enter into the adaptation by families to their circumstances and meeting the needs of their children. This study, combined with our earlier findings (A. E. Gottfried *et al.*, 1988), suggests that one adaptational mechanism is the greater participation of fathers in dual-earner families. Children's developmental level also plays a role in family adaptation. The longitudinal analyses showed that the fathers' involvement when the children were ages 8 and 12 was predicted by maternal employment status in earlier years, a finding indicating that patterns of time involvement tend to be established when the children are young.

The concept of adaptation is a flexible one that may be applied to every family. We believe that the issues concerning maternal employment and children's development have evolved, and that the task facing researchers is to understand and delineate the means of adaptation that support the resilience of family members. It is truly time for researchers to discontinue their search for detriment caused by maternal employment, and to turn their efforts toward understanding the interplay of the complex processes that operate between parental employment, home environment, and children's development.

ACKNOWLEDGMENTS

Over the course of this longitudinal study, this research was supported in part by the Thrasher Research Fund, Spencer Foundation, AMC Theaters, and California State Universities at Fullerton and

Northridge. Our statements and views do not necessarily represent the views of these agencies.

We wish to extend our appreciation to Diana Guerin, Jaki Coffman, Pam Oliver, Craig Thomas, Benita Zuniga, Leigh Hobson, and other members of the research staff of the Fullerton Longitudinal Study, who, over the years, have diligently committed themselves to making this project a success. The continuing interest and participation of the children and families in the Fullerton Longitudinal Study are deeply appreciated.

REFERENCES

Achenbach, T. M. (1991a). *Manual for the Child Behavior Checklist/4-18 and 1991 Profile.* Burlington: University of Vermont, Department of Psychiatry.

Achenbach, T. M. (1991b). *Manual for the Teacher's Report Form and 1991 Profile.* Burlington: University of Vermont, Department of Psychiatry.

Baruch, G. K., & Barnett, R. C. (1983). *Correlates of fathers' participation in family work: A technical report* (Working Paper 106). Wellesley, MA: Wellesley College, Center for Research on Women.

Bathurst, K. (1988). The Inventories of Family Functioning: A psychometric analysis. *Dissertation Abstracts International, 49,* 2918B. (University Microfilms No. DA 88-22158)

Biernat, M., & Wortman, C. B. (1991). Sharing of home responsibilities between professionally employed women and their husbands. *Journal of Personality and Social Psychology, 60,* 844–860.

Bohen, H. H., & Viveros-Long, A. (1981). *Balancing jobs and family life.* Philadelphia: Temple University Press.

Bradley, R. H., Caldwell, B. M., Rock, S. L., Hamrick, H. M., & Harris, P. (1988). Home observation for measurement of the environment: Development of a home inventory for use with families having children 6 to 10 years old. *Contemporary Educational Psychology, 13,* 58–71.

Burchinal, L. G. (1963). Personality characteristics of children. In F. I. Nye & L. W. Hoffman (Eds.), *The employed mother in America* (pp. 106–124). Chicago: Rand McNally.

Caldwell, B., & Bradley, R. (1984). *Home Observation for Measurement of the Environment.* Little Rock: University of Arkansas.

Cohen, J., & Cohen, P. (1983). *Applied multiple regression/correlation analysis for the behavioral sciences* (2nd ed.). Hillsdale, NJ: Erlbaum.

Crouter, A. C., Perry-Jenkins, M., Huston, T. L., & McHale, S. M. (1987). Processes underlying father involvement in dual-earner and single-earner families. *Developmental Psychology, 23,* 431–440.

Darling-Fisher, C. S., & Tieje, B. (1990). The impact of maternal employment characteristics on fathers' participation in child care. *Family Relations, 39,* 20–26.

Elardo, R., & Bradley, R. H. (1981). The Home Observation for Measurement of the Environment (HOME): A review of research. *Developmental Review, 1,* 113–145.

Galambos, N. L., Petersen, A. C., & Lenerz, K. (1988). Maternal employment and sex typing in early adolescence: Contemporaneous and longitudinal relations. In A. E. Gottfried & A. W. Gottfried (Eds.), *Maternal employment and children's development: Longitudinal research* (pp. 155–189). New York: Plenum Press.

Gilbert, L. A. (1985). *Men in dual-career families: Current realities and future prospects.* Hillsdale, NJ: Erlbaum.

Gilbert, L. A., & Dancer, L. S. (1992). Dual-earner families in the United States and adolescent development. In S. Lewis, D. N. Izraeli, & H. Hootsmans (Eds.), *Dual-earner families: International perspectives* (pp. 151–171). Newbury Park, CA: Sage.

Goldberg, W. A., & Easterbrooks, M. A. (1988). Maternal employment when children are toddlers and kindergartners. In A. E. Gottfried & A. W. Gottfried (Eds.), *Maternal employment and children's development: Longitudinal research* (pp. 121–154). New York: Plenum Press.

Goldsmith, E. B. (Ed.). (1989). *Work and family.* Newbury Park, CA: Sage.

Gottfried, A. E. (1985). Academic intrinsic motivation in elementary and junior high school children. *Journal of Educational Psychology, 77,* 631–645.

Gottfried, A. E. (1986). *Children's Academic Intrinsic Motivation Inventory.* Odessa, FL: Psychological Assessment Resources.

Gottfried, A. E. (1988). Maternal employment and children's development: An introduction to the issues. In A. E. Gottfried & A. W. Gottfried, *Maternal employment and children's development: Longitudinal research* (pp. 3–8). New York: Plenum Press.

Gottfried, A. E., & Gottfried, A. W. (1988). Maternal employment and children's development: An integration of longitudinal findings with implications for social policy. In A. E. Gottfried & A. W. Gottfried (Eds.), *Maternal employment and children's development: Longitudinal research* (pp. 269–287). New York: Plenum Press.

Gottfried, A. E., Gottfried, A. W., & Bathurst, K. (1988). Maternal employment, family environment, and children's development: Infancy through the school years. In A. E. Gottfried & A. W. Gottfried (Eds.), *Maternal employment and children's development: Longitudinal research* (pp. 11–58). New York: Plenum Press.

Gottfried, A. W. (1985). Measures of socioeconomic status in child development research: Data and recommendations. *Merrill-Palmer Quarterly, 32,* 85–92.

Gottfried, A. W., & Gilman, G. (1983). Development of visual skills in infants and young children. *Journal of the American Optometric Association, 54,* 541–544.

Gottfried, A. W., & Gottfried, A. E. (1984). Home environment and cognitive development in young children of middle-socioeconomic-status families. In A. W. Gottfried (1984), *Home environment and early cognitive development: Longitudinal research* (pp. 57–115). New York: Academic Press.

Gottfried, A. W., Gottfried, A. E., Bathurst, K., & Guerin, D. (1994). *Gifted IQ: Early developmental aspects.* New York: Plenum Press.

Hock, E., DeMeis, D., & McBride, S. (1988). Maternal separation anxiety: Its role in the balance of employment and motherhood in mothers of infants. In A. E. Gottfried & A. W. Gottfried (Eds.), *Maternal employment and children's development: Longitudinal research* (pp. 191–229). New York: Plenum Press.

Hoffman, L. W. (1989). Effects of maternal employment in the two-parent family. *American Psychologist, 44,* 283–292.

Hollingshead, A. B. (1975). *Four factor index of social status.* Unpublished manuscript, Yale University (available from Department of Sociology).

Hughes, D., & Galinsky, E. (1988). Balancing work and family lives: Research and corporate applications. In A. E. Gottfried & A. W. Gottfried (Eds.), *Maternal employ-*

ment and children's development: Longitudinal research (pp. 233–268). New York: Plenum Press.

Kanter, R. M. (1977). *Work and family in the United States: A critical review and agenda for research and policy.* New York: Sage.

Lerner, J. V., & Galambos, N. L. (1988). The influence of maternal employment across life: The New York Longitudinal Study. In A. E. Gottfried & A. W. Gottfried (Eds.), *Maternal employment and children's development: Longitudinal research* (pp. 59–83). New York: Plenum Press.

Maret, E. (1983). *Women's career pattern.* New York: University Press of America.

Marsh, H.W. (1988). *Self-Description Questionnaire: 1. Manual* San Antonio: Psychological Corporation.

Marsh, H. W., Parker, J. W., & Smith, I. D. (1983). Preadolescent self-concept: Its relation to self-concept as inferred by teachers and to academic ability. *British Journal of Educational Psychology, 53,* 60–78.

Moos, R. H., & Moos, B. S. (1981). *Family environment scale manual.* Palo Alto, CA: Consulting Psychologists Press.

Mortimer, J. T., & London, J. (1984). The varying linkages of work and family. In P. Voydafoff (Ed.), *Work and family: Changing roles of men and women* (pp. 20–35). Palo Alto, CA: Mayfield.

Nye, F. I., & Hoffman, L. W. (1963). The socio-cultural setting. In F. I. Nye & L. W. Hoffman (Eds.), *The employed mother in America* (pp. 3–17). Chicago: Rand McNally.

Nye, F. I., Perry, J. B., & Ogles, R. H. (1963). Anxiety and anti-social behavior in preschool children. In F. I. Nye & L. W. Hoffman (Eds.), *The employed mother in America* (pp. 3–17). Chicago: Rand McNally.

Owen, M. T., Cox, M. J. (1988). Maternal employment and the transition to parenthood. In A. E. Gottfried & A. W. Gottfried (Eds.), *Maternal employment and children's development: Longitudinal research* (pp. 85–119). New York: Plenum Press.

Russell, G. (1982). Maternal employment status and fathers' involvement in child care. *Australian and New Zealand Journal of Sociology, 18,* 172–179.

Silberstein, L. R. (1992). *Dual-career marriage: A system in transition.* Hillsdale, NJ: Erlbaum.

Simmons, R. G., Rosenberg, F., & Rosenberg, M. (1973). Disturbance in the self-image at adolescence. *American Sociological Review, 38,* 553–568.

Sparrow, S. S., Balla, D. A., & Cicchetti, D. V. (1984). *Vineland Adaptive Behavior Scales.* Circle Pines, MN: American Guidance Service.

Staines, G. L., & Pleck, J. H. (1983). *The impact of work schedules on the family.* Ann Arbor: University of Michigan, Institute for Social Research.

Wechsler, D. (1974). *Manual for the Wechsler Intelligence Scale for Children–Revised.* New York: Psychological Corporation.

Woodcock, R. W., & Johnson, M. B. (1977). *Woodcock-Johnson Psycho-Educational Battery.* Allen, TX: DLM Teaching Resources.

Woodcock, R. W., & Johnson, M. B. (1989). *Woodcock-Johnson Psycho-Educational Battery—Revised.* Allen, TX: DLM Teaching Resources.

Zedeck, S. (1992). Introduction: Exploring the domain of work and family concerns. In S. Zedeck (Ed.), *Work, families, and organizations* (pp. 1–32). San Francisco: Jossey-Bass.

Zedeck, S., & Mosler, K. L. (1990). Work in the family and employing organization. *American Psychologist, 45,* 240–251.

4

Revolution and Reassessment
Child Custody in Context

Charlene E. Depner

INTRODUCTION

Dramatic transformations in family demographics pose unprecedented challenges for family law and policy. Demographers predict that just half of all U.S. children born in the 1980s will grow up residing with both parents (Bumpass & Sweet, 1989). For other girls and boys in this generation, legal custody standards and parental responsibilities are the focus of active policy deliberation. What family environments will best promote the welfare of American children? The last decade witnessed a revolution in child custody standards. Over 40 states have now enacted legislation that permits joint custody or shared parenting (Folberg, 1991). In the wake of this change, custody standards are the subject of rancorous debate among legal theorists and

The observations and conclusions in this article are those of the author and are not meant to represent the position of the Statewide Office Family Court Services or the Judicial Council of California.

Charlene E. Depner • Statewide Office of Family Court Services, San Francisco, California 94107.

Redefining Families: Implications for Children's Development, edited by Adele Eskeles Gottfried and Allen W. Gottfried. Plenum Press, New York, 1994.

policymakers (Bartlett & Stack, 1991). Some argue that joint custody has not fulfilled its promise and has resulted in unintended consequences for family members.

What does social science contribute to a reassessment of custody policy? This chapter critically evaluates research on contemporary alternatives in child custody and argues that many of the basic policy questions remain unaddressed by the social science literature. Empirical research constitutes only a small fraction of the citations yielded in a literature search. Outstripping the pace of rigorous research, a social science fiction of custody has filled the information void. It is difficult to sort out speculation, advocacy rhetoric, and research summary. Although it is not uncommon for journalists to proclaim research evidence to be definitive, comprehensive reviews of the custody literature have appropriately characterized it as preliminary and inconclusive (Benjamin & Irving, 1989; Clingempeel & Reppucci, 1982; Kanoy & Cunningham, 1984).

What future research directions would have the greatest policy utility? The rich array of ideas generated by custody research needs to be tested more rigorously in a new generation of inquiry. Moving beyond a comparison of the relative strengths and weaknesses of families divided into custody subgroups, it is time to reevaluate the essential questions and to create innovative methods for answering them. Trombetta (1989) argued persuasively against an evaluative framework that is designed to assess whether and how a custody arrangement "works," as there is a fundamental lack of ideological consensus on the criteria for what "working" means. In his review of the literature, Coller (1988) proposed a progression of questions, beginning with feasibility (Can alternatives to sole custody work?), then extending to description (How and under what conditions do they work?) and intervention (How can the courts, clinicians, and parents themselves make them work better?). Further developing the intervention objective, Kelly (1991) underscored the complexity of the issues and accentuated the need for research to "move beyond the one-liners." The research question, then, evolves from the simplistic "What works?" to the more useful "What works for whom and under what conditions?" To this end, this chapter introduces a heuristic model that considers custody in the context of a dynamic system of variables that influence family functioning and well-being over the life course.

Definitions

The first obstacle to a synthesis of the custody literature is the absence of definitional precision (Folberg, 1984). Custody research has not adopted consistent conceptual or operational definitions. Some studies focus on *de jure* custody, the official legal assignment of decision-making responsibility for the child. Virtually none confine themselves exclusively to physical custody, which legally establishes the residential status of the child. Most commonly, the term *custody* is used to designate the *de facto* division of time between the two parents. Although operational definitions of *de facto* arrangements have converged on a minimum 30%/70% time-sharing ratio, the definition is far from consistent, and the population labeled *joint* is heterogeneous in several respects (e.g., the way in which time is spent, the longevity of the arrangement, and the parental acceptance of it) that may be consequential in the assessment of child outcomes.

Variations in terminology are not merely semantic. Family psychologists are more likely to adopt behavioral definitions: the *de facto* division of parental responsibilities and its implications for child development. Legal scholars turn their attention to the way in which *de jure* legal provisions reflect and influence the operation of families in our culture.

This review attempts to preserve the distinction between the legal and the behavioral definitions. Although there is some relationship between *de facto* and *de jure* custody status, the correspondence is far from isomorphic (Clark, Whitney, & Beck, 1988; Mnookin, Maccoby, Albiston, & Depner, 1990; Phear, Beck, Hauser, Clark, & Whitney, 1984; Seltzer, 1990), and behavioral and legal indicators change at different rates, the variability in *de facto* status often not being legally ratified.

Prevalence

Joint legal custody appears to covary with geographical variations in family policy. A study of two progressive California counties reported 79% joint legal custody (Albiston, Maccoby, & Mnookin, 1990), whereas a Wisconsin study in the same period charted 22% (Seltzer, 1990). *De jure* and *de facto* shared parenting remain relatively rare, with joint physical custody ranging from 2% (Phear *et al.*, 1984) to 20% (Maccoby & Mnookin, 1992). Although shared-parenting arrangements assign unprecedented intervals in paternal care, time is rarely allocated equally between the parents. (Benjamin & Irving, 1989).

With a paucity of long-term investigations, relatively short-term longitudinal studies detect substantial fluctuation in *de facto* custody arrangements (Steinman, Zemmelman, & Knoblauch, 1985). One clinical sample proclaimed a 66% "failure rate" for shared parenting (Frankel, 1985). According to Maccoby and Mnookin (1992), only half of the children found in shared parenting in their study had sustained that arrangement in the three years following the initiation of the parental divorce. Whether this finding is more indicative of a responsiveness to changing family needs or of a fundamental precariousness in the arrangement remains an empirical question. If borne out across time and situations, the stability findings imply that custody history rather than custody status at a fixed point in time may prove to be a more telling indicator of child development.

FAMILY STRUCTURE AS A RISK FACTOR

The "divorce revolution" of the 1970s prompted profound concerns about potentially adverse consequences for children. This apprehension, in turn, inspired innovations in the postdivorce roles available to parents. Investigations conducted in the 1970s and 1980s endeavored to establish whether children from divorced households were at greater risk of experiencing a range of poor outcomes. Dominated by a group comparison paradigm, this genre of research sought distinctive vulnerabilities of children of divorce, contrasting families in groups defined by a static measure of family structure. This approach yielded a wealth of information about the associations between static family structure and child development but commonly left to *post hoc* speculation the mechanisms responsible for the link.

This section summarizes major findings from the group comparisons paradigm, with particular attention to relationships that may be modified by custody arrangements. In essence, the architects of custody policy have framed custody innovation as a means of intervening in a child development trajectory set by the family dissolution. Custody may intervene in potentially adverse processes (e.g., preventing negative emotional consequences of parental estrangement) or may bolster salubrious influences on the course of child development (e.g., enhancing the likelihood of effective parenting).

An exhaustive review of the effects of divorce on children is beyond the scope of this chapter. Critical summaries of the literature (Barber & Eccles, 1992; Demo & Acock, 1988; Emery, 1988; Kelly, 1988, 1993b; Kitson & Morgan, 1990; Wallerstein, 1991) differ somewhat in the way in which they weigh the evidence, but they generally conclude that small systematic deficits for children of divorce can be detected, at least in the short run. Most reviews also make the caveat that the absence of rigorous multivariate tests precludes an assessment of the unique and shared impact of divorce covariates (e.g., interparental conflict and economic discontinuities) on outcomes for children. That is, although the multiplicity of family structures has different implications for child outcomes, the specific causal agents are often not evaluated.

Crisis-Engendered Reactions

The two- to three-year period following the family dissolution is an interval when acute responses are evident. During this stage, family life may be particularly stressful and volatile, involving disruptions in family routines and functioning; a greater demand on resources; economic stress; adaptive tasks (e.g., relocating, setting up a viable visitation schedule, and completing the legal divorce process); heightened parental distress; and diminished parenting quality. Transitive deleterious reactions, particularly among younger children, have been detected by several investigators. (For reviews, see Amato & Keith, 1991; Demo & Acock, 1988; Emery, 1988; Kelly, 1988, 1993b). These include emotional reactions, such as anxiety or depression, disruptions in concentration, distress about changing parent–child relationships, loyalty conflicts, and preoccupation with reconciliation.

Psychological Well-Being

The weight of empirical evidence does not associate divorce with substantial long-term deficits in most children's emotional well-being (Cashion, 1984). In some studies, the aggregate scores for children of divorce are not as strong as those for other children, but the majority still fall well within normal ranges. That is, divorce may increase the risk of scoring lower relative to peers but is less likely to affect the odds on exceeding clinical cutoffs (Kelly, 1993b). Findings of "internalizing" problems (e.g., depression, anxiety, and poor self-concept) are equivocal but are generally attributed to the causal agents (e.g., parental conflict) that accompany changing family structure. "Externalizing" problems (e.g., aggression and lack of self-control), particularly among boys, have been documented repeatedly in studies of divorce, but some investigators ascribe such behavioral problems to family conflict rather than family structure (Emery, 1988).

Social Functioning

Children from divorced families evince disproportionately higher rates of antisocial behavior (e.g., deviance and delinquency) (Demo & Acock, 1988; Matsueda & Heimer, 1987), although the gap is not sizable. Differences in parental supervision (Dornbusch, Carlsmith, Bushwall, Ritter, Leiderman, Hastorf, & Gross, 1985) have been cited as one cause underlying the effects, although the independent role of several causal agents remains to be clarified (Rutter & Giller, 1983).

Gender-Role Orientation

It has been speculated that divorce may have adverse effects on the gender-role development of little boys because it reduces exposure to the father, an agent who models and reinforces normative male gender-role identity (Demo & Acock, 1988). A meta-analysis of the literature on paternal exposure and gender-role development, however, found little systematic evidence to support the perceived advantage of same-sex custody assignment (Stevenson & Black, 1988).

Cognitive Development

Relative to their peers, children from single-parent households consistently perform more poorly on measures of cognitive functioning ranging from standardized achievement tests to scholastic performance (Demo & Acock, 1988; McLanahan, 1985), and children of divorce score worse than children from other single-parent households (Emery, 1988). Nonetheless, the differences are typically quite small (Hetherington, Camera, & Featherman, 1981) and may prove transient when longer range investigations are available (Barber & Eccles, 1992). The differences also diminish or disappear when socioeconomic status is controlled for (Guidubaldi & Perry, 1984; Smith, 1990).

Accelerated Life-Course Transitions

Weiss (1979) observed that children of divorce "grow up a little faster." They must negotiate the complexities of parental relationships and sometimes assume adult responsibilities for household chores and child care. There is evidence that individuals who experience parental divorce are more likely to make adult transitions early in life. Parental divorce leads to earlier departure from the family home, cohabitation, and childbearing. These effects are decelerated if the parents remarry (Furstenberg & Teitler, 1991; Kiernan, 1992; Thornton, 1991).

Adaptive Skills

Resilience theorists underscore the striking variability in children's responses to adverse circumstances (Rutter, 1989). Consistent with the dominant emphasis on pathology in the divorce literature, insufficient attention has been directed toward factors that may help children thrive in the presence of the challenges posed by family disruption. Perhaps it is in this arena, rather than in the abatement of pathology, that alternative access and custody arrangements hold their greatest promise. Hetherington (1989) concluded that a "substantial minority" of children cope constructively with divorce and strengthen their adaptive skills as a result of the experience. This notion is consistent with the finding that exposure to a gradient of manageable challenges can build self-efficacy (O'Leary, Ickovics, & Ryan, 1992).

CHILD CUSTODY INNOVATION

The foregoing summary suggests that family disruption poses risks for children, particularly in the areas of transitive reactions engendered by the dissolution and its aftermath and of longer range associations with antisocial behavior, cognitive functioning, and accelerated life-course transitions. Conversely, some work suggests that, when children are able to cope effectively with the challenges of changing family structure, a sense of self-efficacy is cultivated. Custody innovation has been promoted as a means of averting the potentially adverse effects of family dissolution by approximating the advantages of two-parent households (e.g., economic support, coparenting, supervision, role modeling, and sustained loving relationships). Nonetheless, few empirical investigations directly evaluate the role of custody in reducing the established risks of family dissolution. That is, rather than measuring the way in which custody intervenes in a potentially adverse course of development and/or potentiates beneficial influences, most of the custody literature itself assumes a group-difference paradigm, this time comparing the outcomes of children in static custody categories.

Psychological Well-Being

Although few investigations have been conducted, a clear link has not been established between custody status and the psychological well-being of the child. Most comparative studies reveal few custody-related assets or liabilities for children's emotional well-being (Camera & Resnik, 1988; Kline, Tschann, Johnston, & Wallerstein, 1989; Luepnitz, 1982; Nunan, 1980; Welsh, 1982; Wolchik, Braver, & Sandler, 1985). McKinnon and Wallerstein (1987) observed distress in a sample of 26 preschool children in shared parenting. With age, the incidence of distress diminished, but the severity increased. Shiller (1986a,b) found that boys in shared parenting exhibited fewer problems than those in sole parenting on the Achenbach Child Behavior Checklist, but both groups were above test norms. Among adolescents, somewhat better adjustment was observed in time-sharing arrangements, although most adolescents were well within normal ranges (Buchanan, Maccoby, & Dornbusch, 1992). Although some early research (Warshak, 1986; Warshak & Santrock, 1983) raised interest in the potential advantages of placing children with the same-sex parent, such benefits as enhanced well-being have been replicated for girls, but not boys (Buchanan et al., 1992).

The absence of custody effects appears to be consistent with the observation that few children of divorce experience clinical levels of maladjustment. Most children are within normal ranges of psychological well-being, and some arrangements appear to improve the general pattern for some children, although the effects are not profound. Viewed from a policy perspective, what is the impact of the custody intervention? Divorce poses no clear risks to children's long-range well-being (see above), so custody would not, in this case, be intervening in a negative trajectory. Instead, it is enhancing possibilities for children in some situations.

Other Outcomes

The custody literature introduces its own array of outcome measures (i.e., adaptation to transitions, satisfaction with the arrangements, and parent–child relations). Indeed, a wider range of outcomes are salient in the evaluation of the effects of custody.

Logistics

As noted earlier, some families with joint legal custody have distributions of parental time that are indistinguishable from those of families with sole custody. Supplemental financial demands may face families that embark on genuine time-sharing arrangements (e.g., accommodations for overnight stays and transportation). The extent to which such costs can be absorbed or offset by other savings (e.g., child-care costs) is not known. Although one projection (Patterson, 1982) estimated additional annual expenses of $12,000–$15,000, other studies (Irving, Benjamin, & Trocme, 1984; Maccoby & Mnookin, 1992) have found joint custody and time sharing at all socioeconomic strata. This finding suggests that all low-income families are not precluded from shared parenting on economic grounds. Possibly, there are more cost-effective methods of covering joint custody expenses.

Children must also adapt to the unique logistical demands of time sharing. Most accommodate to the transitions and discontinuities in parental households, but several studies note that a minority of children experience problems negotiating the demands of two households (Arbanel, 1979; Nehls & Morgenbesser, 1980; Steinman, 1981; Watson, 1981). Steinman (1981) reported that 25% of the children in shared parenting were confused by residential transition and 30% felt "overburdened" by it. Transitional difficulties have been linked to the temperament of the child (Hetherington, 1989).

Children's Perspectives on Time Sharing

Although reconciliation fantasies are often observed among children in sole custody, Benjamin and Irving (1989) pointed out that the comparative literature on custody includes few studies that have directly assessed the subjective evaluations of the children involved. Those that have, have found strong endorsements of shared parenting, often on the grounds that the arrangement permits children to maintain relationships with both parents (Buchanan, Maccoby, Mnookin, & Dornbusch, 1993; Irving, Benjamin, & Trocme, 1984; Luepnitz, 1982; Shiller, 1986a; Steinman, 1981). When children are interviewed directly, two thirds (Rothberg, 1983) to three quarters (Ahrons, 1980; Benjamin & Irving, 1989) report satisfaction with shared-parenting arrangements. One exception to this general trend is the case of parents who are locked in higher levels of conflict. In this situation, the children report feeling "caught in the middle" (Buchanan, Maccoby & Dornbush, 1991) and may become deeply enmeshed in an ongoing struggle between their parents (Johnson, Kline, & Tschann, 1989).

Parental Investment in Children

Contact

Fathers who are awarded joint legal custody have more overnight visits with their children immediately following the marital disruption (Albiston, et al., 1990). Wolchik et al. (1985) reported that fathers with joint legal custody spend more time with their children.

Decision Making

Three years after the marital disruption, fathers with joint legal custody were more likely to be involved in discussions of the child's school progress and extracurricular activities, but no more likely to take part in major decisions involving medical treatment, school placement, or religious training (Albiston et al., 1990).

Support

When the mother is the sole caretaker, noncompliance with child support orders is rampant (Weitzman, 1985). Advocates of joint custody suggest that the formal recognition of paternal rights enhances the likelihood that fathers will contribute to the financial well-being of their children by honoring child obligations and providing funds for educational expenses, extracurricular activities, or travel. Contact provides information about the economic needs of the child (Chambers, 1979), and during visitation, children may make direct requests (Tropf, 1984).

Some studies report more consistent financial support under joint legal custody (Pearson & Thoennes, 1988; Seltzer, Schaeffer, & Charng, 1989) or shared parenting (Ahrons, 1983; Irving & Benjamin, 1991; Luepnitz, 1986; S. B. Steinman et al., 1985), although it may be a source of conflict (Rothberg, 1983). Other research does not demonstrate an advantage in shared parenting (Phear et al., 1984). Pearson and Thoennes (1988) found that legal custody had little effect on child support payments, once patterns of visitation were controlled for. Thus, the impact of custody may be attributable to enhanced contact.

The causal sequence of the relationship between contact and support payment is not well established (Seltzer, 1991). Fathers who make child support payments may be motivated to visit in order to ensure that the money will be spent on approved items (Weiss & Willis, 1985); some fathers who do not pay may feel too guilty to visit; mothers may be more willing to permit and facilitate the visitation of fathers who have a good record of meeting their financial responsibilities (Furstenberg, 1988a; Wright & Price, 1986).

Summary

Comparisons of the responses of children in different custody arrangements suggest certain advantages and concerns. Several investigators suggest that the differences observed in custody groups may be attributable, at least in part, to precursing characteristics of the children and the family that lead to the election of one form of custody or another. Moreover, a review of the divorce and custody literature accentuates the fact that child outcomes are multiply determined. Grave misconceptions may result from a failure to consider child custody in the context of the wide range of factors that have a bearing on child adjustment, including family characteristics, circumstances, process, and change. What is needed is a unifying theory that links such determinants of adjustment and multivariate investigations of the way in which they operate independently and jointly with custody arrangements.

TOWARD A BROADER INQUIRY

The challenge of keeping pace with the staggering rate of change in laws and public receptivity to new parenting roles renders the corpus of research understandably limited in scope. This section points out significant barriers to the policy utility of the foregoing generation of social science investigations of custody and argues that a circumscribed analysis confined to family structure, parental roles, and child outcomes may lead to erroneous conclusions about causation and misguided directions for intervention and policy. Indeed, a more sophisticated research paradigm is required to determine the mechanisms underlying superficial observations of the relationships between custody and family outcomes. The remainder of this chapter suggests some potentially consequential reformulations of custody inquiry.

The existing body of custody research is severely limited with respect to the information that it can offer to the architects of social policy. Although policy and practice demand rigorous solutions of such issues as prevalence, diversity, and long-term outcomes, the research base is, at this juncture, at a far more preliminary stage, composed primarily of small exploratory and descriptive studies that were never designed for such applications. Methodological limitations, recounted in every literature review, compromise the policy utility of the results. For example, Benjamin and Irving's review (1989) noted that the field is dominated by small descriptive studies that do not adopt rigorous methods of sampling, measurement, or statistical analysis. The dominance of advocacy scholarship further undermines the credibility of some investigations (Felner & Terre, 1987). *Post hoc* speculation is cited as data, and estimates of prevalence are drawn from small convenience samples that were never designed to generate population statistics.

The underlying complexities in this rich system of variables require more sophisticated statistical modeling. For example, the system needs to empirically capture nonlinearities (e.g., parental estrangement has negative outcomes, but there is no evidence of a monotonic relationship between parental contact and child outcomes) and heterogeneity (e.g., economic polarization has inherent implications for child outcomes, and ethnicity implies different patterns of dissolution and access to social and material resources).

Extension and Inclusion

Perhaps the most crippling shortcoming of custody research to date is the narrow generality of the findings of many investigations.

Sampling techniques often truncate racial and economic diversity and rarely permit subgroup comparisons. Demo & Acock's sobering assessment (1988) was that the literature did not include sufficient studies to allow any conclusions about racial differences. It is not an exaggeration to state that what we do know about custody is based primarily on the experience of white middle-class parents who are divorcing for the first time. The concentration on relatively elite populations, with the virtually systematic exclusion of the wider population for whom custody is an issue (e.g., people of color, the financially disadvantaged, the never-married, or those modifying existing custody orders), compromises the information base from which practice and policy can draw.

Equally alarming is the dearth of empirical studies of the custody issues for families in crisis (e.g., those grappling with substance abuse and/or violence). We have no assurance that findings based on relatively well-functioning families can be generalized to those facing severe and often life-threatening difficulties. Although some of the literature on family conflict and custody incorporates families in which violence has occurred, there is a pressing need to study family violence as a distinct dynamic. More important, because initial descriptive studies have found that families often simultaneously grapple with multiple problems, research models need to move beyond simple absence–presence dichotomies and to capture the full complexity of a system of problems requiring intervention.

Also absent from most custody inquiry are the never-married, who are increasingly likely to develop *de facto* and *de jure* custodial arrangements (Bray & Depner, 1993). Very little is known about the custody situations of these populations or the advisability of extending models developed for divorcing parents. Another population excluded from custody research is those who modify custody arrangements. Arrangements revised in response to changing family needs or structures are not differentiated in the literature and may have a unique dynamic.

This line of thinking underscores the imperative for a broader and more complex vision of family dissolution (Depner & Bray, 1993). A strong, monolithic stereotype of divorcing families pervades the current conceptualization and research. Pioneers in custody research have called for recognition of the vast differences in family histories, circumstances, and resources (Kelly, 1988, 1993b) and of the variations in the responses of parents and children (Hetheringon, 1989).

Moving beyond the Group-Comparison Paradigm

Regardless of the caliber of methodological execution, the group-comparison paradigm imposes conceptual limitations that can generate misleading results. Fundamentally, the emphasis on designs involving the comparison of subgroups with different custody orders or parenting arrangements presupposes the preeminence of *de jure* or *de facto* custody *vis-à-vis* other variables. A fundamental question remains to be evaluated: Is custody a more potent determinant than ongoing attributes of the family and its members?

It can also be argued that defining groups by custodial status may introduce a good deal of imprecision into the analysis. A gross categorization may mask important combinations in *de jure* and *de facto* status. Moreover, evidence that *de facto* custodial status is highly volatile (Maccoby & Mnookin, 1992) alerts us to the time dependence of the group classification; the same family may appear in a different custody category in a classification made at a different time in the life course. For example, one popular methodological approach involves dividing a classroom of children into groups based on custodial status. The time since the marital disruption is highly variable. With the recognition that a high proportion of access arrangements change over time, it is clear that the children in any particular group may have very different custodial histories or prospects.

Another problem is that defining group status by *de facto* time sharing demands that an otherwise continuous variable (time with the child) must be arbitrarily divided into segments that define the groups. The choice of these cutoff points may influence the outcome of the group comparisons.

The group-comparison approach is useful in identifying associations between custodial status and another variable, but it does not reveal the causal hierarchy among variables (e.g., a relationship between custody and parental cooperation may mean that joint custody engenders cooperation or that cooperative parents elect joint custody). Further, although *post hoc* speculation may offer hypotheses about the reasons that account for the association, the group-comparison method does not evaluate the mechanisms driving the relationship.

What are the advantages of moving away from a group-comparison paradigm altogether? Causal modeling can allow us to address more interesting questions: Is the legal label the engine that drives family outcomes? Are there common factors that affect both custody and outcomes? Are there synergistic effects of family dynamics and custody labels that ratify commitments to children and/or establish contexts that facilitate favorable outcomes?

Extending the Temporal Dimension

Virtually all custody research is cast within a "divorce-event paradigm." The dominant framework casts custody as a variable that intervenes between the trauma of divorce and the adaptation of the family. New research suggests that this model may lead to quite erroneous conclusions by accentuating some events, such as the custody decision, and failing to measure others, such as the events and the family dynamics that preceded the divorce. An alternative approach would stretch the time frame in both directions, to precede the custody decision and measure the factors that mold it as well as to evaluate its consequences as the family continues to evolve over time.

Recent research underscores the wisdom of extending the time frame for custody analysis into the past. Prospective studies have demonstrated that some differences in children's behavioral and cognitive adjustment that might otherwise be attributed to marital dissolution are, in fact, evident well before the divorce takes place (Block, Block, & Gjerde, 1986; Cherlin, Furstenberg, Chase-Lansdale, Kiernan, Robins, Morrison, & Teller, 1991). Family dynamics and individual differences may precede rather than flow from custodial choice.

The need to measure long-term outcomes has also been emphasized (Wallerstein, 1991). Partly because alternative custodial options have only recently been legally formalized, empirical studies of custody status are of limited time duration. Most are cross sectional or confined to outcomes within five years of marital disruption. As custodial arrangements establish longer tenure, empirical models can factor in the complexities of temporal dynamics. For example, it will be possible to see if the effects observed in short-term observations are transient reactions to family change or enduring effects that set a new trajectory for child development.

The evaluation of child outcomes must consider at least two "clocks," one marking child development and the other marking family experience over time (Bray & Berger, 1993). Still other clocks may be relevant to a particular analysis, such as the rate of assimilation of minority parents or the pace of change in custodial ideology in particular geographical location. Moreover, there are competing hypotheses about the temporal mechanisms underlying custodial relationships. For example, an observed relationship between custodial status and child adjustment may be attributed to the duration of a particular form of custody (e.g., children may initially have difficulty adapting to the logistics of joint custody), to timing (e.g., the alternation schedule may be poorly coordinated with the developmental needs of the child), or to cumulative effects (e.g., the number of ecological changes in the child's environment). Such hypotheses can be differentiated empirically.

Elucidating More Complex Causal Mechanisms

Causal inferences are routinely yet inappropriately drawn from the custody research base. For example, early descriptive studies noted that joint-custody parents showed lower conflict and higher cooperation. The strong possibility that low-conflict families may have been more likely to elect joint custody was overlooked in the enthusiastic speculation that imposing joint custody may force parents to resolve conflicts.

The foregoing research has strong utility in laying the groundwork for dynamic models of the individual, family, and social-context variables that may be consequential in custodial outcomes. Such variables, often unmeasured in the foregoing research, may affect the links between custodial status and an outcome by different mechanisms: precursing, intervening, or potentiating. For example, a consideration of *precursing* family circumstances, such as interparental conflict, may illuminate the spurious relationship between custody and outcome (i.e., the precursor is the causal agent that affects both custody and outcome). Other variables may *intervene* to determine custodial outcomes. For example, joint custody may lead to another variable, such as a sustained father–child contact, which may in turn have salubrious effects. *Potentiating* effects are factors that condition the outcomes of custody. For example, the impact of custody may be especially strong for children of a particular age or for families with certain emotional or financial resources.

A HEURISTIC MULTIVARIATE MODEL: CHILD CUSTODY IN CONTEXT

Figure 1 is a heuristic model, drawn from foregoing theory and research, that places custody and access arrangements in the

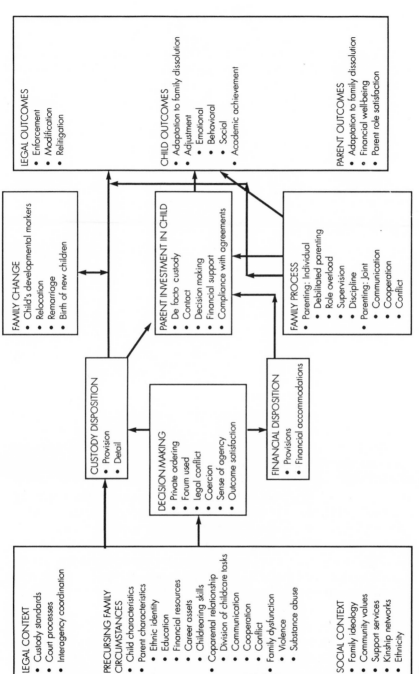

Figure 1.

The figure is a flowchart diagram (rotated sideways on the page) containing the following boxes and contents:

LEGAL OUTCOMES
- Enforcement
- Modification
- Relitigation

CHILD OUTCOMES
- Adaptation to family dissolution
- Adjustment
  - Emotional
  - Behavioral
  - Social
- Academic achievement

PARENT OUTCOMES
- Adaptation to family dissolution
- Financial wellbeing
- Parent role satisfaction

FAMILY CHANGE
- Child's developmental markers
- Relocation
- Remarriage
- Birth of new children

PARENT INVESTMENT IN CHILD
- De facto custody
- Contact
- Decision making
- Financial support
- Compliance with agreements

FAMILY PROCESS
- Parenting: Individual
  - Debilitated parenting
  - Role overload
  - Supervision
  - Discipline
- Parenting: Joint
  - Communication
  - Cooperation
  - Conflict

CUSTODY DISPOSITION
- Provision
- Detail

DECISION MAKING
- Private ordering
- Forum used
- Legal conflict
- Coercion
- Sense of agency
- Outcome satisfaction

FINANCIAL DISPOSITION
- Provisions
- Financial accommodations

LEGAL CONTEXT
- Custody standards
- Court processes
- Interagency coordination

PRECURSING FAMILY CIRCUMSTANCES
- Child characteristics
- Parent characteristics
  - Ethnic identity
  - Education
  - Financial resources
  - Career assets
  - Childrearing skills
- Coparental relationship
  - Division of childcare tasks
  - Communication
  - Cooperation
  - Conflict
- Family dysfunction
  - Violence
  - Substance abuse

SOCIAL CONTEXT
- Family ideology
- Community values
- Support services
- Kinship networks
- Ethnicity

context of the life-course family process. The system of variables is fruitful ground for model development. Connections among the classes of variables included in the boxes are just beginning to be established. Illustrative findings will be cited as the model is reviewed.

Custody Disposition

Up to this point, the chapter has touched on some of the components of the model. *Custody disposition* refers to the formal legal provisions of the legal decree. *De facto* custody is one aspect of *parental investment in the child*, a category that also includes a broad range of roles, including financial support and compliance with agreements about parenting activities. A number of investigations report links among the indicators of parental investment, particularly visitation and maintenance of child support (Furstenberg, 1985; 1988a,b; Furstenberg, Morgan, & Allison, 1987; Furstenberg, Nord, Peterson, & Zill, 1983; Maccoby & Mnookin, 1992; Seltzer, 1991).

Financial Disposition

Although custody and time-sharing arrangements have financial implications for parents, the connections between custody and financial dispositions are rarely studied. The claim that custody is used as a bargaining chip to reduce child support demands is commonly cited but rarely evaluated. Nonetheless, some states are now introducing "visitation credits" that may operate as financial disincentives to sole custody. Research is needed to test assumptions about the relationship between the proportion of time a parent spends with a child and the costs incurred. Virtually no research has been devoted to compliance with *de facto* and *de jure* visitation agreements. We know that substantial proportions of children are affected by low (or nonexistent) awards and delinquent payment. Research is needed to measure directly the accuracy of the claims that shared custody increases the likelihood that support will be paid.

Further, as some research suggests that child outcomes are moderated by the distress or adaptation of the custodial parent (Longfellow, 1979), the relationship between financial stress and custody is particularly worthy of further study.

Contextual Variables

On the left side of the model, the *legal and social contexts* affect custody decision making by introducing options, constraints, support, and entitlement. Surprisingly little empirical attention has been directed toward the role of the legal and social contexts in the custody dynamic; yet differences in time and place suggest that the cultural ethos and the legal framework furnish an influential backdrop for family structure and dynamics.

First and foremost, legal doctrine affects the options available for custody and financial dispositions. Despite the initial enthusiasm, a reappraisal of joint custody has sparked rancorous debate about the merits of adopting a primary parenting presumption. Chesler's work (1986) alleges that there is a double standard for evaluating the parental competence of men and women. Fathers' rights advocates argue that custodial opportunities should not be revoked for all fathers, even if they are abused by some fathers, and point out that the estrangement of fathers from their children is a damaging and common outcome of sole custody. Coller (1988) characterized mother-custody presumptions as "the state-sanctioned destruction of father-child relationships" (p. 465).

More generally, it appears that legal options endorse and popularize particular parental roles. Furstenberg *et al.*'s national study (1983) of over 800 families who divorced in the 1970s—before joint custody was legally sanctioned—found shared parenting virtually nonexistent. By the mid-1980s, a study of two California counties recorded joint legal custody orders in 76% of the families (Mnookin *et al.*, 1990). In a similar period in Wisconsin, the rate of joint legal custody was just 15%. Father participation is on the rise, particularly in places with high rates of joint custody. Furstenberg's study of divorce and separation in the 1970s revealed that 50% of the fathers had not seen their children in the past year. The Wisconsin study showed 30% paternal disengagement; and the California study, 13%.

Similarly, community values and support systems may influence the acceptability and viability of particular custody and access arrangements. Kurdek (1981) argued that a child's adaptation to divorce is affected by social attitudes about divorce, custody, and postdivorce parenting. Depner and Bray (1993) suggested that the stigmatization of children of divorce may be a self-fulfilling prophecy. Del Carmen and Virgo (1993) suggested that kinship norms and networks exert a powerful influence on paternal roles.

Precursing Family Circumstances

Precursing variables set the stage for the family disruption as well as for the custody and access arrangements that will be feasible and desirable. Of all the variables that affect relationships among custody and outcomes, precursing family circumstances have received the most attention in the literature. Many studies of custody have had a limited range on family background variables because they used small convenience samples or were based on selective sub-populations, such as clients in counseling (Clingempeel & Repucci, 1982). Only recently have large community and national surveys made it possible to identify general population characteristics that covary with custody type. Recently available prospective longitudinal studies will also be useful in teasing out causal sequences. This line of inquiry is of particular significance because it may be that the presumed links between custody and outcomes are, in reality, attributable to common predictors. That is, is the custodial placement itself an outcome of family circumstances and processes that, in and of themselves, have consequences for family members? From this perspective, the effects of custody are more accurately understood as operating within the family context.

The available research reveals, despite considerable diversity within custody types, certain custody-linked prototypes. Time sharing has been more common among better educated, high-earning parents and families that include male children, only children, and youngsters in the 2–9 age range (Maccoby, Depner, & Mnookin, 1988; Maccoby & Mnookin, 1992). Higher paternal incomes have been found among families with *de jure* and *de facto* custody. Seltzer (1990) found that economic factors have a stronger bearing on legal custody, whereas family composition is more strongly linked to physical custody.

To illustrate how a consideration of precursing variables may change our understanding of the causal significance of custody, let us examine one line of research that has recently been elaborated empirically: the role of financial resources in the system of variables affecting outcomes for children. Joint custody families have, on average, higher incomes. Higher incomes are associated, in some studies, with higher support payments (Albiston *et al*, 1990; Seltzer, 1991; Seltzer *et al.*, 1989). Does joint custody have a causal impact on support behavior after income level has been taken into account?

It might be hypothesized that joint custody fathers are most motivated to invest both time and money in their children, or it is possible that joint custody enhances the opportunities to observe and address financial need. If these theories are true, then the custody–award link will hold, regardless of level of income. In fact, relationships between custody and parental investment in time and money disappear after paternal income is controlled for. Using different statistical techniques, two studies (Albiston *et al.*, 1990; Seltzer, 1991) each found that, when income was held constant, joint legal custody had no impact on the level of the award. However, higher income fathers with joint custody were more likely to pay support. This finding suggests that custody may potentiate some family circumstances that hold promise for child well-being.

Decision Making

Proximate decision-making processes set the stage for future family processes, including opportunities and expectations for parental investment in the child. Not surprisingly, most parents report considerable trepidation about broaching discussions about parenting arrangements, and avoidance behavior is widespread (Kelly, 1993a). The trend away from judicial intervention and toward private ordering (Mnookin & Kornhauser, 1979) has increased the prevalence of parenting plans forged between the parties themselves, or with the assistance of lawyers or mediators. Many parents cannot afford to hire professionals to give them the information or the representation that they need to strike an equitable agreement. Other parents pay the high financial and emotional price of protracted litigation.

The genesis of the custody plan has long-standing implications, particularly if the arrangement was not the product of mutual consent. It is certainly conducive to the best interest of children to study the role of the decision-making dynamic in the fate of the custody arrangement. Such an approach would get closer to the meaning of the arrangement for each family member. Is the custody arrangement the product of a prudent and well-advised planning process? Is it an act of coercion or vengeance? Does it maintain the power of one parent to abuse the other?

Allegations of gender bias, leveled at legal presumptions and legal decision-making arenas, deserve careful scrutiny. A strong concern among mothers' advocates is that joint custody can be used as a bargaining chip to negotiate lower child-support awards (Bruch, 1986; Fineman, 1988; Weitzman, 1985). That is, by seeking or obtaining more time with the child, a father can reduce his financial obligations. Conversely, fathers cite the distribution of custodial awards to argue that the law is gender-neutral in spirit, but not in practice.

The various modes used by parents to work out parenting plans (litigation, mediation, and a host of other innovative programs) need to be evaluated against comparable criteria, including their capacity to foster informed, equitable agreements, as well as the emotional climate that they foster between parents. Third parties play an influential role in the process and outcome. For example, Mnookin *et al.* (1990) reported that parties with lawyers are more likely to elect joint legal custody. Kelly (1993b) found that the use of mediation results in parenting plans that specifically delineate the rights and responsibilities of each parent. She suggested that the opportunity for a planning process clarifies parental expectations and establishes basic ground rules. Noncustodial parents may continue to invest time in their children because a clear and consensual plan has been set in place.

Family Process

The fate of any parenting plan is highly dependent on the capability of the mothers and the fathers to master the new demands of parenting apart (Hetherington, 1989). This mastery involves the difficult task of transforming a painful and, in some cases, dysfunctional personal relationship into a "business relationship" on behalf of the child (Ricci, 1989).

To illustrate the potential role of family process, we touch on a frequently studied variable: family conflict. Although intense and protracted conflict is far from universal (Kelly, 1988), it has been consistently linked to poor outcomes for children (Depner, Leino, & Chun, 1992; Emery, 1982) and is often a more powerful determinant of poor outcome than family dissolution itself (Emery, 1988).

Countering the association of parental investment with salubrious effects for children is the observation that such an investment also enhances the opportunity for conflict through increased parental interaction and negotiation (Hodges, 1986; Rothberg, 1983). Even so, a direct link between investment and conflict has not been established in multivariate assessment (Seltzer, 1990). That is, the investment–conflict link is spurious when other relevant factors are built into the analysis. Neither contact nor support enhanced conflict when precursing factors of parental education were controlled for. These findings are consistent with those of other investigations that have simultaneously evaluated the relative effects of custody and investment in time with other predictors of child adjustment. For example, Kline, Tschann, Johnston, and Wallerstein (1989) found that family process variables and parent short-term outcomes (anxiety and depression) were more consequential for child outcomes than custody status.

A more fully elaborated model could also clarify the offsetting advantages of family process and parental investment for a spectrum of possible outcomes. For example, Buchanan *et al.* (1993) observed that interparental conflict is associated with adolescents' feeling "caught in the middle," which in turn materializes into poor psychological adjustment. Adolescents in shared-parenting arrangements were more likely than those in other custodial arrangements to feel "caught in the middle" when parental hostility was high. Nonetheless, being in a time-sharing arrangement was not, in and of itself, connected with adjustment problems.

Family Change

Over the life course of the family, it is reasonable to assume that parental roles will vary (e.g., as a result of the changing needs of the growing child, mobility, of remarriage, and of new children). The complexity is increased, as noted above, because individual and family changes proceed on different timetables. For example, child adjustment may be considered the joint effect of simultaneous progression through developmental markers and unfolding events in family dissolution and reorganization (Bray, 1991; Wallerstein, 1991).

Approximately one child in three will spend some part of childhood in a stepfamily (Glick, 1989; Hofferth, 1985). Throughout the minority of the child, the parents are likely to form relationships with a series of romantic partners. Cohabitation is common, but it eventuates in a marital union in only about half of all cases (Bumpass, Castro-Martin, & Sweet, 1991; London, 1991). Both parents are likely to remarry eventually, but because men remarry at a faster rate (London, 1991; Norton & Moorman, 1987), children are first likely to experience stepmothers. Because the divorce rate for remarriage is higher than for first marriages, many children experience a second marital disruption (Brody, Neubaum, & Forhand, 1988; Glick, 1989).

The remarriage of noncustodial fathers has been linked to a reduced financial and emotional investment in their children (Furstenberg et al., 1987; Peterson & Nord, 1990). The remarriage of custodial mothers prompts changes in parental roles as well as competition and loyalty conflicts (Bray, 1988). Crosbie-Burnett's study of remarried families (1988) suggested that poor outcomes are more likely as the family structure increases in complexity. Adolescents were less happy in remarried families and less likely to regard their stepfathers as family members when two conditions applied: The family had joint custody, and the stepfather had offspring from a previous relationship. Neither condition alone brought about the effects.

Legal Outcomes

From the perspective of the legal system, a successful custody arrangement is one that all family members can live with and one that is flexible enough to accommodate to changing family circumstances. Low rates of compliance and high rates of relitigation are viewed as poor outcomes. Findings of lower relitigation rates for joint custody families in California (Ilfeld, Ilfeld, & Alexander, 1982) and Canada (Benjamin & Irving, 1989) were not replicated in Massachusetts (Phear et al., 1984).

Child Outcomes

Various outcomes for children have been considered in the foregoing review. Excessive emphasis on negative and pathological outcomes has been noted by several investigators. In an extensive review of the literature, Demo and Acock (1988) called for attention to a wider spectrum of child outcomes that includes adaptive and beneficial aspects.

In addition, close examination of the research in the "Child Outcome" category dictates the extension of research designs to include direct and in-depth studies of children (Benjamin & Irving, 1989) as well as an examination of individual differences among children that affect the advisability of certain custody measures (Hetherington, 1989).

Parent Outcomes

Families comprise systems of individuals whose interests differ and often conflict in the event of a custody decision. How do the process and outcome of custody decision making affect the perceived rights and responsibilities of each family member? Few studies simultaneously capture the ramifications of custody for multiple family members. By looking at the full family system, inequities would be elucidated (Depner, 1985).

The discussion of legal context and decision-making variables reviewed some of the concerns about gender inequities. In addition, custody decisions may have different implications for the financial well-being and relocation opportunities of different family members (Bartlett & Stack, 1991; Bruch, 1988; Shulman & Pitt, 1982).

CONCLUSIONS

Empirical research has generated a roster of variables that deserve consideration in the determination of the consequences of custody status. Initial findings that have begun to link the components of this model suggest that conclusions about custody need to factor in the influence of variables often omitted from simplistic designs. The sheer weight of these variables may be daunting to some scholars and practitioners, but at this juncture, an expansive approach will facilitate the evaluation of alternative causal paths. For example, a clearer understanding of the role of custody develops when other pertinent variables, such as percursing family circumstances, parent investment, and family process, are incorporated into the analysis.

The research evidence to date suggests that the answer to the question "Does joint custody work?" will depend on a complex system of factors and will therefore be different for individuals who vary along the dimensions defined by these factors. Although simple answers allude us, a contextual understanding of custody dynamics should alert us to the factors pertinent to policy and practice.

REFERENCES

Ahrons, C. R. (1980). Joint custody arrangements in the postdivorce family. *Journal of Divorce, 3,* 533–540.

Ahrons, C. R. (1983). Predictors of paternal involvement post-divorce: Mothers' and fathers' perceptions. *Journal of Divorce, 6,* 55–69.

Albiston, C. R., Maccoby, E. E., & Mnookin, R. (1990). Does joint legal custody matter? *Stanford Law and Policy Review,* 167–179.

Amato, P., & Keith, B. (1991). Parental divorce and adult well being: A meta-analysis. *Journal of Marriage and the Family, 53*(1), 43–58.

Arbanel, A. (1979). Shared parenting after separation and divorce: A study of joint custody. *American Journal of Orthopsychiatry, 49,* 320–329.

Barber, B. L., & Eccles, J. S. (1992). Long-term influence of divorce and single parenting on adolescent family- and work-related values, behaviors, and aspirations. *Psychological Bulletin, 111*(1), 108–126.

Bartlett, K. T., & Stack, C.B. (1991). Joint custody, feminism, and the dependency dilemma. In J. Folberg (Ed.), *Joint custody and shared parenting* (2nd ed., pp. 63–88). New York: Guilford Press.

Benjamin, M., & Irving, H. H. (1989). Shared parenting: Critical review of the research literature. *Family and Conciliation Courts Review, 27*(2), 21–35.

Block, J., Block, J., & Gjerde, P. (1986). The personality of children prior to divorce: A prospective study. *Child Development, 57,* 827–840.

Bray, J. H. (1988). Children's development in early marriage. In E. M. Hetherington & J. A. Arasteh (Eds.), *The impact of divorce, single-parenting and step-parenting on children* (pp. 279–298). Hillsdale, NJ: Erlbaum.

Bray, J. H. (1991). Psychosocial factors affecting custodial and visitation arrangements. *Behavioral Science and the Law, 9,* 419–437.

Bray, J. H., & Berger, S. H. (1993). Nonresidential parents after remarriage. In C. E. Depner & J. H. Bray (Eds.), *Nonresidential parenting: New vistas in family living* (pp. 156–181). Newbury Park, CA: Sage.

Bray, J. H., & Depner, C. E. (1993). Perspectives on nonresidential parenting. In C. E. Depner & J. H. Bray (Eds.), *Nonresidential parenting: New vistas in family living* (pp. 3–12). Newbury Park, CA: Sage.

Brody, G. H., Neubaum, E., & Forhand, R. (1988). Serial marriage: A heuristic analysis of an emerging family form. *Psychological Bulletin, 103,* 211–222.

Bruch, C. S. (1986). And how are the children? The effects of ideology and mediation on child custody law and children's well-being in the United States. *International Journal of Law and the Family, 2,* 106–126.

Bruch, C. S. (1988). Problems inherent in designing child support guidelines. In *Essentials of child support guidelines development: Economic issues and policy considerations* (pp. 41–64). Proceedings of the Women's Legal Defense Fund's National Conference on the Development of Child Support and Guidelines, Queenstown, MD. Washington, DC: Women's Legal Defense Fund.

Buchanan, C. M., Maccoby, E. E., & Dornbusch, S. M. (1991). Caught in between parents: Adolescent's experience in divorced homes. *Child development, 62*(5), 1008–1029.

Buchanan, C. M., Maccoby, E. E., & Dornbusch, S. M. (1992). Adolescents and their families after divorce: Three residential arrangements compared. *Journal of Research in Adolescence, 2*(3), 261–291.

Buchanan, C. M., Maccoby, E. E., Mnookin, R. H., & Dornbusch, S. M. (1993). Post-divorce roles of mothers and fathers in the lives of their children. *Family Psychology, 7*(1), 24–38.

Bumpass, L. L., & Sweet, J. A. (1989). Children's experience in single-parent families: Implications of cohabitation and marital transitions. *Family Planning Perspectives, 21*, 256–260.

Bumpass, L. L., Castro-Martin, T., & Sweet, J. A. (1991). The impact of family background and early marital factors on marital disruption. *Journal of Family Issues, 12*(1), 22–42.

Camera, K., & Resnik, G. (1988). Interparental conflict and cooperation: Factors moderating children's post divorce adjustment. In E. M. Hetherington & J. A. Arasteh (Eds.), *The impact of divorce, single-parenting and step-parenting on children* (pp. 169–196). Hillsdale, NJ: Erlbaum.

Cashion, B. G. (1984). Female-headed families: Effects on children and clinical implications. In D. H. Olson & B. C. Miller (Eds.), *Family studies review yearbook* (pp. 481–489). Beverly Hills, CA: Sage.

Chambers, D. L. (1979). *Making fathers pay*. Chicago: University of Chicago Press.

Cherlin, A. J., Furstenberg, F. F., Chase-Lansdale, P. L., Kiernan, K. E., Robins, P. K., Morrison, D. R., & Teller, J. O. (1991). Longitudinal studies of effects of divorce on children in Great Britain and the United States. *Science, 252*, 1386–1389.

Chesler, P. (1986). *Mothers on trial*. New York: McGraw-Hill.

Clark, S. C., Whitney, R. A., & Beck, J. C. (1988). Discrepancies between custodial awards and custodial practices: De jure and de facto custody. *Journal of Divorce, 11*(3–4), 219–229.

Clingempeel, W. G., & Reppucci, N. D. (1982). Joint custody after divorce: Major issues and goals for research. *Psychological Bulletin, 91*(1), 102–127.

Coller, D. R. (1988). Joint custody: Research, theory, and policy. *Family Process, 27*, 459–469.

Crosbie-Burnett, M. (1988). Impact of joint versus maternal legal custody, sex and age of adolescent, and family structure complexity on adolescents in remarried families. *Family and Conciliation Courts Review, 26*(2), 47–52.

Del Carmen, R., & Virgo, G. N. (1993). Marital disruption and nonresidential parenting: A multicultural perspective. In C. E., Depner & J. H. Bray (Eds.), *Nonresidential parenting: New vistas in family living* (pp. 156–181). Newbury Park, CA: Sage.

Demo, D. H., & Acock, A. C. (1988). The impact of divorce on children. *Journal of Marriage and the Family, 50*, 619–648.

Depner, C. E. (1985, August). *Assessing the impact of divorce on family structure and functioning*. Paper presented at the annual meeting of the American Psychological Association, Los Angeles.

Depner, C. E., & Bray, J. H (1993). Nonresidential parenting: Multidimensional approaches in research, policy, and practice. In C. E. Depner & J. H. Bray (Eds.), *Nonresidential parenting: New vistas in family living* (pp. 156–181). Newbury Park, CA: Sage.

Depner, C. E., Leino, V., & Chun, A. (1992). Interparental conflict and child development: A decade review and meta-analysis. *Family and Conciliation Courts review, 30*(3), 323–342.

Dornbusch, S. M., Carlsmith, J. M., Bushwall, S. J., Ritter, P. L., Leiderman, H., Hastorf, A. H., & Gross, R. T. (1985). Single parents, extended households, and the control of adolescents. *Child Development, 56*, 326–341.

Emery, R. E. (1982). Interpersonal conflict and the children of discord and divorce. *Psychological Bulletin, 92*(2), 310–330.

Emery, R. E. (1988). *Marriage, divorce, and children's adjustment.* Newbury Park, CA: Sage

Felner, R. D., & Terre, L. (1987). Child custody dispositions and children's adaptation following divorce. In L. Weithorn (Ed.), *Psychology and child custody determinants: Knowledge, roles and expertise.* Lincoln: University of Nebraska Press.

Fineman, M. (1988). Dominant discourse, professional language, and legal change in child custody decision-making. *Harvard Law Review, 101,* 727–774.

Folberg, J. (1984). Issues and trends in the law of joint custody. In J. Folberg (Ed.), *Joint custody and shared parenting* (pp. 159–167). Washington, DC: BNA Books.

Folberg, J. (1991). Custody overview. In J. Folberg (Ed.), *Joint custody and shared parenting* (2nd ed., pp. 3–10). New York: Guilford Press.

Frankel, S. A. (1985). Joint custody awards and children: A theoretical framework and some practical considerations. *Psychiatry, 48,* 318–328.

Furstenberg, F. F., Jr. (1985). Sociological ventures in child development. *Child Development, 56,* 281–288.

Furstenberg, F. F., Jr. (1988a). Good dads-bad dads: Two faces of fatherhood. In A. J. Cherlin (Ed.), *The changing American family and public policy* (pp. 193–218). Washington, DC: Urban Institute.

Furstenberg, F. F., Jr. (1988b). Marital disruptions, child custody, and visitation. In A. J. Kahn & S. B. Kammerman (Eds.), *Child support: From debt collection to social policy.* Beverly Hills, CA: Sage.

Furstenberg, F. F., Jr., & Teitler, J. O. (1991, October). *Reconsidering the effects of marital disruption: What happens to children of divorce in early adulthood?* Paper presented at the European Population Conference, Paris.

Furstenberg, F. F., Nord, C. W., Peterson, J. L., & Zill, N. (1983). The life course of children of divorce: Marital disruption and parental contact. *American Sociological Review, 48,* 656–668.

Furstenberg, F. F., Jr., Morgan, S. P., & Allison, P. D. (1987). Paternal participation and children's well-being after marital dissolution. *American Sociological Review, 52,* 595–601.

Glick, P. C. (1989). Remarried families, stepfamilies, and stepchildren: A brief demographic profile. *Family Relations, 38,* 24–27.

Guidubaldi, J., & Perry, J. D. (1984). Divorce, socioeconomic status, and children's cognitive-social competence at school entry. *American Journal of Orthopsychiatry, 54*(3), 459–468.

Hetherington, E. M. (1989). Coping with family transitions: Winners, losers, and survivors. *Child Development, 60,* 1–14.

Hetherington, E. M., Camera, K. A., & Featherman, D. L. (1981). Achievement and intellectual functioning of children in one-parent households. In J. Spence (Ed.), *Assessing achievement.* New York: Freeman.

Hodges, W. F. (1986). *Interventions for children of divorce.* New York: Wiley.

Hoffreth, S. L. (1985). Updating children's life course. *Journal of Marriage and the Family, 47,* 93–115.

Ilfeld, F. W., Jr., Ilfeld, H. Z., & Alexander, J. R. (1982). Does joint custody work? A first look at outcome data or relitigation. *American Journal of Psychiatry, 131*(1), 62–66.

Irving, H. H., & Benjamin, M. (1991). Shared and sole-custody parents: A comparative analysis. In J. Folberg (Ed.), *Joint custody and shared parenting* (2nd ed., pp. 114–132). New York: Guilford Press.

Irving, H. H., Benjamin, M., & Trocme, N. (1984). Shared parenting: An empirical analysis utilizing a large data base. *Family Process, 23,* 561–569.

Johnston, J., Kline, M., & Tschann, J. M. (1989). Ongoing post-divorce conflict: Effects on children of joint custody and frequent access. *American Journal of Orthopsychiatry, 59*(4), 576–592.

Kanoy, K. W., & Cunningham, J. L. (1984). Consensus or confusion in research on children and divorce: Conceptual and methodological issues. *Journal of Divorce, 7,* 45–71.

Kelly, J. (1988). Long-term adjustment in children of divorce: Converging findings and implications for practice. *Journal of Family Psychology, 2*(1), 119–140.

Kelly, J. (1991). Parent interaction after divorce: Comparison of mediated and adversarial divorce processes. *Behavioral Sciences and the Law, 9,* 387–398.

Kelly, J. (1993a). Developing and implementing post-divorce parenting plans: Does the forum make the difference? In C. E. Depner & J. H. Bray (Eds.), *Nonresidential parenting: New vistas in family living* (pp. 156–181). Newbury Park, CA: Sage.

Kelly, J. (1993b). Current research on children's postdivorce adjustment: No simple answers. *Family and Conciliation Courts Review, 31*(1), 29–49.

Kiernan, K. (1992). The impact of family disruption in childhood on transitions made in young adult life. *Population Studies, 46*(3), 363–380.

Kitson, G. C., & Morgan, L. A. (1990). The multiple consequences of divorce: A decade review. *Journal of Marriage and the Family, 52,* 913–924.

Kline, M., Tschann, J. M., Johnston, J. R., & Wallerstein, J. S. (1989). Children's adjustment to joint and sole physical custody families. *Developmental Psychology, 25*(3), 430–438.

Kurdek, L. A. (1981). An integrative perspective on children's divorce adjustment. *American Psychologist, 36*(8), 856–866.

London, K. A. (1991). Cohabitation, marriage, marital dissolution, and remarriage: United States, 1988. *Advance data from vital and health statistics; no 194.* Hyattsville, MD: National Center for Health Statistics.

Longfellow, C. (1979). Divorce in context: Its impact on children. In G. Levinger & O. C. Moles (Eds.), *Divorce and separation: Context, causes and consequences* (pp. 287–306). New York: Basic Books.

Luepnitz, D. A. (1982). *Child custody: A study of families after divorce.* Lexington, MA: Lexington Books.

Luepnitz, D. (1986). A comparison of maternal, paternal and joint custody: Under the varieties of post-divorce family life. *Journal of Divorce, 9*(3), 1–12.

Maccoby, E., & Mnookin, R. H. (1992). *Dividing the child: The social and legal dilemmas of custody.* Cambridge: Harvard University Press.

Maccoby, E. E., Depner, C. E., & Mnookin, R. H. (1988). Child custody following divorce. In E. M. Hetherington & J. D. Arasteh (Eds.), *Impact of divorce, single parenting and stepparenting on children* (pp. 91–114). Hillsdale, NJ: Erlbaum.

Matsueda, R. L., & Heimer, K. (1987). Race, family structure, and delinquency. *American Sociological Review, 52,* 826–840.

McKinnon, R., & Wallerstein, J. S. (1987). Joint custody and the preschool child. *Conciliation Courts Review, 25,* 39–47.

McLanahan, S. (1985). Family structure and the reproduction of poverty. *American Journal of Sociology, 90,* 873–901.

Mnookin, R. H., & Kornhauser, L. (1979). Bargaining in the shadow of the law: The case of divorce. *Yale Law Journal, 88*, 950–997.

Mnookin, R. H., Maccoby, E., Albiston, C. R., & Depner, C. E. (1990). Private ordering revisited: What custodial arrangements are parents negotiating? In S. D. Sugarman & H. Hill Kay (Eds.), *Divorce reform at the crossroads* (pp. 37–74). New Haven: Yale University Press.

Nehls, N. M., & Morgenbesser, M. (1980). Joint custody: An exploration of the issues. *Family Process, 19*, 119–125.

Norton, A. J., & Moorman, J. E. (1987). Marriage and divorce patterns of U.S. women. *Journal of Marriage and the Family, 49*, 3–14.

Nunan, S. (1980). Joint custody versus single effects on child development. *Dissertation Abstracts International, 41*, 4680B–4681B.

O'Leary, V., Ickovics, J. R., & Ryan, M. (1992, January). Resilience in women. In *The resilient woman: Strength in the face of adversity*, conference sponsored by the Spring Foundation, Stanford, CA.

Patterson, G. R. (1982). *Coercive family processes: A social learning approach* (Vol. 3). Eugene, OR: Castalia.

Pearson, J., & Thoennes, N. (1988). Supporting children after divorce: The influence of custody on support levels and payments. *Family Law Quarterly, 22*, 319–339.

Peterson, J. L., & Nord, C. W. (1990). The regular receipt of child support: A multistep process. *Journal of Marriage and the Family, 52*, 539–551.

Phear, W. P. C., Beck, J. C., Hauser, B. B., Clark, S. C., & Whitney, R. A. (1984). An empirical study of custody arrangements: Joint versus sole legal custody. In J. Folberg (Ed.), *Joint custody and shared parenting* (pp. 142–158). Washington, DC: BNA Books.

Ricci, I. (1989). Mediation, joint custody and legal agreements: A time to review, revise and refine. *Family and Conciliation Courts Review, 27*(1), 47–55.

Rothberg, B. (1983). Joint custody: Parental problems and satisfaction. *Family Process, 22*, 43–52.

Rutter, M. (1989). Intergenerational continuities and discontinuities in serious parenting difficulties. In D. Cichetti & V. Carlson (Eds.), *Child maltreatment: Theory and research on the causes and consequences of child abuse and neglect* (pp. 317–348). Cambridge: Cambridge University Press.

Rutter, M., & Giller, H. (1983). *Juvenile delinquency: Trends and perspectives*. New York: Guilford Press.

Seltzer, J. A. (1990). Legal and physical custody arrangements in recent divorces. *Social Science Quarterly, 71*(2), 250–266.

Seltzer, J. A. (1991). Legal custody arrangements and children's economic welfare. *American Journal of Sociology, 96*(4), 895–929.

Seltzer, J. A., Schaeffer, N. C., & Charng, H. (1989). Family ties after divorce: The relationship between visiting and paying child support. *Journal of Marriage and the family, 51*(4), 1013–1031.

Shiller, V. M. (1986a). Joint versus maternal custody for families with latency age boys: Parent characteristics and child adjustment. *American Journal of Orthopsychiatry, 56*, 486–489.

Shiller, V. M. (1986b). Loyalty conflicts and family relationships in latency age boys: A comparison of joint and maternal custody. *Journal of Divorce, 9*(4), 17–38.

Shulman, J., & Pitt, V. (1982). Second thoughts on joint custody: Analysis of legislation and its implications for women and children. *Golden Gate Law Review, 12*, 539–577.

Smith, T. (1990). Parental separation and the academic self-concepts of adolescents: An effort to solve the puzzle of separation effects. *Journal of Marriage and the Family, 52*(1), 107–118.

Steinman, S. D. (1981). The experience of children in a joint custody arrangement: A report of a study. *American Journal of Orthopsychiatry, 51*, 403–414.

Steinman, S. B., Zemmelman, S. E., & Knoblauch, T. M. (1985). A study of parent who sought joint custody following divorce: Who reaches agreement and sustains joint custody and who returns to court. *Journal of the American Academy of Child Psychiatry, 24*, 545–554.

Stevenson, M. R., & Black, K. N. (1988). Paternal absence and sex-role development: A meta analysis. *Child Development, 59*, 793–814.

Thornton, A. (1991). Influence of the marital history of parents on the marital and cohabitational experiences of children. *American Journal of Sociology, 86*(1), 868–894.

Trombetta, D. (1989). Shared parenting: Is it working? *Family and Conciliation Courts Review, 27*(2), 17–21.

Tropf, W. (1984). An exploratory examination of the effects of remarriage on child support and personal contacts. *Journal of Divorce, 7*(3), 57–73.

Wallerstein, J. (1991). The long-term effects of divorce on children: A review. *Journal of the American Academy of Child Adolescent Psychiatry, 30*(3), 349–360.

Warshak, R. A. (1986). Father-custody and child development: A review and analysis of psychological research. *Behavioral Science and the Law, 4*(2), 185–202.

Warshak, R. A., & Santrock, J. W. (1983). The impact of divorce in father-custody homes: The child's perspective. In L. A. Kurdek (Ed.), *Children and divorce.* San Francisco: Jossey-Bass.

Watson, M. A. (1981). Custody alternatives: Defining the best interests of the children. *Family Relations, 30*, 474–479.

Weiss, R. S. (1979). Growing up a little faster: The experience of growing up in a single-parent household. *Journal of Social Issues, 35*, 97–111.

Weiss, Y., & Willis, R. J. (1985). Children as collective goods and divorce settlements. *Journal of Labor Economics, 3*, 268–292.

Weitzman, L. J. (1985). *The divorce revolution: The unexpected social and economic consequences for women and children in America.* New York: Free Press.

Welsh, O. (1982). The effects of custody arrangements on children of divorce. *Dissertation Abstracts International, 42*, 4946B.

Wolchik, S. A., Braver, S. L., & Sandler, I. W. (1985). Maternal versus joint custody: Children's postseparation experiences and adjustment. *Journal of Clinical Child Psychology, 14*, 5–10.

Wright, D. W., & Price, S. J. (1986). Court-ordered child support payment: The effects of the former spouse relationship on compliance. *Journal of Marriage and the Family, 48*, 869–874.

5

The Gap between Psychosocial Assumptions and Empirical Research in Lesbian-Mother Child Custody Cases

Patricia J. Falk

The phrase "lesbian mother" is still viewed as a contradiction in terms (Hitchens, 1979–1980; Hitchens & Price, 1979) by some segments of our society[1]: "Until recently, the existence of lesbian mothers

[1] The following analysis focuses primarily on lesbian mothers who have children as the result of heterosexual marriage because this is the population most often involved in child custody disputes. Of course, lesbian women can become mothers in a number of other ways, including adoption (see Ricketts & Achtenberg, 1989) and artificial insemination by a known or unknown donor (AID) (See Pies, 1989). In this connection, it is important to note that the number of lesbian women electing to have children by artificial insemination has increased dramatically, the increase causing Pies (1987) to comment that there has been a "baby boom" in the lesbian community since the late 1970s. In addition, lesbian women can become foster parents (see Ricketts & Achtenberg, 1989), "stepparents" to their partner's children from a previous relationship (see Baptiste, 1987), or "second mothers" to children planned and conceived within a lesbian relationship (see Delaney, 1991; Polikoff, 1990).

Patricia J. Falk • Cleveland-Marshall College of Law, Cleveland, Ohio 44115.

Redefining Families: Implications for Children's Development, edited by Adele Eskeles Gottfried and Allen W. Gottfried. Plenum Press, New York, 1994.

was almost unrecognized in American society, for most people believe that homosexuality is inconsistent with the ability or desire to procreate" (Riley, 1975, p. 799). However, since the late 1970s, there has been a dawning appreciation that lesbianism and motherhood are not mutually exclusive categories. This trend has been noted in society in general (DiLapi, 1989; Riley, 1975) in the courts (Basile, 1974), and in the social science community (Gottman, 1989). Further evidence of the recognition of this "increasingly present population" (Gottman, 1989, p. 193) is the virtual explosion in the legal and social-scientific literature on lesbian mother families (for reviews, see Cramer, 1986; "Developments in the Law," 1989; Gibbs, 1988; Gottman, 1989; Kleber, Howell, & Tibbits-Kleber, 1986; Steckel, 1987; Susoeff, 1985).

Given the nascent recognition of lesbian motherhood, it is not surprising that accurate appraisals of the number of women who fall into this category or the number of children being raised by lesbian mothers or gay fathers are unavailable. The estimates of the number of lesbian mothers who reside with their children range from 3 million (Kirkpatrick, 1987; Pies, 1987) to 5 million (Rivera, 1979). The estimates of the number of children living with gay parents are even more substantial: from 6 million (Gottman, 1989) to 14 million (Turner, Scadden, & Harris, 1990).

LEGAL ASSUMPTIONS

In recent years, there has been a significant increase in the number of reported cases involving the custody rights of lesbian mothers in divorce or child protection proceedings and in the related scholarly discussion in both law and social science. Many cases involving the rights of lesbian mothers have previously been unpublished. Even when they were published, the courts often eliminated or truncated their discussions concerning the mother's sexual orientation (Basile, 1974; Rivera, 1979). Thus, one reason for the "increase" in these cases may simply be that the topic is more discussable and therefore that more cases are being reported. Also, with the growth of the gay rights movement, more lesbian women are willing to admit their sexual orientation and to fight in court for the custody of their children (Hitchens, 1979–1980). According to Rivera (1980–1981), child custody cases are the most litigated area of homosexual rights.

Nonetheless, lesbian mothers, especially those who "admit" their sexual orientation, still have a difficult time obtaining the custody of their children (Browne & Giampetro, 1985). Commentators (e.g., Davies, 1979; Moses & Hawkins, 1982; Rand, Graham, & Rawlings, 1982) have estimated that a lesbian mother's likelihood of success is no more than 50%. Although the general prospects are not encouraging, there appears to be a trend in the direction of granting custody to lesbian mothers (Kraft, 1983).

In most jurisdictions, the legal criterion used in child custody cases is the so-called best-interests-of-the-child standard. This standard is ambiguous and highly subjective, and legal decision makers, therefore, wield a considerable degree of discretion. Furthermore, because the trial judge's decision is given great deference by the reviewing courts and is reversed only if there is a clear abuse of discretion, the judge's decision is essentially final. Some states have attempted to articulate, through legislation, the factors bearing on this standard, including parental fitness; the grounds for divorce; the age, health, and sex of the child; the quality of the home environment; the mental and physical health of the parents; and the preferences of the child and the parents (Basile, 1974).

The major problem encountered by lesbian mothers in child custody cases appears to be the attention paid by legal decision makers to the issue of homosexuality, to the exclusion of their consideration of the other factors commonly associated with a determination of the child's best interests ("Burden on Gay Litigants," 1984; Hitchens & Price, 1979). Once the issue of parental homosexuality is raised, other factors and issues become secondary (Hitchens, 1979–1980). Also, the courts tend to base their decisions more on their attitudes toward or stereotypes of gay individuals than on the facts in any particular case ("Burdens on Gay Litigants," 1984; Hitchens & Price, 1979).

Legal decision makers often focus on the mother's homosexuality without even attempting to establish a causal relation between the mother's sexual orientation and the child's welfare. Not only should this connection be made, but it should be substantiated by more than mere supposition (Kraft, 1983). However, when the courts do attempt to articulate a relation between a mother's sexual orientation and her child's development, they often rely on general assumptions and not on expert testimony or empirical research findings.

Before we examine these assumptions, three caveats are in order:

1. I will focus only on the most common and salient psychosocial assumptions.
2. It is important to note that assumptions relating to the morality of homosexuality (Basile, 1974; "Developments in the Law," 1989; Harris, 1977) and the physical well-being of children in light of the AIDS epidemic (Rivera, 1987) also appear in many court opinions, but because these are not empirical psychological assumptions, they will not be directly addressed in the following discussion.
3. The courts often do not articulate, with any degree of specificity, their assumptions regarding the impact on a child of being raised by a homosexual parent. Instead, the courts couch their decisions in general language about the "harm" of the custody arrangement or environment (Irish v. Irish, 1980). Thus, the following assumptions are overtly present only when the court seeks to specify the nature of the harm resulting from a lesbian mother's retaining custody of her children.

There are two major categories of psychosocial empirical assumptions that appear in lesbian-mother child custody cases: (a) those concerning the lesbian mother and her lifestyle and (b) those concerning the effect of the lesbian mother and her lifestyle on the development of the child.

The courts make two general assumptions about lesbian mothers themselves. First, they often express the belief that all homosexual individuals, including lesbian mothers, are mentally ill (Davies, 1979; Mucklow & Phelan, 1979; Rand et al., 1982, Riley, 1975) and therefore supposedly incapable of being good parents. In Thigpen v. Carpenter (1987), for example, the court highlighted an expert witness's testimony that the mother had been found to be "emotionally stable," thus implying that this issue is one to be resolved in a case involving a lesbian mother.

Second, it is commonly assumed that lesbian women are less maternal than their heterosexual counterparts and thus are poor mothers (Miller, Jacobsen, & Bigner, 1981; Moses & Hawkins, 1982; Mucklow & Phelan, 1979). "Because the sexual aspect of their lesbianism is perceived to be the overwhelming focus of their lives, it is assumed to extend [sic] into their roles as mothers" (Erlichman, 1988, p. 209). The court in DiStefano v. DiStefano (1978; see also Bark v. Bark, 1985;

Hall v. Hall, 1980) pointed out that the mother had failed to keep her lesbian relationship separate from her role as mother and that this failure had had a detrimental effect on her children. The underlying assumption was that lesbian women are less maternal because, it is asserted, their chief priority is their relationship with another adult, rather than their children.

Assumptions about the parent–child interaction tend to be more specific than those about lesbian mothers *per se*. This second set of assumptions can be further subdivided into two categories: (1) those dealing with the child's general health and welfare and (2) those dealing with the child's gender or sexual development. One common assumption falling into the first category is that children raised by lesbian mothers are more likely to develop psychological or mental problems (Golombok, Spencer, & Rutter, 1983; see, e.g., *Doe v. Doe*, 1981; *In re Jane B.*, 1976; *In re Mara*, 1956; *S.E.G. v. R.A.G.*, 1987).

The courts often assume that lesbian women are sexually perverse and that children raised by them are more likely to be sexually molested by the custodial parent, her partner, or her acquaintances (Davies, 1979; DiLapi, 1989; Hall, 1978; Harris, 1977; Kraft, 1983; Miller *et al.*, 1981; Moses & Hawkins, 1982). One example of a court's assumption that a child with a lesbian mother (or a gay father) is more likely to be sexually molested was presented in *J.L.P.(H.) v. D.L.P.* (1982). In that case, a gay father had presented expert testimony that child molestation was more common in the heterosexual population than among gay persons. The court was extremely skeptical of all the evidence but was particularly critical of testimony on the molestation issue: "Every trial judge, or for that matter, every appellate judge, knows that molestation of minor boys by adult males is not as uncommon as the psychological experts' testimony indicated" (p. 869).

With regard to the gender or sexual development of a child with a lesbian mother, the courts have made two assumptions. First, judges have stated their belief that the gender-role development of the child will be significantly impaired. For example, in *N.K.M. v. L.E.M.* (1980), the court denied a lesbian mother custody of her daughter and supported its decision, in part, by stating that it was concerned that the child would experience sexual disorientation as a result of living with the mother. The same issue arose in *Spence v. Durham* (1973), in which the court expressed fear about the danger that the mother would "instill tendencies toward 'sexual aberrations' in the girls" (p. 551).

The second assumption with respect to gender or sexual development, and perhaps the most uniformly cited assumption, is that the child will be more likely to become homosexual than a child raised by heterosexual parents (for reviews, see Basile, 1974; Campbell, 1978; Davies, 1979; Golombok et al., 1983; Green, 1978, 1982; Hall, 1978; Harris, 1977; Hitchens, 1979–1980; Hitchens & Price, 1979; Kirkpatrick, Smith, & Roy, 1981; Kraft, 1983; Moses & Hawkins, 1982; Riley, 1975; Weeks, Derdeyn, & Langmon, 1975). Riley (1975) pointed out that this assumption is based on the questionable value judgment that having a child become homosexual is a negative consequence. In this connection, the opinion in *N.K.M. v. L.E.M.* (1980) is also instructive: "Allowing that homosexuality is a permissible lifestyle—an 'alternate life style,' as it is termed these days—if voluntarily chosen, yet who would place a child in a milieu where she may be inclined toward it?" (p. 186). It is interesting that several courts either have rejected this assumption outright (see e.g., *Bezio v. Patenaude,* 1980) or have stated that they were unable to determine the accuracy of this assumption (see, e.g., *Jacobson v. Jacobson,* 1981). One of the best examples of the former approach is the majority opinion in *Conkel v. Conkel* (1987): "The court takes judicial notice that there is no consensus on what causes homosexuality, but there is substantial consensus among experts that being raised by a homosexual parent does not increase the likelihood that a child will become homosexual" (p. 986).

One final assumption that does not fit neatly into either of the previous categories, but that appears to be based on the broader impact of having a lesbian mother, is that children of such mothers are going to be traumatized or stigmatized by society or their peers (Basile, 1974; Campbell, 1978; Hall, 1978; Hitchens, 1979–1980; Hitchens & Price, 1979; Kraft, 1983; Moses & Hawkins, 1982). The "stigma" assumption is remarkably common in legal opinions involving lesbian mothers. In *S.E.G. v. R.A.G.* (1987), the court wrote, "We wish to protect the children from peer pressure, teasing, and possible ostracizing they may encounter as a result of the 'alternate life style' their mother has chosen" (p. 166). Similarly, the court in *Thigpen v. Carpenter* (1987) commented that "homosexuality is generally socially unacceptable, and the children will be exposed to ridicule and teasing by other children" (p. 514). The courts in *N.K.M. v. L.E.M.* (1980) and *Jacobson v. Jacobson* (1981) also indicated their concern about possible stigma. In addition to these opinions, at least three cases relied on an article by Lewis (1980), which is discussed in the next section, to support the assumption that discrimination against gay parents may cause the child to be isolated from his or her peers (*Constant A. v. Paul C.A.*, 1985; *Dailey v. Dailey*, 1981; *S. v. S.*, 1980). But compare the opinions in *M.A.B. v. R.B.* (1986), *M.P. v. S.P.* (1979), *S.N.E. v. R.L.B.* (1985), and *Doe v. Doe* (1981), in which the courts eschewed the effect of stigma.

SOCIAL SCIENCE RESEARCH

Mental Health of Lesbian Mothers

One of the best studied of the assumptions used to deny lesbian mothers custody is the notion that lesbians are apt to be mentally ill. First, it is important to note that homosexuality itself is not considered a mental illness.[2] With respect to the mental health of lesbian women, Harris (1977) summarized the present "state of the art" as follows: "Numerous studies geared specifically to testing the 'lesbian' psyche have found lesbians to have the same or lower incidence of psychiatric disorder than matched heterosexual controls" (p. 85). Armon (1960) found no differences in psychological adjustment between homosexual and heterosexual women. Thompson, McCandles, and Strickland (1971) discovered that gay women are more self-confident, independent, composed, and self-sufficient than their heterosexual counterparts (Harris, 1977; Rand *et al.*, 1982; Riley, 1975) and that lesbian women do not differ in important ways from heterosexuals on measures of defensiveness, personal adjustment, and self-evaluation (Harris, 1977). Siegelman (1972) found that lesbian women score higher on tendermindedness and lower on depression, submission, and anxiety than heterosexual women.

In a more recent review of the available literature, Gibbs (1988) concluded that current research had disclosed "many similarities and few differences between lesbians and heterosexual women. Studies

---

[2] In 1973, the American Psychiatric Association deleted homosexuality from the list of mental illnesses, except in cases in which it was ego-dystonic. In 1975, the American Psychological Association adopted a resolution to the effect that homosexuality is not a mental illness. In 1987, homosexuality was removed from the diagnostic classification system altogether (see Erlichman, 1988; Gibbs, 1988).

have been unable to document the stereotypes of lesbian women as more mentally disturbed, lacking in self-esteem, or more prone to alcohol abuse or suicide" (p. 67).

Rand et al. (1982) studied 25 lesbian mothers, using interviews, subscales of the California Psychological Inventory (Gough, 1957), and the Affectometer (Kamman, Christie, Irwin, & Dixon, 1978), and they found that the lesbian mothers were at least as psychologically healthy as the larger standardized sample. Rand et al. (1982) also found correlations between psychological health and the expression of lesbianism, lending partial support to their hypothesis that mothers who expressed their lesbianism would be psychologically healthier than those who did not. Some clinicians (e.g., Krestan, 1987) have echoed this sentiment.

In comparing lesbian and heterosexual mothers and their children, Green, Mandel, Hotvedt, Gray, and Smith (1986) found that lesbian mothers scored higher on self-confidence, dominance, and exhibition on the Adjective Checklist (Gough & Heilbrun, 1965) than their heterosexual counterparts, whereas heterosexual mothers scored higher on abasement and deference. There were no significant differences between the groups on the Bem Sex Role Inventory (Bem, 1974) and various attitude scales.

Thus, the available research tends to negate the assumption that lesbian women are commonly mentally ill. Furthermore, if the courts are truly concerned about the psychological welfare of lesbian mothers, then they should be cognizant of the potentially damaging consequences of placing restrictions on their associational and expressive rights in light of Rand et al.'s findings (1982).

Parenting Ability of Lesbian Mothers

Mucklow and Phelan (1979) studied the self-concepts and maternal attitudes of lesbian and heterosexual mothers and found no significant differences between the groups. Although cautious about the generalizability of their findings, Mucklow and Phelan suggested that lesbian and heterosexual mothers may be more alike than different in their maternal attitudes and self-concepts.

Rees (1979) compared children in 12 lesbian-headed households and 12 heterosexual-headed households and assessed the mothers' parenting styles. Using the Parent Attitude Research Instrument, Rees found that there were no significant differences between the lesbian and heterosexual mothers in child-rearing practices or attitudes.

Miller *et al.* (1981) found that lesbian mothers were more child-oriented, as opposed to task- or adult-oriented, than their heterosexual counterparts and that lesbian mothers tended to assume a principal role in child-care responsibility. Miller *et al.* concluded that their study tended to negate the stereotype that heterosexual mothers are more child-oriented than lesbian mothers.

Kirkpatrick *et al.* (1981) assessed 20 children and their lesbian mothers and 20 children and their single-heterosexual mothers on a number of measures. Although the main focus of this research was on the children and their development, the authors did interview both sets of mothers and found them to be very similar in their maternal interests, lifestyles, and child-rearing practices. Kirkpatrick *et al.* also reported that the lesbian mothers were more concerned about providing male role models for their children than their heterosexual counterparts.

Lewin and Lyons (1982) conducted in-depth, semistructured interviews with 43 lesbian and 37 heterosexual mothers and found that the mothers were more similar than different in their parenting experiences. The greatest commonality between the two groups of women was the salience of motherhood: "Mothers in both groups report that motherhood influences the conduct of their lives in ways which generally overshadow the influences of other factors" (p. 260).

Harris and Turner (1985–1986) used an anonymous questionnaire to survey 23 lesbian and gay male parents and 16 single heterosexual parents about their relationships with their children. The researchers found no differences between the two groups on their self-reported parenting behaviors, except that the heterosexual parents in their study, in contrast to those in the Kirkpatrick *et al.* (1981) study, made a greater effort to provide an opposite-sex role model for their children. Although Harris and Turner (1985–1986) were cautious about the representativeness of their sample, they concluded that their findings tended to refute the assumption that homosexuality is incompatible with effective parenting.

Finally, writing about an unpublished study by Riddle, Moses and Hawkins (1982) suggested that homosexual individuals make as good parents as heterosexuals and that they must be highly motivated. Riddle had commented that " 'Sexual orientation has little to do with whether or not one wants to be a parent, but it has a lot to do with motivation because of the high costs of being a gay parent at this time' " (Moses & Hawkins, 1982, p. 200).

In summary, the research on the maternal attitudes and care-giving behaviors of lesbian mothers indicates either that there are no substantial differences between this group and their heterosexual counterparts or that lesbian mothers may actually be more child-oriented than heterosexual mothers. Thus, no research to date has substantiated the courts' assumptions that lesbian women make poor mothers or that a gay sexual orientation weakens or undermines a woman's parenting ability.

Mental Health of Children Raised by Lesbian Mothers

There have been several empirical studies of the mental or psychological health of children reared by lesbian mothers. Using various questionnaires to assess the children's emotions, behavior, and relationships, Golombok *et al.* (1983) compared 27 lesbian and 27 heterosexual families and found no significant differences in psychological health between the two groups of children. Additionally, Golombok *et al.* used interviews with the mothers to determine the presence of psychiatric problems in their children and found that only a small minority of the children had significant psychiatric problems. Notably, the proportion was substantially greater in the heterosexual single-parent group than in the homosexual group. More children in the heterosexual group had been referred for psychiatric care than in the homosexual group.

In an unpublished doctoral dissertation, Smith (1981) used two projective tasks to assess the psychological health of 20 children raised by lesbian mothers and 20 children raised by heterosexual mothers. Smith found that there were no significant differences between the two groups of children in the prevalence, degree, or type of emotional disturbance.

Kirkpatrick *et al.* (1981) compared the psychological functioning of children raised by lesbian and single heterosexual mothers and found no significant differences in the type or frequency of psychopathology between the two groups of children. Given that the subjects had been recruited by the offer of free psychological evaluations, it is not surprising that Kirkpatrick *et al.* found that over half of the children in both groups had moderate or severe emotional problems. However, the authors cautioned that this result may also have been due to the children's having experienced marital discord, parental separation, and frequent moves and changes in child-care arrangements.

Using the Draw-A-Person Test to assess the presence of emotional problems, Green et al. (1986) found no significant differences in scores between children raised by lesbian and single heterosexual mothers. Green et al. concluded that there was no evidence of childhood psychopathology related to the mother's sexual orientation: "The children in our study, similar to those of Kirkpatrick et al., are characterized as having reactions typical of children who have experienced parental separation and divorce" (p. 180).

Reporting on her own unpublished doctoral dissertation (Schwartz, 1985), Gottman (1989) found no significant differences between 105 adult daughters of remated lesbian, remated heterosexual, and non-remated heterosexual mothers in their scores on the California Psychological Inventory, except on one scale. The scores on this scale varied in relation to the presence or absence of older brothers in the home.

Researchers using other eclectic measures of psychological functioning have also failed to identify differences between the children of lesbian and heterosexual mothers. Rees (1979) found no significant differences on three measures of socialization, including a measure of moral development, between children raised by lesbian and single heterosexual mothers. Using a family relations test and a structured interview, Mandel and Hotvedt (1980) found no significant differences between the children of lesbian and heterosexual mothers. Mandel and Hotvedt's subjects did exhibit problems common to the children of divorced parents. Puryear (1983) compared children in 15 lesbian and 15 heterosexual households and discovered no significant differences in self-concept and family view between the two groups of children. Reporting on her unpublished dissertation (Steckel, 1985), Steckel (1987) compared independence, ego functions, and object relations in 22 three- and four-year-old children raised by lesbian and heterosexual couples. Steckel (1985) had found no significant differences between the groups of children in the amount of psychopathology or difficulties in the separation–individuation process, but she noted that the process had been a qualitatively different experience for the two groups.

In addition to these empirical studies, some clinical reports are also available. Lewis (1980) interviewed 21 children from eight families with lesbian mothers and found that the families with teenagers appeared to have the most adjustment problems. In a few of these families, the children had exhibited gross maladaptive behavior at the time of the mother's disclosure of her lesbianism. The youngest child in each family seemed the least able to deal with his or her ambivalence toward the mother. Lewis also found that the children believed that the break up of their parents' marriage had been more traumatic than learning of their mother's sexual orientation. According to Lewis, it was virtually impossible to segregate the impact of the mother's homosexuality from the effects of the parents' divorce.

Reporting on two cases of children with gay parents, Weeks *et al.* (1975) found some evidence of sexual and emotional difficulties but cautioned that it was hard to distinguish specific problem areas that were directly related to parental homosexuality. In particular, Weeks *et al.* noted that the children in their study had problems common to the children of divorced parents. Similarly, Osman (1972) reported on a case of an adolescent boy experiencing psychological problems after his mother's partner had moved into the home but suggested that factors other than the mother's sexual orientation were more significant determinants of his problems.

Summarizing these results, there is no empirical support for the assumption that children raised by lesbian mothers are more prone to mental or psychological problems. Other factors, such as marital discord and divorce, appear to be more highly correlated with a child's psychological adjustment than the mother's sexual orientation.

Sexual Molestation of Children Raised by Lesbian Mothers

Given the difficulty of gathering accurate information on the incidence of sexual molestation, it is hardly surprising to discover a dearth of data on its rate of occurrence in lesbian versus heterosexual households. However, research on patterns of child sexual abuse has disclosed that women rarely molest children. DiLapi (1989) provided this summary by the National Gay Task Force (1979): "'Every authoritative study on arrests for sex crimes including children indicates that over 90% of such incidents involve female children and male adults, and that incidents involving adult women with children of either sex are statistically insignificant (1979, p. 14)'" (in DiLapi, 1989, p. 117). Similarly, Hall (1978) noted the absence in judicial records of incidents between lesbian women and minor children, and Richardson (1981) found no cases of female pedophilia, homosexual or heterosexual, reported in the literature.

In addition, the available statistics have disclosed that sexual molestation occurs with much greater frequency in the heterosexual male versus homosexual male population, leading one commentator to characterize sexual molestation in the United States as "essentially a heterosexual male act" (Riley, 1975, p. 862). Groth and Birnbaum (1978), for example, studied 175 males convicted of sexual assault and found that none of them had a primary homosexual orientation. The authors concluded, "It appears, therefore, that the adult heterosexual male constitutes a greater sexual risk to underage children than does the adult homosexual male" (p. 181).

Briefly, then, there is no evidence either that homosexual parents are more likely to seduce or allow their children to be seduced than their heterosexual counterparts or that lesbian mothers or their acquaintances molest children more often than heterosexual individuals.

Gender-Role Development of Children Raised by Lesbian Mothers

In contrast to the amount of research on some of the assumptions discussed above, there have been a considerable number of empirical studies on the effects of lesbian mothers on their children's gender-role development. In a comparison of lesbian and heterosexual families using a number of measures, including structured interviews and questionnaires, Golombok et al. (1983) found no evidence of inappropriate gender identity in any of the children and showed that the sexes were clearly differentiated on sex-typed behavior scales. There were no differences between children reared in lesbian households and those in heterosexual households with respect to gender identity, sex-role behavior, or sexual orientation. However, the authors cautioned that their findings might not be generalizable to lesbian families in which the mother had adopted or conceived by artificial insemination because almost all the children in their sample had been in heterosexual households for at least two years.

In their study of households with lesbian and heterosexual mothers, Green et al. (1986) found no significant differences between the two groups of children on various personality and gender identity measures. Green et al. found that the sons in both groups were traditionally masculine. Although the girls showed a wider variety of gender-role behavior than the boys, their behavior was still within the normal range. The daughters of lesbian mothers were less traditionally feminine on various measures, including dress and activity preference.

Schwartz (1985) compared the adult daughters of mated lesbian, mated heterosexual, and single heterosexual mothers on various measures of gender identity, gender role, and sexual orientation. Schwartz found no significant difference in gender identity in the three groups of daughters. The groups did differ in gender role, but only in relation to the number of older brothers in the household, and when the effects of this variable were partialed out, no significant differences were found in the groups.

Steckel (1985) found that there were no significant differences in gender-role behavior between preschool-aged children raised by lesbian couples and those raised by heterosexual couples. The daughters of the lesbian couples were not significantly more androgynous or masculine than the daughters of the heterosexual couples, but the sons of the heterosexual couples appeared to be slightly more aggressive than their counterparts in the lesbian group.

Using a variety of measures, including questionnaires, attitude scales, and interviews, Hotvedt and Mandel (1982) compared 50 lesbian and 20 single heterosexual mothers and their preadolescent children. On measures of gender identity, Hotvedt and Mandel found that the boys in the two groups preferred traditionally masculine toys and games. The daughters of the lesbian mothers were less traditionally feminine than their counterparts from the heterosexual households, although both groups of daughters showed more flexibility in sex roles than the boys.

Hoeffer (1981) studied 40 matched lesbian and heterosexual mothers and their children. She discovered no significant differences between the two groups of children on measures of gender-role behavior, including their choice of toys. The lesbian mothers preferred a more nearly equal mixture of sex-typed masculine and feminine toys than the heterosexual mothers, although both groups were more likely to encourage play with neutral toys than with sex-typed ones. Hoeffer noted that the mothers' influence on their children's gender-role behavior was limited to the extent that they were involved in their children's play activities and that the children's choices were influenced by models other than their mothers, notably their peers.

Kirkpatrick et al. (1981) found no significant differences in gender-role development between children raised by lesbian mothers and those raised by unmarried heterosexual mothers. One interesting finding of this study was that the children giving answers suggestive of gender problems were more likely to share a history of some physical difficulty in early life than to have in common mothers with a particular sexual orientation.

Kweskin and Cook (1982) compared lesbian and heterosexual women on their self-described gender-role behaviors and their ratings of ideal gender-role behaviors in children and found that there was a significant relationship between the two measures; that is, the mother's own classifications were better indicators of the ideal child's ratings than the mother's sexual orientation or the child's gender. In this sense, the authors suggested, sexual orientation may not be a meaningful research variable.

In his unpublished doctoral dissertation, Rees (1979) studied the socialization of children raised in lesbian and heterosexual households and used the Bem Sex Role Inventory to assess gender-role identity. Rees found that there was no significant difference in scores between the two groups of children.

Turner et al. (1990) conducted structured interviews with 10 single gay fathers and 11 single lesbian mothers and found, "Nearly all subjects reported that their children seemed to be developing a normal sex-role identification, and the parents perceived their children's behaviors to be no different from those of other children their age and sex" (p. 61).

Finally, in an unpublished study reported in Moses and Hawkins (1982) and Nungesser (1980), Ostrow (1977) found that the sexual preference of the parent had no direct effect on the children's play choices:

> The results do indicate that regardless of the parents's sexuality, some of the play choices conformed to traditional patterns of sex-typing and some did not. . . . . These findings are not surprising since a majority of the parents are committed to non-sexist child-rearing. The children are still influenced to great degree, however, by television, peers, teachers, and relatives. This would explain their conformity to societal standards of behavior considered appropriate for boys and girls (Ostrow, 1977). (In Moses & Hawkins, 1982, p. 185)

Thus, even when the most conservative view is taken of this relatively well-developed area of research, it is apparent that lesbian mothers do not exert a detrimental influence on their children's gender-role development. As Ostrow and others have noted, this finding is understandable, given the diversity of influences on the child, only one of which is his or her mother.

Sexual Orientation of Children Raised by Lesbian Mothers

One of the most widely used assumptions in lesbian-mother child custody cases is that children brought up by a homosexual parent will also become gay, what Riley (1975) called the "universal latency fear." It is hardly surprising that this assumption is so common considering the homophobic attitudes that many legal decision makers exhibit toward lesbian mothers (Goldyn, 1981). Judges often view the possibility of a child's becoming homosexual as one of the most undesirable and perhaps even "tragic" outcomes of awarding custody to lesbian mothers.

Surprisingly, little research has been done in this area. Perhaps the best known study was conducted by Green (1978), who interviewed children being raised by lesbian and by transsexual parents to determine their sexual identity and sexual orientation. For the younger children, Green used toy and game preference, peer-group composition, clothing preference, roles in fantasy games, vocational aspiration, and the Draw-A-Person Test. Green assessed the adolescents' sexual identity by obtaining information on the child's romantic crushes, erotic fantasies, and interpersonal sexual behavior. Green found that psychosexual development appeared to be typical or normal in 36 of the 37 studied children. In explaining this result, Green pointed out that children do not live in a universe composed entirely of the home environment; they are also influenced by television, reading, school, and nonschool recreation with peers and their families. Green concluded tentatively that children raised by transsexual or homosexual parents do not differ appreciably, in terms of sexual identity, from children raised in heterosexual families.

In a later article, Green (1982) reported on the results of interviews with 21 children who had been raised in households with lesbian mothers for about 3.5 years. Of the older children, 5 reported sexual experiences, and all were heterosexual. Green also found that none of the children were experiencing sexual identity conflict.

Golombok et al. (1983) found, vis-à-vis the sexual orientation of the prepubertal children in their sample, the children of heterosexual women and those of lesbian women showed no significant differences in their patterns of childhood friendships. All the children tended to have predominantly same-sexed friends. These authors also investigated the sexual orientation of the pubertal and postpubertal adolescents in lesbian households and heterosexual-mother households by asking them about romantic crushes and friendships. They found that there was no difference between the two groups of children in terms of sexual orientation and that the patterns were typical for the age groups.

Schwartz (1985) used the Sexual Orientation Method questionnaire to compare adult daughters of mated lesbian and heterosexual mothers and also single heterosexual mothers. Schwartz found that there were no significant differences between the daughters in sexual orientation. The vast majority of the subjects in all three groups were heterosexual.

Although Huggins's study (1989) of 36 adolescents raised by divorced lesbian and divorced heterosexual mothers was not specifically designed to investigate the sexual orientation of the children, she found that only one of the adolescents was homosexual and that this adolescent was in the heterosexual-mother group.

Turner *et al.* (1990) interviewed 21 gay parents about relationships with their children and also asked them about their children's sexual orientation. Of the 21 children, who were 12 years old and older, only 1 child was reported as being homosexual. Finally, two clinical case studies reported that adolescents with lesbian mothers were heterosexual in orientation, although the children had encountered problems in the course of development (Javaid, 1983; Ross, 1988).

In short, research on the sexual orientation of the children of lesbian mothers does not confirm the "contagion" assumption inherent in so many court decisions. This finding is consistent with the research literature on the etiology of homosexuality; researchers have been unable to identify one family pattern associated with the development of a homosexual orientation.

Social Stigma

Unlike the six assumptions examined so far, the assumption that children reared in lesbian households will be harmed by the stigma associated with homosexuality is not based on the quality of the mother's parenting ability or on the parent–child interaction but derives from an external societal source. Because stigma is a societal by-product, it is not within the mother's or the child's ability to change. Nonetheless, the courts have frequently based their denial of custody on the possibility of stigma, even when they have recognized that a lesbian mother can hardly be expected to eliminate societal homophobia singlehandedly (Kraft, 1983).

Some commentators (e.g., Basile, 1974) have argued that the use of the stigma assumption in lesbian-mother child custody cases is a denial of equal protection because the courts have refused to consider the impact of stigma in interracial custody disputes (e.g., *Palmore v. Sidoti*, 1984), and lesbian mothers merit the same consideration. As Moses and Hawkins (1982) noted:

> We must certainly expect that the children of gay parents will have to cope with prejudice, misunderstanding, and possibly even negative peer reactions. But then, so may the children of black parents, poor Appalachian parents, divorced parents, and parents with physical impairments such as blindness, deafness, or paraplegia. The fact that a child's parents are different from the majority of white middle-class unimpaired parents is not usually considered an appropriate reason for removing a child from the home. We see no reason why sexual preference should be any different in this respect, unless it can be shown that there is some clear and consistent impairment because of this. (p. 200).

Assuming, for argument, that social stigmatization does have legal relevance in lesbian-mother child custody cases, it is unfortunate that so little research has been undertaken on its rate of occurrence or its degree of severity. Data on the number of children of lesbian mothers who are teased by their peers or are otherwise given negative feedback on their mother's homosexuality vary widely. Reporting on the limited research in this area, Susoeff (1985) stated that only 5% of children living with openly gay parents were harassed by other children. Green (1978) found that only 4 of 21 children raised by lesbian mothers had been teased and that each case had been an isolated incident. Riddle and Arguelles (1981) administered a questionnaire to 60 lesbian mothers and 22 gay fathers and found that children in 63% of the families had received some "negative input" on homosexuality, 79% of this input coming from peers.

The fact that social stigmatization may occur in some degree, however, does not end the inquiry. It is necessary to determine the potential consequences of such stigmatization. As Richardson (1981) pointed out:

> In addition we should note that it is unlikely that a child will be stigmatized by all of her or his peers, or that all occasions of teasing will have serious consequences for the child in terms of his self esteem and social

relationships. The possible effects of teasing will obviously depend on many factors, such as the form the teasing takes, how often and under what circumstances it occurs and who does it, as well as the particular personality of the individual child concerned. (p. 157)

A number of researchers have investigated the potential consequences of stigmatization by assessing peer-group relationships, social adjustment, popularity, and levels of self-esteem in children raised by lesbian mothers. Hotvedt and Mandel (1982) found that there was no significant difference in peer-group relationships between children of lesbian and heterosexual mothers. When the children were asked to rate their own popularity with their peers, there was no significant difference between the boys in each group. However, Hotvedt and Mandel found that the daughters of the lesbian mothers had higher self-ratings of popularity than their counterparts in the heterosexual group.

Green et al. (1986) used a variety of measures, including interviews, questionnaires, and psychological tests, to compare children and mothers in lesbian and heterosexual households and found that there was no difference between the two groups of children in terms of peer-group relationships, popularity, and social adjustment: 80% of the daughters of lesbian mothers and 75% of their counterparts in the heterosexual group reported that they were liked "much more," "somewhat more," or "as much" by their same-sex peer group. More than 80% of the sons in both groups gave similar popularity ratings with their male classmates.

In the only empirical study specifically designed to test the stigma assumption, Huggins (1989) compared the self-esteem of 18 adolescent children raised by divorced lesbian mothers and 18 adolescent children raised by divorced heterosexual mothers. She found no significant differences between the groups of adolescents based on their mother's sexual orientation. Huggins concluded, "Therefore, the assumption that children of lesbian mothers are socially stigmatized by their mother's sexual choice is not borne out by this study" (p. 132). Huggins also suggested that sexual orientation may not be a valid criterion on which to base child custody decisions.

In a more clinical context, Lewis's interviews (1980) with children of lesbian mothers revealed that the younger children focused on the need for secrecy, felt a sense of separation or "differentness" from their peers, and feared being ostracized by them. However, Lewis also found that "almost without exception, the children were

proud of their mothers for challenging society's rules and for standing up for what she believed. Problems between the mother and
children seemed secondary to the children's respect for the difficult
steps she had taken." (p. 203)

Pennington (1987) reported similar findings based on her 10 years
of clinical experience with 32 children from 28 lesbian families. The
younger children were more concerned about their parents' separation or divorce than about their mother's sexual orientation. As the
children grew older and became increasingly aware of their mother's
sexual orientation, they worried that their peers would find out and
that they would be ostracized. However, Pennington also found that
this reaction tended to subside as the children achieved firmer sexual
identities and separation from their mothers.

Reporting on the results of Bryant's unpublished study of lesbian mothers (1975), Nungesser (1980) stated that the majority of
children were not conscious of society's negative attitudes toward
their mothers. Those who were aware tended to resemble the children in Lewis's study (1980):

> In some cases, children are embarrassed for their friends or the general
> public to know their mother is a lesbian, but the majority of children
> combine any embarrassment or initial uncomfortableness with an under-
> standing that society has created the prejudice; that it is society, and not
> their mothers that should re-examine its position (Bryant, 1975, p. 73A).
> (In Nungesser, 1980, p. 184)

Other commentators (e.g., Gottman, 1989) have also remarked on
the ability of children with lesbian mothers to cope with the potential
effects of social stigmatization:

> Children may have issues to contend with concerning how society per-
> ceives them when a parent's homosexuality is revealed. However, it appears
> that children develop strategies to protect themselves when necessary.
> Judicial courts may want to consider these findings when resolving a
> custody dispute involving a homosexual parent. (Gottman, 1989, p. 191)

Finally, a few authors have approached the question of stigma
from a more theoretical perspective. Some have maintained that the
possible stigma associated with being reared in a lesbian household
may have its compensations. Kraft (1983) noted that, in one court's
view, "a child who struggles with societal disapproval may be better equipped in adulthood to form independent moral convictions"
(p. 184). Miller et al. (1981) suggested that lesbian mothers may compensate for the potential stigma their children may suffer by being

more child-oriented than single heterosexual mothers. Thus, stigmatization may be offset in some cases by lesbian mothers who recognize its occurrence and make efforts to counteract its influence. Riley (1975) attempted to deflate the importance of the stigma assumption by pointing out that lesbian women's index of recognition is low, and that therefore the stigma problem may never surface in any particular case. Nevertheless, when the courts focus on the supposed stigma encountered by the children of lesbian women, they merely perpetuate the very stigma that they find detrimental (Kraft, 1983).

In summary, although some of the evidence suggests that the children of lesbian mothers may be affected by social stigma, the available research and theory also indicate that children's self-esteem and peer-group relationships are not severely damaged, and that the children learn to develop coping mechanisms to combat societal homophobia. Thus, legal decision makers may be overemphasizing the severity, and even perpetuating the effect, of this stigma.

CONCLUSIONS

Because research on lesbian mothers and their children is still in its "seed state" (Gottman, 1989, p. 193) and there are methodological problems associated with this work, conclusions must remain tentative. Nonetheless, it is important to note that a rapidly growing and highly consistent body of empirical work has failed to identify significant differences between lesbian mothers and their heterosexual counterparts or the children raised by these groups. Researchers have been unable to establish empirically that detriment results to children from being raised by lesbian mothers.

The highly consistent and coherent results of research on lesbian mothers and their children has been recognized by some legal decision makers. For example, one Justice of the New Hampshire Supreme Court, dissenting from an opinion that disenfranchised homosexual individuals from being adoptive or foster parents, wrote:

> The legislature received no meaningful evidence to show that homosexual parents endanger their children's development of sexual preference, gender role identity, or general physical and psychological health any more than heterosexual parents. The legislature received no such evidence because apparently the overwhelming weight of professional study on the subject concludes that no difference in psychological or psychosexual development can be discerned between children raised by heterosexual

parents and children raised by homosexual parents. (Opinion of the Justices, 1987, p. 28, citing Golombok *et al.*, 1983; Green *et al.*, 1986; Harris & Turner, 1985–1986; 1985; Susoeff, 1985)

Thus, it appears that there is a considerable gap between many of the assumptions on which legal decision makers have traditionally based their decisions and the corresponding empirical and theoretical literature on lesbian mothers and their children. The major implication for legal decision makers is that they should focus less or not at all on the sexual orientation of a potential custodian and more on other factors commonly associated with the best-interests-of-the-child standard, such as the quality of the parent–child relationship. By returning to a more traditional and balanced application of the best-interests standard, judges are likely to arrive at better and more informed decisions: "Rather than promoting prejudice by basing decisions on false stereotypes or perceived community intolerance, courts and legislatures should instead further the children's welfare by focusing on their need for stable and supportive home environments" ("Developments in the Law," 1989, p. 1660). "The best interests of the child lay [*sic*] with a loving parent, not with a heterosexual parent or a homosexual parent" (Basile, 1974, p. 18).

ACKNOWLEDGMENTS

I wish to thank the American Psychological Association for permission to use portions of a previously published article (Falk, 1989) in this book chapter. I also wish to acknowledge with gratitude the financial support of the Cleveland-Marshall Fund.

REFERENCES

Armon, V. (1960). Some personality factors in overt female homosexuality. *Journal of Projective Techniques, 26,* 292–309.
Baptiste, D. A. (1987). Psychotherapy with gay/lesbian couples and their children in "stepfamilies": A challenge for marriage and family therapists. *Journal of Homosexuality, 14*(1–2), 223–238.
Bark v. Bark, 479 So.2d 42 (Ala. Civ. App. 1985).
Basile, R. A. (1974). Lesbian mothers: 1. *Women's Law Reporter, 2*(2), 3–18.
Bem, S. (1974). The measurement of psychological androgyny. *Journal of Consulting and Clinical Psychology, 42,* 155–162.
Bezio v. Patenaude, 381 Mass. 563, 410 N.E.2d 1207 (1980).
Browne, M. N., & Giampetro, A (1985). The contribution of social science data to the adjudication of child custody disputes? *Capital University Law Review, 15,* 43–58.

Bryant, B. S. (1975). *Lesbian mothers*. Unpublished master's thesis, California State University, Sacramento. Burdens of gay litigants and bias in the court system: Homosexual panic, child custody, and anonymous parties [Note]. (1984). *Harvard Civil Rights and Civil Liberties Law Review, 19*, 497–559.

Campbell, R. W. (1978). Child custody when one parent is a homosexual. *Judges' Journal, 7*, 38–41, 51–52.

Conkel v. Conkel, 31 Ohio App.3d 169, 509 N.E.2d 983 (1987).

Constant A. v. Paul C. A., 334 Pa.Super. 49, 496 A.2d 1 (1985).

Cramer, D. (1986). Gay parents and their children: A review of research and practical implications. *Journal of Counseling and Development, 64*, 504–507.

Dailey v. Dailey, 635 S.W.2d 391 (Tenn. App. 1981).

Davies, R. C. (1979). Representing the lesbian mother. *Family Advocate, 1*(3), 21–23, 36.

Delaney, E. A. (1991). Statutory protection of the other mother: Legally recognizing the relationship between the nonbiological lesbian parent and her child. *Hastings Law Journal, 43*, 177–216.

Developments in the law: Sexual orientation and the law. (1980). *Harvard Law Review, 102*, 1508–1671.

DiLapi, E. M. (1989). Lesbian mothers and the motherhood hierarchy. *Journal of Homosexuality, 18*(1–2), 101–121.

DiStefano v. DiStefano, 60 A.D.2d 976, 401 N.Y.S.2d 636 (1978).

Doe v. Doe, 222 Va. 736, 284 S.E.2d 799 (1981).

Erlichman, K. L. (1988). Lesbian mothers: Ethical issues in social work practice. *Women and Therapy, 8*(1–2), 207–224.

Falk, P. J. (1989). Lesbian mothers: Psychological assumptions in the family law. *American Psychologist, 44*(6), 941–947.

Gibbs, E. D. (1988). Psychosocial development of children raised by lesbian mothers: A review of the research. *Women and Therapy, 8*(1–2), 65–75.

Goldyn, L. (1981). Gratuitous language in appellate cases involving gay people: "Queer baiting" from the bench. *Political Behavior, 3*, 31–48.

Golombok, S., Spencer, A., & Rutter, M. (1983). Children in lesbian and single-parent households: Psychosexual and psychiatric appraisal. *Journal of Child Psychology and Psychiatry, 24*, 551–572.

Gottman, J. S. (1989). Children of gay and lesbian parents. *Marriage and Family Review, 14*(3–4), 177–196.

Gough, H. G. (1957). *California Psychological Inventory*. Palo Alto, CA: Consulting Psychologists Press.

Gough, H. G., & Heilbrun, A. (1965). *The Adjective Checklist*. Palo Alto, CA: Consulting Psychologists Press.

Green, R. (1978). Sexual identity of 37 children raised by homosexual and transsexual parents. *American Journal of Psychiatry, 135*, 692–697.

Green, R. (1982). The best interest of the child with a lesbian mother. *Bulletin of the American Academy of Psychiatry and the Law, 10*, 7–15.

Green, R., Mandel, J. B., Hotvedt, M. E., Gray, J., & Smith, L. (1986). Lesbian mothers and their children: A comparison with solo parent heterosexual mothers and their children. *Archives of Sexual Behavior, 15*, 167–184.

Groth, A. N., & Birnbaum, H. J. (1978). Adult sexual orientation and attraction to underage persons. *Archives of Sexual Behavior, 7*(3), 175–181.

Hall v. Hall, 95 Mich.App. 614, 291 N.W.2d 143 (1980).

Hall, M. (1978). Lesbian families: Cultural and clinical issues. *Social Work, 23*, 380–385.

Harris, B. S. (1977). Lesbian mother child custody: Legal and psychiatric aspects. *Bulletin of the American Academy of Psychiatry and the Law, 5*, 75–89.

Harris, M. B., & Turner, P. H. (1985–1986). Gay and lesbian parents. *Journal of Homosexuality, 12*(2), 101–113.

Hitchens, D. (1979–1980). Social attitudes, legal standards and personal trauma in child custody cases. *Journal of Homosexuality, 5*(1–2), 89–95.

Hitchens, D., & Price, B. (1979). Trial strategy in lesbian mother custody cases: The use of expert testimony. *Golden Gate University Law Review*, 451–479.

Hoeffer, B. (1981). Children's acquisition of sex-role behavior in lesbian-mother families. *American Journal of Orthopsychiatry, 51*, 536–544.

Hotvedt, M. E., & Mandel, J. B. (1982). Children of lesbian mothers. In W. Paul, J. D. Weinrich, J. C. Gonsiorek, & M. E. Hotvedt (Ed.), *Homosexuality: Social, psychological, and biological issues* (pp. 275–285), Beverly Hills, CA: Sage.

Huggins, S. L. (1989). A comparative study of self-esteem of adolescent children of divorced lesbian mothers and divorced heterosexual mothers. *Journal of Homosexuality, 18*(1–2), 123–133.

In re Jane B., 85 Misc.2d 515, 380 N.Y.S.2d 848 (N.Y.Sup.Ct. 1976).

In re Mara, 3 Misc.2d 174, 150 N.Y.S.2d 524 (N.Y.Fam.Ct. 1956).

Irish v. Irish, 102 Mich.App.75, 300 N.W.2d 739 (1980).

J.L.P.(H.) v. D.L.P., 643 S.W.2d 865 (Mo. App. 1982).

Jacobson v. Jacobson, 314 N.W.2d 78 (N.D. 1981).

Javaid, G. A. (1983). The sexual development of the adolescent daughter of a homosexual mother. *Journal of the American Academy of Child Psychiatry, 22*(2), 196–201.

Kamman, R., Christie, D., Irwin, R., & Dixon, G. (1978). *The Affectometer: An inventory of subjective well-being*. Punedin, New Zealand: University of Ontago.

Kirkpatrick, M. (1987). Clinical implications of lesbian mother studies. *Journal of Homosexuality, 14*(1–2), 201–211.

Kirkpatrick, M., Smith, C., & Roy, R. (1981). Lesbian mothers and their children: A comparative survey. *American Journal of Orthopsychiatry, 51*, 545–551.

Kleber, D. J., Howell, R. J., & Tibbits-Kleber, A. L. (1986). The impact of parental homosexuality in child custody case: A review of the literature. *Bulletin of the American Academy of Psychiatry and Law, 14*(1), 81–87.

Kraft, P. (1983). Recent developments: Lesbian child custody. *Harvard Women's Law Journal, 6*, 183–192.

Krestan, J. (1987). Lesbian daughters and lesbian mothers: The crisis of disclosure from a family systems perspective. *Journal of Psychotherapy and the Family, 3*(4), 113–130.

Kweskin, S. L., & Cook, A. S. (1982). Heterosexual and homosexual mothers' self-described sex-role behavior and ideal sex-role behavior in children. *Sex Roles, 8*, 967–975.

Lewin, E., & Lyons, T. A. (1982). Everything in its place: The co-existence of lesbianism and motherhood. In W. Paul, J. D. Weinrich, J. C. Gonsiorek, M. E. Hotvedt (Eds.), *Homosexuality: Social, Psychological, and Biological Issues* (pp. 249–273). Beverly Hills, CA: Sage.

Lewis, K. G. (1980). Children of lesbians: Their point of view. *Social Work, 25*, 198–203.

M.A.B. v. R.B., 134 Misc.2d 317, 510 N.Y.S.2d 960 (N.Y.Sup.Ct. 1986).

M.P. v. S.P., 169 N.J.Super. 425, 404 A.2d 1256 (1979).

Mandel, J. B., & Hotvedt, M. E. (1980). Lesbians as parents. *Huisarts and Praktyk, 4,* 31–34.

Miller, J. A., Jacobsen, R. B., & Bigner, J. J. (1981). The child's home environment for lesbian v. heterosexual mothers: A neglected area of research. *Journal of Homosexuality, 7(1),* 49–56.

Moses, A. E., & Hawkins, R. O., Jr. (1982). *Counseling lesbian women and gay men: A life-issues approach.* St. Louis: C. V. Mosby.

Mucklow, B. M., & Phelan, G. K. (1979). Lesbian and traditional mothers' responses to adult response to child behavior and self-concept. *Psychological Reports, 44,* 880–882.

National Gay Task Force (1979). Twenty questions about homosexuality. New York: Author.

N.K.M. v. L.E.M., 606 S.w.2d 179 (Mo.App. 1980).

Nungesser, L. G. (1980). Theoretical bases for research on the acquisition of social sex-roles by children of lesbian mothers. *Journal of Homosexuality, 5(3),* 177–187.

Opinion of the Justices, 129 N.H. 290, 530 A.2d 21 (1987).

Osman, S. (1972). My stepfather is a she. *Family Process, 11,* 209–218.

Ostrow, D. (1977). *Gay and straight parents: What about the children?* Unpublished bachelor's thesis, Hampshire College, Amherst, MA.

Palmore v. Sidoti, 466 U.S. 429 (1984).

Pennington, S. B. (1987). Children of lesbian mothers. In F. W. Bozett (Ed.), *Gay and lesbian parents* (pp. 58–74). New York: Praeger.

Pies, C. (1987). Lesbians choosing children: The use of social group work in maintaining and strengthening the primary relationship. *Journal of Social Work and Human Sexuality, 5(2),* 79–88.

Pies, C. A. (1988). Lesbians and the choice to parent. *Marriage and Family Review, 14(3–4),* 137–154.

Polikoff, N. D. (1990). This child does have two mothers: Redefining parenthood to meet the needs of children in lesbian-mother and other nontraditional families. *Georgetown Law Journal, 78,* 459–575.

Puryear, D. (1983). *A comparison between the children of lesbian mothers and the children of heterosexual mothers.* Unpublished doctoral dissertation, California School of Professional Psychology, Berkeley.

Rand, C., Graham, D. L. R., & Rawlings, E. I. (1982). Psychological health and factors in the court seeks to control in lesbian mother custody trials. *Journal of Homosexuality, 8(1),* 27–39.

Rees, R. L. (1979). *A comparison of children of lesbian and single heterosexual mothers on three measures of socialization.* Unpublished doctoral dissertation, California School of Professional Psychology, Berkeley.

Richardson, D. (1981). Lesbian mothers. In J. Hart & D. Richardson (Eds.), *The theory and practice of homosexuality* (pp. 149–158). London: Routledge & Kegan Paul.

Ricketts, W., & Achtenberg, R. (1989). Adopting and fostering parenting for lesbians and gay men: Creating new traditions in family. *Marriage and Family Review, 14(3–4),* 83–118.

Riddle, D., & Arguelles, M. (1981). Children of gay parents: Homophobia's victims. In I. Stuart & L. Abt (Eds.), *Children of separation and divorce: Management and treatment* (pp. 174–197). New York: Van Nostrand Reinhold.

Riley, M. (1975). The avowed lesbian mother and her right to child custody: A constitutional challenge that can no longer be denied. *San Diego Law Review, 12,* 799–864.

Rivera, R. R. (1979). Our straight-laced judges: The legal position of homosexual persons in the United States. *Hastings Law Journal, 30,* 799–955.

Rivera, R. R. (1980–1981). Recent developments in sexual preference law. *Drake Law Review, 30,* 311–346.

Rivera, R. R. (1987). Legal issues in gay and lesbian parenting. In F. W. Bozett (Ed.), *Gay and lesbian parents* (pp. 199–227). New York: Praeger.

Ross, J. L. (1988). Challenging boundaries: An adolescent in a homosexual family. *Journal of Family Psychology, 2*(2), 227–240.

S. v. S., 608 S.W.2d 64 (Ky.App. 1980), *cert. denied,* 451 U.S. 911, *reh'g denied,* 452 U.S. 910 (1982).

S.E.G. v. R.A.G., 735 S.W.2d 164 (Mo. App. 1987).

S.N.E. v. R.L.B., 699 P.2d 875 (Alaska 1985).

Schwartz, J. (1985). *An exploration of personality traits in daughters of lesbian mothers.* Unpublished doctoral dissertation, California School of Professional Psychology, San Diego.

Siegelman, M. (1972). Adjustment of homosexual and heterosexual women. *American Journal of Psychiatry, 120,* 477–481.

Smith, K. V. (1981). *Children raised by lesbian mothers.* Unpublished doctoral dissertation, University of California, Los Angeles.

Spence v. Durham, 16 N.C.App. 372, 191 S.E.2d 908 (1972), *rev'd,* 283 N.C. 671, 198 S.E.2d 537 (1973), *cert. denied,* 415 U.S. 918 (1974).

Steckel, A. (1985). *Separation-individuation in children of lesbian and heterosexual couples.* Unpublished doctoral dissertation, Wright Institute, Berkeley, CA.

Steckel, A. (1987). Psychosocial development of children of lesbian mothers. In F. W. Bozett (Ed.), *Gay and lesbian parents* (pp. 75–85). New York: Praeger.

Susoeff, S. (1985). Assessing children's best interests when a parent is gay or lesbian: Toward a rational custody standard. *UCLA Law Review, 32,* 852–903.

Thigpen v. Carpenter, 21 Ark.App. 194, 730 S.W.2d 510 (1987).

Thompson, N., McCandles, B., & Strickland, B. (1971). Personal adjustment of male and female homosexuals and heterosexuals. *Journal of Abnormal Psychology, 78,* 237–240.

Turner, P. H., Scadden, L., & Harris, M. B. (1990). Parenting in gay and lesbian families. *Journal of Gay and Lesbian Psychotherapy, 1*(3), 55–66.

Weeks, R. B., Derdeyn, A. P., & Langmon, M. (1975). Two cases of children of homosexuals. *Child Psychiatry and Human Development, 6,* 26–32.

6

Gay Dads

Robert L. Barret and Bryan E. Robinson

In recent years, the idea of men being more active in the father role has become commonplace. Formerly restricted to being breadwinners, men are learning that they can find much satisfaction as fathers, and it is not uncommon to see fathers awarded primary custody when a divorce occurs (Robinson & Barret, 1986). New on the horizon are the many gay men who are now choosing to be more active and more visible as fathers. It was not very long ago that the idea of a gay man being a father seemed quite strange. Today, as our culture becomes more familiar with the variety of lifestyles within the gay community, many have come to see that gay men can make good dads, too (Barret & Robinson, 1990). This chapter gives the answers to three main questions: Who are gay fathers? How do gay fathers become parents? And how do the children of gay fathers turn out?

PROFILE OF GAY FATHERS

Perhaps fueled by the AIDS epidemic's lessons about the brevity of life and the importance of families, gay men and women are

Robert L. Barret and Bryan E. Robinson • Human Services Department, University of North Carolina at Charlotte, Charlotte, North Carolina 28223.

Redefining Families: Implications for Children's Development, edited by Adele Eskeles Gottfried and Allen W. Gottfried. Plenum Press, New York, 1994.

Case Study

Boyce: Gay Father of Two

Boyce, married at 26 and the father of two by age 32, left his family when he was 41 years old. A schoolteacher, he had realized he was gay after becoming involved as a volunteer at an AIDS service organization. His first sexual experience with a man happened four months before he left his wife and convinced him that his concerns about his sexuality were valid. For the first several months following their separation, Boyce and his wife saw each other about every other week, and he was able to have his children visit him every other weekend.

All of that changed once he told his wife he was gay. Their divorce was contentious, as Boyce tried unsuccessfully to get joint custody of his son and daughter. Telling his children about his sexual orientation was the most difficult part of the entire separation process. At first, they joined in their mother's struggle to deny him visitation with them. But over the months, they began to realize that he was just about the same dad they had loved for years, and they began to initiate contact. Boyce was careful not to expose them to many of his gay friends, but he was frequently frustrated by his family's unwillingness to participate more fully in his life. As the years passed, his wife remarried, and as teenagers, his children began to spend more and more time with him.

---

opting for parenthood in increasing numbers. Although there are no statistics to tell us how many gay parents there are, cities with large gay populations often have many support systems in place for gay fathers. For example, the San Francisco *Bay Times,* a gay, lesbian, and bisexual newspaper, advertises opportunities for coparenting as well as the following support groups for gay fathers: Gay/Lesbian Parenting Group, Prospective Queer Parents, Southbay Gay Parents, and Adoption Support Groups. As more and more services are made available to assist gay fathers, it is probable that these men will become more visible in schools, churches, and the other social service agencies that routinely interact with parents.

Gay fathers are men like any other fathers. They are young, old, professionals, blue-collar workers, stable, unstable, financially secure, on welfare, in committed couple relationships, and single. As we talked with gay fathers across the country, it became clear that they have a strong commitment to their children and that the primary focus of their lives is their children's well-being. They struggle as

Finally, he and his lover, Tom, became full-time parents when Boyce's ex-wife moved across the country with her new family.

This gay couple struggles with how visible to be in Boyce's children's lives. Although Boyce attends teacher conferences alone, the whole family attends sports events together, and the teenagers have got comfortable introducing Tom as their father's "partner."

Tom never thought he would be a parent but has developed close feelings for the kids. He does not always like living in the suburbs, though, and he talks about being unsure exactly how to be a "stepfather." Being parents has definitely created some strains on Boyce and Tom's relationship. But the communication between the pair seems strong, and they have an obvious commitment to providing a stable home environment. Like heterosexual stepfamilies, Tom and Boyce work hard to keep the children out of the crossfire between the two natural parents. The coparenting demands are not unlike those on any couple.

A recent breakthrough in family relations occurred when Tom found himself the sole "parent" who was available during a medical emergency. Contacting both Bryce and the children's mother as decisions were made enabled this extended family to learn how to use their strengths to cooperate. Events such as these enhance the ability of extended families to trust the effectiveness and commitment of gay parents.

they encounter the homophobia (fear of homosexuals) that prevails in our country, yet they attempt to minimize its negative impact on their children. Some go so far as to go back into the closet once they become parents. Others live openly with their partners, often in the suburbs alongside heterosexual parents.

Exact figures on the numbers of gay fathers do not exist, and projections are just guesses. The Kinsey data (1948) that suggested that 10% of the adult U.S. population is gay informed us that there are many gay fathers in every community. Harry (1983) projected that 20% of the homosexual population is composed of heterosexually married gay men. And Bell and Weinberg (1978) suggested that, of these marriages, approximately half result in children. In sum, it is estimated that over 1 million gay fathers live in the United States and Canada (Bozett, 1984).

In the few studies that exist, most gay fathers, like Boyce (Figure 1), have formerly been married to women (Bozett, 1980; Miller, 1979; Skeen & Robinson, 1984) and live separately from their spouses and see their children only periodically. But gay men become fathers in other ways, too. Some gay men in long-standing homosexual relationships choose to have a child with a woman found through friendship networks or through payments to surrogate mothers. Others choose private adoptions, often through adoption agencies in foreign countries. Although in the past the most common type of gay father was the previously married man, more and more gay men are opting for fatherhood because they want to have the experience of raising children in stable homes.

The number of gay men who want to become fathers is growing. From observing formerly married gay men raise their children and desiring to participate more fully in the whole range of family activities that accompany adulthood, gay men are finding creative ways to experience fatherhood. Unfortunately, this does not happen without controversy. Heterosexual former spouses, social service agencies, and the legal system are not altogether comfortable with the idea of gay men as parents. However, there is a growing body of research that indicates that gay men can serve very adequately in the fathering role (Barret & Robinson, 1990).

Often, gay men must turn to the courts to gain access to their children. In some of these cases, custody is awarded reluctantly when it is clear that the natural mother is an inadequate parent. Although the court may be uneasy about awarding custody to a gay father, there are more cases where sole or joint custody is awarded to these fathers, many of whom are openly gay, and some legal systems are placing homosexual kids who have been abandoned by their natural parents with gay foster parents. The hope in these instances is that the gay parents will provide a positive role model for the gay youth (Harry, 1983).

More conservative groups, threatened by the growing gay-rights movement, serve as watchdogs in the legal system and challenge these changes by depicting the gay rights movement as antifamily. In California and Colorado, recent advances in antidiscrimination legislation have been challenged in the courts or before the electorate (in Colorado, successfully). This same homophobia can be seen among some professionals who are uninformed about the strengths of gay fathers and retain the belief that homosexuality is a sin or a sickness rather than an alternate lifestyle. Gay men who are biological fathers find it almost impossible to secure custody or even visitation rights from the legal system (Hitchens, 1980). Sometimes, the court addresses this concern directly. In a North Carolina case, *Woodruff v.*

Woodruff (1979), the gay father retained alternate weekend, summer, and holiday visitation rights with his son, while granting the mother primary custody. But changes do seem to be coming as states and communities enact antidiscrimination legislation that can be used to block the courts from preventing visitation and custody solely on the basis of sexual orientation.

There remain many significant barriers for gay fathers to overcome before their role will have wide acceptance. Public concern about the ability of gay fathers to have the primary responsibility for child care focuses on two main concerns: gay fathers will "recruit" their children into the homosexual lifestyle, and sons of gay fathers will become incest victims (Barret & Robinson, 1990). Let's take a look at these two myths about gay fathers.

HOMOSEXUAL INCEST

As we begin to examine the research findings about gay fathers, it is important to remember that the number of studies of gay fathers is small. By and large, the studies that exist involve few subjects, and most of the data have been gathered from the fathers themselves as they report their experiences. Still, the studies that do exist illuminate how gay men act as fathers.

Recent interest in incest has led to the speculation that it is not uncommon for children to be sexually abused by their parents. Incest research that focuses on gay fathers is virtually absent from the literature. The reason may be that few gay fathers have been studied at all, or that few gay fathers have molested their children, or that the incest taboo is so strong among gay men that they do not speak of their experiences. However, it is generally believed that the vast number of child molesters identify as heterosexual. Gay parents and their lovers are involved in virtually no reported cases of child sexual abuse (DeFrancis, 1976; Gebhard, Gagnon, Pomeroy, & Christenson, 1965; Geiser, 1979; Richardson, 1981). Although the evidence is scant, at this time it appears that children living with heterosexual parents are more at risk of incest than children living with gay fathers.

Similarly, research suggests that children living with gay fathers do not "catch" homosexuality from their parents. Miller (1979) reported that some worry that the children of gay parents have a biological predisposition toward homosexuality that can be curbed only by placing them with heterosexual households. But many homosexuals were raised by heterosexual parents, and many heterosexuals have grown up in single-parent families. Homosexuality does not seem to be a sexual orientation that is "caught." (Green, 1978; Miller, 1979).

The concerns that gay fathers will pass along their homosexuality or molest their children suggest the general negative attitudes that exist toward homosexuality: that gay men are less sexually reliable with their children than heterosexual parents, and that homosexuality would be a "bad" thing to "catch." Gay fathers usually point to their heterosexual parents to refute both of these concerns. One gay father said, "I get so annoyed when the people claim that I will be the cause of my child's homosexuality. My own parents are straight, and if their logic is correct, I would be straight, too. Using this concern as the basis to keep me from my children is blatant homophobia!"

CHILDREN OF GAY FATHERS

The children of gay fathers are like children from all families. Some are academically talented, some struggle to get through school, some are model students, and some are constantly in trouble. In thinking about the children of gay fathers, it is essential to recognize that many of them have experienced the divorce of their parents, others have grown up in single-parent homes, and still others have been caught in major crossfire between their parents, grandparents, and perhaps their community over the appropriateness of gay men serving in the father role. Much of any distress that one sees in a child living with a gay father may, in fact, be the result of the divorce or other family tensions. Legitimate concerns about the impact of living with a gay father include the developmental impact of the knowledge that one's father is gay, reasonable worries about the timing of coming out to children, and creating sensitivity to how the children will experience society's generally negative attitudes toward homosexuality.

Coming out to children is usually an emotion-laden event for gay fathers. The disclosure of one's homosexuality creates anxiety about rejection, fear of hurting or damaging the child's self-esteem, and grieving over the loss of innocence. Some gay fathers never accomplish this task and remain deeply closeted, citing legal and emotional reasons (Bozett, 1980, 1981; Humphreys, 1979; Spada, 1979). Recent publications report the intricacies of this question (Corley, 1990). Those who never disclose their homosexuality often lead deeply conflicted lives and present parenting styles that are characterized by psychological distance (Miller, 1979). Those who do come out to their children do so in the desire to be more of a whole person as a father. As they try to merge their gayness with the father role, they encounter a different kind of conflict: deciding how open to be about their sexual relationships and how much exposure to the gay community to offer their children (Robinson & Barret, 1986).

Fathers report that the first concern they have about coming out is the well-being and healthy adjustment of their children. Many gay fathers seek the help of counselors or specialists in child development as they decide when and how to tell their children about their homosexuality. Research studies indicate that fathers and children report that they are closer after self-disclosure about the father's sexual orientation (Bozett, 1980; Miller, 1979). Bigner and Bozett (1989) studied the reasons that gay fathers give for coming out to their children. Among the most cited were wanting their children to know them as they are, being aware that children will usually discover for themselves if there is frequent contact, and the presence of a male lover in the home.

Gay fathers may come out indirectly by showing affection to men in front of their children or by taking them to gay community events. Others choose to come out verbally or by correspondence (Maddox, 1982). Factors in disclosure are the degree of intimacy between the father and his children and the obtrusiveness of his gayness (Bozett, 1988). By and large, the research suggests that children who are told at an earlier age have fewer difficulties with the day-to-day issues that accompany their father's homosexuality (Bozett, 1989).

The parenting styles of gay fathers are not markedly different from those of other single fathers, but gay fathers try to create a more stable home environment and more positive relationships with their children than traditional heterosexual parents (Bigner & Jacobsen, 1989a; Bozett, 1989). One study found that homosexual fathers differed from their heterosexual counterparts in providing more nurturing and in having less traditional parenting attitudes (Scallen, 1981). Another study of gay fathers found no differences in paternal involvement and amount of intimacy (Bigner & Jacobsen, 1989b). In general, investigators have found that gay fathers feel an additional responsibility to provide effective fathering because they know their homosexuality causes others to examine their parenting styles more closely (Barret & Robinson, 1990). This is not to say that no risk is involved in gay fathering. Miller (1979) found that six daughters of the gay fathers in his study had significant life problems. Others have reported that the children of gay fathers must be prepared to face

ridicule and harassment (Bozett, 1980; Epstein, 1979) or may be alien-
ated from their agemates, may become confused about their sexual identity, and may express discomfort with their father's sexual
orientation (Lewis, 1980). Most researchers have concluded that being
homosexual is compatible with effective parenting and is not usually a major issue in parental relationships with children (Harris &
Turner, 1986).

As Chip reveals (Figure 2), dealing with the outside world is a
task that gay fathers and their children must master. Gay families live
in a social system that is generally uncomfortable with homosexuality
and that certainly does not overtly support gay parenting. One reality
for gay fathers is figuring out how to interact successfully with the
world of the schools, after-school activities, PTAs, churches, and their
children's social networks. Many gay fathers see no choice other than
to continue living relatively closeted lives (Bozett, 1988; Miller, 1979).
Others, fearing the damage that exposure may bring to their children and/or possible custody battles involving their homosexuality,
live rigidly controlled lives and may never develop a gay identity.
Those who are more open about their gayness struggle to help their
children develop a positive attitude toward homosexuality while simultaneously cautioning them about the dangers of disclosure to
teachers and friends. Teaching their children to manage these two
tasks is a major challenge for gay fathers (Morin & Schultz, 1978;
Riddle, 1978). Accomplishing this task when there are virtually no
visible role models frequently leaves these fathers and their children
feeling extremely isolated.

Bozett (1988) identified several strategies that these children use
as they experience both their own and the public's discomfort with
their gay fathers. The children of gay fathers in his study used boundary control, nondisclosure, and disclosure as they interacted with
their fathers and the outside world. For example, some children limited or attempted to control the content of their interactions with
their father. One father we talked with (Barret & Robinson, 1990)
reported that he had offered to introduce his teenaged daughter to
some of his gay friends in the hope that she would see how normal
they were. Her reply was a curt "Dad, that will never happen!"
Another father told of trying to reconcile with his son but being
rebuffed by the comment, "I don't want to hear anything about your
personal life. I can't handle it." Such boundary control limits the
ability of the relationship to grow. Other ways that children control

boundaries are by not introducing their friends to their fathers or by carefully managing the amount of time they spend together, as Chip reveals in his interview.

Some children do learn to let their friends know carefully about their fathers' homosexuality. These disclosures have a potential for both increased intimacy and rejection. Helping children discriminate when and how to inform their friends is a critical challenge of gay parenting. As children grow up, these issues may become more complex, as families struggle to involve gay fathers in events such as weddings, graduations, and birth celebrations, where the presence of the gay father and his partner may raise questions.

Children of gay fathers do sometimes worry that their sexual orientation may become contaminated by their fathers' homosexuality. Either they or their friends may begin to question whether they are gay as well. Those children who do disclose their fathers' homosexuality report being harassed by the use of such terms as *queer* and *fag*. Naturally, this concern is greatest during their teenage years (Riddle & Arguelles, 1981). Obviously, the children of gay fathers need to consider carefully the consequences of disclosure. Keeping this aspect of their lives secret may have the same negative impact on their development as isolation, alienation, and compartmentalization does on gay men.

This is not to say that the responses of social support networks are universally negative. Many children with gay fathers report that their friends are both curious and supportive. It is important to recognize that coming out is a process rather than a discrete event. Fathers, children, and their friends need time to move into the process, and to examine their own feelings and attitudes so that acceptance and understanding replace confusion and fear. One child of a gay father said:

> At first, I was really angry at my dad. I couldn't figure out how to tell my friends what was going on, so I said nothing. My dad and I had terrible fights as he put pressure on me to say it was OK. I thought what he was doing was sinful and embarrassing. But over time, I began to realize that he is the same dad he has always been, and now we are closer than ever. My friends have also got used to the idea and like to spend time with him, too.

STATE OF RESEARCH ON CHILDREN OF GAY FATHERS

In reviewing the impact of gay fathering on children, it is important to acknowledge that most children who live with gay fathers

Case Study

Chip Speaks

My name is Chip and I'm seventeen and in twelfth grade. When we first moved to Indianapolis, I learned my dad was gay. I was twelve. I didn't really think much about it. There was a birthday coming up and Dad said we were going to go out and buy a birthday card. He went out, drove around the block and then parked in front of our house. Then he took me to the park and told me the facts of life. He asked me if I knew what it meant to be gay. I told him, "Yeah, it means to be happy and enjoy yourself." Then he started to explain to me about being homosexual. I really didn't know what it was at that point, until he explained it to me.

It's an accepted part of my life now. I've been growing up with it almost five years. When he invites another guy into the house it's OK. I don't bring other kids home then. One of my friends is extremely homophobic and he lets that fact be known. I wouldn't dare risk anything or it would be like "goodbye" to my friend. My other two friends, I don't know how they would react. So I have to be careful about having certain friends over. To me it's blatantly obvious. Having been exposed to so many gay people, I know what to look for and what I'm seeing. Sometimes it's kind of hard because people make fun of gay people. And, if I stick up for their rights, then I get ridiculed. So I just don't say anything at school. It's kind of hard sometimes.

The good thing is that you get a more objective view of people in general, being raised by someone who's so persecuted by society. You begin to sympathize with anyone who is persecuted by society. You tend not to be as prejudiced. You need to appreciate people for what they are personally, not just in terms of color, religion, or sexual preference. That's the best thing. The hardest thing is hearing all those people making cracks or jokes on TV or at school and not being really able to do anything about it. Because he's my dad after all, it makes me kind of sad. I never feel ashamed or embarrassed, but I do feel a little pressured because of this. One time a friend of mine made a joke about gay people. I just played it off like I thought it was funny, but I didn't.

are also the products of divorce and may show the psychological distress that typically accompanies the experience of marital dissolution. All too often, the emotional distress of children with gay parents is solely attributed to the parents' sexual orientation and is not

You have to pretend you think the same thing they do when you don't. That makes me feel like a fraud.

When my dad puts his arm around another man, the first thing I think is, "I could never do that." It makes me a little bit uncomfortable, but I'm not repulsed by it. There are times I wish he wouldn't do it, but other times I'm glad he can have the freedom to do it. When he first came out to me, the only question I asked him was, "What are the chances of me being gay?" He couldn't answer it. But today, to the best of my knowledge, I'm not gay. I like chasing after girls.

Sometimes I feel like I'm keeping a big secret. My dad had a holy union with a man once. My friends had big plans and we were all going out on the day of the big event. And I couldn't go and couldn't explain why. Things like that have happened a number of times. I can't go and I can't tell why. They start yelling at me and get mad. They'll get over it; it's none of their business.

As fathers go, mine tends to be a little nicer—almost a mother's temperament. A friend of mine's father doesn't spend much time with him. They just seem to have stricter parents than mine. I don't know if that's just because of his personality in general or if it's because he's gay. He's a very emotional person; he cries easily. I love him. He's a good dad. He's more open than other dads. He doesn't let me get away with a lot. He tends to be more worried about me and a girl together than some other fathers are about their sons—more worried about my having sex. Whenever I go out on a date, he always says something like, "Don't do anything I wouldn't do," only he doesn't say it jokingly. Sometimes he's just overly cautious.

If I could change my dad and make him straight, I wouldn't do it. It might make things easier for me in some ways, but I wouldn't have grown up the way I have. Being exposed to the straight world and gay world equally has balanced me out more than some of the other people I know. The only things I'd want to change is society's treatment of him. (Barret & Robinson, 1990, pp. 14–15)

(*Note:* Chip's dad died of AIDS two years after this interview took place.)

seen as a complex mixture of family dynamics, divorce adjustment, and the incorporation of the parents' sexual coming out.

Only two studies have directly addressed the children of gay fathers (Green, 1978; Weeks, Derdeyn, & Langman, 1975). In both studies, the researchers gave psychological tests to the children. The findings from this testing have been used to support the notion that a parent's homosexuality has little bearing on the child's sexual orientation. Children showed clear heterosexual preferences or were developing them. Green concluded that "The children I interviewed were able to comprehend and verbalize the atypical nature of their parents' lifestyles and to view their atypicality in the broader perspective of the cultural norm" (p. 696). Our interviews with children have also supported this finding (Barret & Robinson, 1990). Still, the problem is that the observations of Weeks and his colleagues (1975) are based on the clinical assessment of only two children, and the Green study (1978) observed only the children of lesbian mothers and the children of parents who had experienced sex-change surgery. None of the parents in that sample were classified as gay fathers. The findings of these two studies and others of lesbian mothers (e.g., Goodman, 1973; Hoeffer, 1981; Kirkpatrick, Smith, & Roy, 1981) are frequently generalized to include the gay father's children, even though important differences exist between transsexuals and gay men as well as between gay men and lesbians.

CONCLUSIONS

The profile we use to understand and describe gay fathers and their children is far from conclusive. Clearly, the literature has improved, after 1982, in its use of comparison groups and a more diverse, nationwide sampling. Still, until researchers can obtain larger, more representative samples and use more sophisticated research designs, caution must be exercised in making sweeping generalizations about gay fathers and their families. Meanwhile, it is possible to speculate from some limited data that, although not fully developed, provides an emerging picture of the children of gay fathers:

1. They are like all kids. Some do well in just about all activities; some have problems, and some are well adjusted.
2. They live in family situations that are unique and must develop strategies to cope with these situations.
3. They need help sorting out their feelings about homosexuality and their anxieties about their own sexual orientation.
4. They may be isolated and angry and may have poor relationships with their fathers.

5. They are in little danger of sexual abuse and unlikely to "catch" homosexuality.
6. Many of them adjust quite well to their family situation and use the family as a means to develop greater tolerance of diversity.
7. Some of them become involved in the human rights movement as they promote gay rights.
8. Their relationships with their fathers have a potential for greater honesty and openness.

REFERENCES

Barret, R., & Robinson, B. (1990). *Gay fathers.* New York: Free Press.

Bell, A., & Weinberg, M. (1978). *Homosexualities: A study of diversity among men and women.* New York: Simon & Schuster.

Bigner, J., & Bozett, F. (1989). Parenting by gay fathers. *Marriage and Family Review, 14,* 155–175.

Bigner, J., & Jacobsen, R. (1989a). Parenting behaviors of homosexual and heterosexual fathers. *Journal of Homosexuality, 18,* 173–186.

Bigner, J., & Jacobsen, R. (1989b). The value of children to gay and heterosexual fathers. *Journal of Homosexuality, 18,* 163–172.

Bozett, F. (1980). Gay fathers: How and why they disclose their homosexuality to their children. *Family Relations: Journal of Applied Family and Child Studies, 29,* 173–179.

Bozett, F. (1981). Gay fathers: Evolution of the gay father identity. *American Journal of Orthopsychiatry, 51,* 552–559.

Bozett, F. (1984). Parenting concerns of gay fathers. *Topics in Clinical Nursing, 6,* 60–71.

Bozett, F. (1988). Social control of identity of gay fathers. *Western Journal of Nursing Research, 10,* 550–565.

Bozett, F. (1989). Gay fathers: A review of the literature. *Journal of Homosexuality, 18,* 137–162.

Corley, R. (1990). *The final closet: The gay parent's guide to coming out to their children.* Miami: Editech Press.

DeFrancis, V. (1976). *Protecting the child victim of sex crimes committed by adults.* Denver: American Humane Society, Children's Division.

Epstein, R. (1979, June). Children of gays. *Christopher Street,* 43–50.

Gebhard, P., Gagnon, J., Pomeroy, W., & Christenson, C. (1965). *Sex offenders: An analysis of types.* New York: Harper & Row.

Geiser, R. (1979). *Hidden victims: The sexual abuse of children.* Boston: Beacon Press.

Goodman, B. (1973). The lesbian mother. *American Journal of Orthopsychiatry, 43,* 283–284.

Green, R. (1978). Sexual identity of 37 children raised by homosexual or transsexual parents. *American Journal of Psychiatry, 135,* 692–697.

Harris, M., & Turner, P. (1986). Gay and lesbian parents. *Journal of Homosexuality, 18,* 101–113.

Harry, J. (1983). Gay male and lesbian relationships. In E. Macklin & R. Rubin (Eds.), *Contemporary families and alternative lifestyles* (pp. 216–234). Beverly Hills, CA: Sage.

Hitchens, D. (1980). Social attitudes, legal standards, and personal trauma in child custody cases. *Journal of Homosexuality, 5,* 89–95.

Hoeffer, B. (1981). Children's acquisition of sex-role behavior in lesbian-mother families. *American Journal of Orthopsychiatry, 51,* 536–544.

Humphreys, L. (1979). *Tearoom trade.* Chicago: Aldine.

Kinsey, A. C., Pomeroy, W. B., & Martin, C. E. (1948). *Sexual behavior in the human male.* Philadelphia: W.B. Saunders.

Kirkpatrick, M., Smith, C., & Roy, R. (1981). Lesbian mothers and their children. *American Journal of Orthopsychiatry, 51,* 545–551.

Lewis, K. (1980). Children of lesbians: Their point of view. *Social Work, 25,* 200.

Maddox, B. (1982, February). Homosexual parents. *Psychology Today,* 62–69.

Miller, B. (1979, October). Gay fathers and their children. *The Family Coordinator, 28,* 544–551.

Morin, S., & Schultz, S. (1978). The gay movement and the rights of children. *Journal of Social Issues, 34,* 137–148.

Richardson, D. (1981). Lesbian mothers. In J. Hart & D. Richardson (Eds.), *The theory and practice of homosexuality.* London: Routledge & Kegan Paul.

Riddle, D. (1978). Relating to children: Gays as role models. *Journal of Social Issues, 34,* 38–58.

Riddle, D., & Arguelles, M. (1981). Children of gay parents: homophobia's victims. In I. Stuart & L. Abt (Eds.), *Children of separation and divorce.* New York: Van Nostrand Reinhold.

Robinson, B., & Barret, R. (1986). *The developing father.* New York: Guilford Press.

Scallen, R. (1981). *An investigation of paternal attitudes and behaviors in homosexual and heterosexual fathers.* Doctoral dissertation, California School of Professional Psychology, San Francisco, CA. (*Dissertation Abstracts International, 42,* 3809B).

Skeen, P., & Robinson, B. (1984). Family background of gay fathers: A descriptive study. *Psychological Reports, 54,* 999–1005.

Spada, J. (1979). *The Spada report.* New York: Signet Books.

Weeks, R. B., Derdeyn, A. P., & Langman, M. (1975). Two cases of children of homosexuals. *Child Psychiatry and Human Development, 6,* 26–32.

Woodruff v. Woodruff (1979). 44 N.C. App. No 7921 DC 456.

7

Custodial Grandparenting
Implications for Children's Development

R. Jerald Shore and Bert Hayslip, Jr.

OVERVIEW OF GRANDPARENTING AND INTERGENERATIONAL RELATIONSHIPS

Implications of Sociodemographic Changes

Many professionals and laypersons can verify that families are in a state of flux. Traditional, well-defined roles that men, women, and children play have been altered by divorce, teenage pregnancy, dual-career families, and single parenthood. Consequently, a redefinition of family forms has taken place, brought about by the necessity to fulfill the unique role responsibilities associated with changing family composition. Bengtson, Rosenthal, and Burton (1990) have underscored the fact that traditional expectations about families have been altered by demographic factors such as increased longevity and reduced fertility, as well as a diversity of family forms.

R. Jerald Shore • Department of Rehabilitation Science, University of Texas Southwestern Medical School, Dallas, Texas 75235.   Bert Hayslip, Jr. • Department of Psychology, University of North Texas, Denton, Texas 76203.

Redefining Families: Implications for Children's Development, edited by Adele Eskeles Gottfried and Allen W. Gottfried. Plenum Press, New York, 1994.

A critical dimension of the changing family is intergenerational relationships. Because of increased longevity and reduced fertility, older persons are increasingly likely to be members of four- and five-generation families, in contrast to the three-generation family structure that was common during the early 20th century (Hagestad, 1986, 1988a,b). For example, as life expectancy increases, persons will be spending more time together in the postparental phase of their lives. Women, who currently outlive their husbands by 5–10 years, will be spending an increasing portion of their lives as widows. Whereas parents and children used to share 20–30 years together, and grandparents and grandchildren perhaps 10 years (Juster & Vinorskis, 1987), parents, children, and grandchildren may now be a part of one another's lives for anywhere between 20 and 50 years (Hagestad & Burton, 1985; Preston, 1984). As women are having fewer children, and couples are spacing their children more closely, the number of persons per generation has become smaller.

Because persons often become grandparents in their mid-40s (Sprey & Matthews, 1982), women can easily spend half their lives as grandparents. Collectively, these changes have created what has been termed the *beanpole family*, in which there is an increase in the number of generations within family lineages; that is, the family is "verticalized" while the breadth of each generation constricts (Hagestad, 1986). Thus, in the future, individuals are likely to have more vertical lineage relationships (i.e., parents and grandparents) than horizontal lineage relationships (e.g., siblings, aunts, and uncles).

In light of these demographic changes as well as changes in the timing of fertility such as teenage childbearing (Burton & Martin, 1987) and delays in childbearing or childlessness due to career demands (Connidis, 1989; Parke, 1988), the salience of single parenting and divorce has increased (Bengtson & Dannefer, 1987).

This enhanced role of divorce and single parenting, combined with our awareness of caregiving as a life task faced by both younger and older adults (Gatz, Bengtson, & Blum, 1990), has numerous implications. The greater life span of older adults suggests that more elderly persons will be available to whom caregiving responsibilities can be allocated. On the other hand, smaller generations of younger persons lessen the size of the caregiver pool for ill or dependent parents or grandparents (Bengtson *et al.*, 1990). This new pattern has special implications for women, who outlive men.

With divorce rates that have been increasing since the early 1970s

(Bengston *et al.*, 1990), the likelihood of new family forms becomes greater. Obviously, should remarriage occur, the role of a stepparent or stepgrandparent is acquired. Should an adult child not receive custody of his or her child, the opportunity for the grandparent to be centrally involved and influential in this child's life may be lost (Bengston *et al.*, 1990). If, however, custody is granted, child-care responsibilities must be responsibly assumed. Most single parents, by necessity, must work, and of course, their children must be cared for, too. Moreover, should this parent become ill, die, or desert the child, the grandparents, who are a valued resource in the family, may assume either temporary or permanent child-care responsibility. Ideally, the grandparents serve as viable role models for their grandchildren and also represent an important link to the past and to the history of the family (Cherlin & Furstenberg, 1986b).

In view of the changing demographics of aging, questions such as "What does being a grandparent mean?" or "Is grandparenting satisfying?" are now more relevant than ever. The once-popular image of the grandparent as a kindly elderly person in a rocking chair is now clearly inaccurate; grandparents are more likely to be men and women who are much younger, who are employed, or who even have adult children still at home. Moreover, they may also be caring for a mother or a father who is quite old. Although the frequency of contact between grandparents and their grandchildren is fairly regular (often daily), it is rare for grandparents, adult children, and grandchildren to live under the same roof (Bengtson *et al.*, 1990; Troll, Miller, & Atchley, 1979). Further, it is important to note that grandparent styles and contact with grandchildren are affected by forces such as age, gender, divorce, and family separation (Strom & Strom, 1987).

Being a grandparent is often considered a developmental task of middle or late adulthood (Newman & Newman, 1990), and for many, having a grandchild may be considered a marker of middle age or aging. As the relative proportion of persons who are older increases, grandparenthood as a normative experience will become more commonplace. Of all older persons, 70% can expect to become grandparents (Barranti, 1985).

Attitudes of Grandparents toward the Grandparental Role

Interestingly, though most persons have experienced a relationship of some sort with their grandparents, the literature on grandparenting is not extensive. What literature does exist suggests, however, that grandparenthood can have *many* meanings, and that there are many styles or types of grandparenting, which are affected by a number of individual, environmental, and socioeconomic factors. Grandparent is a *tenuous role*, having no clear criteria for its entry or exit (Rosow, 1985). Tenuous roles are characterized by less activity and are somewhat ambiguous. Middle-aged and especially older persons increasingly suffer from role loss and role constriction, with a consequent loss of status and, often, increased dependency (Rosow, 1985). For women, this pattern may be signaled by the departure of the children from the home, and for men, it may be precipitated by retirement. Relative to active parenting, grandparenting is typically a more narrow, less active role, whose definition is consequently an individual matter. One may be unsure regarding the extent to which continued involvement in a grandchild's life is appropriate (Bengtson, 1985). In this light, Rosow (1985) suggested that the tenuous nature of the grandparent role is due to a lack of normative expectations about appropriate behavior. It is for this reason that grandparenting is largely an individual experience. Despite the ambiguous status of grandparenthood, programs designed with the needs of grandparents in mind are available. These programs help persons to define their roles more clearly and to improve the quality of their relationships with their grandchildren (Strom & Strom, 1987, 1989, 1990).

Whether one finds grandparenting satisfying or not depends on numerous factors, for example, the race, gender, and life stage of the grandchild, and the age and health of the grandparent (Kivett, 1985; Thomas, 1986b; Wilson, 1986). Positive, yet voluntary, relationships with their grandchildren and close relations with their adult child who is the parent also contribute to how grandparents perceive their role (Johnson, 1988). Thomas (1989b) found that, when viewed from the perspective of the grandparent, the presence of the parents appeared to interfere with the quality of the grandparent–grandchild relationship. This is especially important if the grandparent–adult child relationship is conflictual (Thomas, 1990). It thus appears that parents can interfere with, but not necessarily enhance, the grandparent–grandchild relationship (Thomas, 1989a; Thomas et al., 1988).

The grandparents who derive the most satisfaction from their role are female and married, express positive feelings toward their grandchild, see their relationship with their grandchild as central to them, and express greater caretaking responsibility (Thomas, Bence, & Meyer, 1988). It is important to note that such responsibilities are not primary in nature. In the Thomas *et al.* (1988) study, the *parents* had the primary child-care and child-rearing responsibility. Interestingly, proximity to the grandchildren and the quality of the relationship with the adult parent failed to predict satisfaction with grandparenting in this study.

Examining grandparenting from the perspective of the grandchild, King and Thomas (1989) found that adult grandchildren who saw their parents as encouraging them to be close to their grandparents saw their grandparents as role models as well as sources of advice and support in the family. Mickus and Hirsch (1991) also found that adolescents saw their grandparents as significant influences in their lives, particularly in the areas of personal growth and academics. Recent studies of young adult grandchildren have confirmed these findings (Hodgson, 1992; Roberto & Stroes, 1992).

Meanings of Grandparenthood

What do grandparents value about their role? Whether grandparenting is satisfying or not seems to depend principally on the relationship with one's adult children (Cherlin & Furstenberg, 1986b). If that relationship is positive and lacks conflict, the grandparent role is likely to be more fulfilling to all involved. At the least, it fails to detract from grandparental satisfaction (see above). In this respect, conflicts, when they exist, often cover three issues: (1) the grandparents' responsibility in raising the grandchildren, (2) relations with their adult children, and (3) their feelings about *being* a grandparent (Thomas, 1990).

As grandparenthood means different things to different people, it most likely influences one's *style* of grandparenting. Meaning is also affected by the quality of one's relationship with the grandchildren (which is a determinant of role satisfaction). Thomas and King (1990) explored the role of numerous sociodemographic factors (i.e., race, gender, geographic proximity, and frequency of contact) in explaining young adult grandchildren's views of their grandparents. When geographic proximity and frequency of contact were controlled for, these authors found that both white and minority young-adult grandchildren gave strong endorsement to the notion that their grandparents were good role models and good sources of advice and support.

Indeed, grandparents and grandchildren both give to one another and receive from one another both tangible and emotional support (Bengtson *et al.*, 1990; Langer, 1990). Such mutually satisfying *reciprocal* relationships strengthen one's convoy (interpersonal network) of support (Antonucci, 1990; Kahn & Antonucci, 1980).

Perhaps the earliest study of grandparenting was by Wood and Robertson (1976), who classified grandparenthood into four types, based on the perceived *meaning* of grandparenthood. These meaning types were based on a grandparent's relative standing on two independent dimensions of grandparenting. The first of these was a social dimension of grandparenting, in which its meaning related to the role's meeting society's needs (i.e., a social-normative definition of grandparenting). For example, carrying on the family line, getting respect, setting a good example,and reinforcing family values all defined this social dimension of grandparenting. The other dimension was a personal one, in which grandparenting fulfilled each individual's internal needs (e.g., having an emotionally satisfying involvement in the grandchildren's lives, feeling young, and being concerned about the grandchild's welfare). Persons who were high in both dimensions were termed *apportioned,* and those who were low in both were termed *remote; symbolic* grandparents were high on a social and low in the personal dimension, and *individualized* persons were high on a personal and low in the social dimension.

Apportional grandparents derived satisfaction from their own personal experiences and social norms, enjoying the role of grandparents, whereas remote grandparents found little meaning either in their personal experience or in meeting social expectations. Symbolic grandparents saw their role as rewarding in terms of social norms (i.e., their involvement was more remote because of their family position and was somewhat stereotypical in nature), whereas individualized persons found satisfaction through their own personal experiences with their grandchildren.

In general, apportioned and individualized grandparents spent more time with their grandchildren. These persons were older and had *more* grandchildren. Wood and Robertson (1976) found, however, that having grandchildren did not substitute for having friends of one's own age.

Robertson (1977) found that the largest percentage of grandmothers surveyed described themselves as being "remote." Most grandmothers enjoyed the role because it made them feel younger, and because they felt they were assisting in carrying on the family line. They got satisfaction primarily from providing "things" for their grandchildren that they had not been able to provide for their own children. Thus, their involvement was more traditional, to the extent that it reflected normative values about the family. Remote grandparents also achieved satisfaction and enjoyment from helping their grandchildren achieve more than their parents or grandparents had been able to achieve.

More recently, based on the essentially individualistic nature of grandparenting, and on the fact that a given behavior associated with the role may mean different things to different individuals, Kivnick (1985) defined five dimensions of grandparental meaning: centrality (relationships with a grandchild are important to oneself); valued elder (feeling needed and helpful, carrying on the family tradition); immortality through clan (being the center of the family and being influential and respected); reinvolvement with one's personal past (reliving one's experiences as a child or parent); and indulgence (spoiling the grandchildren and being tolerant of their mistakes). Although these multiple dimensions have been most useful in understanding grandparenting, they may not be independent of one another (Miller & Cavanaugh, 1990).

Styles of Grandparenting

Perhaps the first detailed analyses of grandparenting styles in the United States was conducted by Neugarten and Weinstein (1964), who identified five distinctive types of grandparenting styles. These styles are termed *formal, fun seeker, surrogate parent, reservoir of family wisdom,* and *distant figure.* The formal style includes grandparents who are highly interested in their grandchildren. Though these grandparents often care for their grandchildren, they should not be viewed as primary or surrogate caretakers. However, they often have authority and control over the children in the absence of the parents.

The fun-seeker style includes individuals who are involved in playful, free relationships with their grandchildren and do not exert any control or authority over them. Grandparents exercising this style look upon being with their grandchildren as a leisure activity.

Surrogate-parent-style grandparents are often the primary caretakers of children; this style is quite common because of the increasing number of single-parent families and families in which both parents work outside the home. For some grandparents, however, caring for a grandchild when the adult child has divorced is a full-time job. We term this dimension of the grandparent role *custodial grandparenting*.

Grandparents with a reservoir-of-family-wisdom style provide special skills, resources, and knowledge to younger members of the family and seem to be comparatively rare. This style is usually associated with the grandfather.

Although the distant-figure style was relatively rare when Neugarten and Weinstein proposed their typology, it is probably somewhat more common now because of society's increased mobility. In this style, contacts with grandchildren are infrequent, usually on holidays, and the grandparents are perceived as benevolent, yet remote, in terms of physical contact and distance.

Based on interviews of over 500 grandparents, Cherlin and Furstenberg (1985) identified two clusters of activities through which the grandparents related to their teenage grandchildren, differing from those in previous studies because of a variation in the ages of both the grandchildren and the grandparents. The first cluster of activities reflected an exchange of a variety of services between the generations, and the second reflected the extent of the parent type of influence that the grandparents were able to exert over their grandchildren.

In a procedure analogous to that used by Wood and Robertson (1976), Cherlin and Furstenberg (1985) derived scores for each grandparent on both exchange of services and parental influence. *Detached* individuals scored low on each and had a minimum of contact with their grandchildren, and *passive* grandparents also scored low on each but had more intergenerational contact. *Active* grandparents scored high on one or both dimensions, regardless of the extent of contact. In turn, active grandparents were subdivided into those who were *supportive* (high exchange of services), *authoritative* (very parentlike in their influence), and *influential* (high in both exchange of services and parental influence). Not surprisingly, the detached and passive grandparents felt less close to their grandchildren than did the supportive, authoritative, and influential (in that order) grandparents.

Cherlin and Furstenberg (1985) found little social class and educational variation in grandparental style, but black grandparents were a great deal more likely to fill an authoritative or influential role, in part because of the relatively high proportion of single-parent black families in this national sample of grandparents. Men were likely to play a more active (supportive, authoritative) role than a passive one in this sample.

Cherlin and Furstenberg (1986b) developed new categories of grandparental styles: *companionette, remote,* and *involved.* Companionette grandparents are described as affectionate but somewhat passive. They do not play an active role in caring for and disciplining the grandchildren. Remote grandparents (as in Neugarten and Weinstein's distant-figure style) are geographically distant, but not necessarily emotionally removed. Involved grandparents appear to be similar to the Neugarten and Weinstein formal and surrogate-parent styles; they enforce discipline and maintain family rules (see Tomlin & Passman, 1989, 1991).

That there is considerable variation in grandparental styles from study to study can be explained by both conceptual and empirical differences in the approaches to defining grandparenthood, as well as by differences across the studies in the age and health status of the grandparents themselves. As Cherlin and Furstenberg (1985) noted, the grandparent role is a dynamic one; it fluctuates with both the age and the individual needs of both the grandchild and the grandparent. As persons age, they tend to be less diverse in their style of grandparenting, usually drifting toward a less involved style (Cherlin & Furstenberg, 1985).

Gender Differences in Grandparenting

The diversity of grandparental roles is supported by the fact that there are substantial gender and kinship-status differences in attitudes toward grandparenting. For example, Kahana and Kahana (1970) found maternal grandmothers and paternal grandfathers to manifest closeness and warmth toward their grandchildren, whereas maternal grandfathers and paternal grandmothers appeared to express the most negative attitudes toward their grandchildren. Thomas (1986b) found grandmothers to be more satisfied with their role than grandfathers. This was perhaps because of their relative familiarity with intimate family relationships, as they had been principally responsible for raising their children. The men who expressed more satisfaction were older, had active relationships with their young grandchildren, and were happy with their involvement in the task of child rearing. Thomas (1986b) and Kivett (1985) have suggested that exposure to such grandfathers may have an impact on their grandchildren's tendency to define themselves androgynously (see also Kivnick, 1985).

That gender influences in perceptions of grandparenthood exist is also illustrated in a study by Thomas (1989b), where the grand-mothers expressed the most satisfaction, irrespective of their kinship position. The grandfathers, however, defined their roles primarily by the symbolic meaning they saw in having a grandchild with the family name, and by the opportunity to indulge their grandchildren (see also Cherlin & Furstenberg, 1985).

A recent study by Kivett (1991) suggests that ethnicity helps to define the grandparent role for men. Kivett found that the grand-father role was more central to black males than to white males, and that this role was more affectionate than functional for older black men. Interestingly, Kivett also found more diversity in how the grandfather role was defined for black males, consistent with the flexible role structure and helping network found in black families. Recall that, in the Cherlin and Furstenberg (1985) study, there were substantial racial differences in grandparental style. In that study, most of those interviewed, however, were women.

GRANDCHILD–GRANDPARENT RELATIONSHIPS

Attitudes of Grandchildren toward Grandparents

Information on grandparent–grandchild contact is important be-cause, for many persons, their contact with older adults and/or at-titudes toward them are influenced in part by their interactions with their grandparents, or with other elderly relatives. Kennedy (1990) reported that college students' perceptions of grandparent and grand-child roles were generally positive, indicating affection and respect for grandparents (see Robertson, 1976). However, in this study, black students saw the grandparent role as a more active one in the fam-ily than did white students, a finding reflecting racial differences in persons' perceptions of the extended-family network (Bengtson *et al.*, 1990).

How children respond to their grandparents is diverse. Whereas younger children may define their grandparents in physical terms (e.g., wrinkles and white hair), older children tend to see their grand-parents first in a functional light (e.g., "Old people don't play with you") and later in more abstract if not generic terms (e.g., sickness, weakness, friendliness, or experience) (Kahana & Kahana, 1970). Other influences are the kinship position and gender of the grandparent (Matthews & Sprey, 1985), the frequency of contact and residential proximity (Cherlin & Furstenberg, 1986b), the quality of the parent–grandparent bond (Johnson, 1983; Matthews & Sprey, 1985), and the nature and degree of influence of the grandparent, varying by the sex of the grandparent (Hagestad, 1988). The perceived closeness and the extent of influence tend to be greater for grandmothers than for grandfathers (Roberto & Stroes, 1992).

Hoffman (1979–1980) found that kinship position influenced adult grandchildren's perceptions of their grandparents when ties were close with the maternal grandparents, particularly the grandmother. Yet, there was a great deal of variability in such relationships.

Shore and Hayslip (1988) also investigated grandchildren's perceptions of their grandparents. They studied younger grandchildren and comprehensively incorporated numerous grandchild and grandparent characteristics into their analyses. Especially critical to the grandchildren's views about their grandparents was the quality of the child's relationship with his or her mother (see King & Thomas, 1989). Additionally, perceived grandparental style predicted relationship quality, and both a companionette and an involved relational style (Cherlin & Furstenberg, 1986b) were most important in this respect.

King and Thomas (1989) studied adult grandchildren's perceptions of their grandparents, specifically focusing on the extent of the grandparents' perceived influence in these adults' lives. Perceived closeness was associated with the view of grandmothers as role models; this was not true of grandfathers. Age and gender were not related to views of grandparent influence. A later study (Thomas & King, 1990) indicated that, for the most part, race did not influence perceptions of grandparental influence when geographic proximity and frequency of contact were taken into account. In addition, Hodgson (1991) found that both men and women saw · their relationships with their grandparents as similarly close and saw themselves as equally supportive of and equally responsible to their grandparents.

Grandparents who reported good health, who were married, and who felt closest to their grandchildren tended to express higher morale, life satisfaction, and self-esteem (Thomas, 1989c). Interestingly, the meaning they attributed to being a grandparent had little to do with their mental health in this study.

On the basis of what we know (largely limited to grandmothers), grandparenthood *can* be satisfying to those persons who value the role, who have the opportunity to interact with their grandchildren, and whose relationships with their adult children are positive. As Troll (1980) noted, the real value that grandparenthood has for many middle-aged and elderly persons is that it reinforces their sense of family. Wilcoxon (1987) termed such persons "significant grandparents." That is, grandparents can derive a great deal of satisfaction in knowing that the "family theme" is being carried on by the grandchildren, even if their contacts with their adult children and their children's children are minimal. That is, grandparents prefer fulfilling voluntary, nonparental relationships with their grandchildren (Shore & Hayslip, 1990).

Bidirectional Influence of Grandparents and Grandchildren

As in parent–child relationships, grandparents can influence *and* are influenced by their grandchildren (Lerner & Spanier, 1978; Parke, 1988). Thus, as in parenthood, we see the bidirectional nature of socialization. An older family member can communicate values, instruct, make history "real," and support his or her grandchildren regarding issues related to work and education. In Hagestad's research (1978), satisfying grandparent–grandchild relations were also characterized by decisions to *avoid* discussing certain topics (sexuality, religion, and political issues) to minimize conflict and enrich the relationship. In many cases, however, the free exchange of views can ease the tensions that may exist with a parent (Robertson, 1977).

Simply being older does not guarantee that one will derive a great deal of personal satisfaction from having grandchildren. Like many things in life, the grandparent role must be actively shaped if it is to have any meaning for both grandchild and grandparent. Despite the obvious dynamic relationship of the grandchild and the grandparent, in virtually no research examining this relationship have data been collected simultaneously from both generations. However, the above literature suggests that satisfying intergenerational ties seem to be viewed as such by both grandparents and grandchildren.

GRANDPARENTS AND DIVORCE

Divorce, of course, dynamically changes the matrix of family relationships. Although much has been written about how grandparents define their relationships with their adult children and grandchildren in the event of a divorce (Johnson, 1985; Novatney, 1990; Thompson, Tinsley, Scalora, & Parke, 1989; Trygstad & Sanders, 1989), comparatively little attention has been directed to the resumption of the parent role late in life as a function of the dissolution of the family.

As noted above, grandparenthood *can* be very rewarding. However, grandparents, many of whom have actually been recruited to assume the child-rearing roles of their adult children, have been thrust into the arena of divorce (Matthews & Sprey, 1984). In many cases, upon the divorce of their adult child, they may not be permitted to visit the grandchild they have been caring for. Legal avenues may need to be pursued to guarantee a grandparent visitation rights, over the objections of the adult child. In times of family crisis, their legal visitation rights are often ambiguous or unenforceable, so that they are cut off from an important source of emotional nourishment—an ongoing warm relationship with a grandchild (Wilson & DeShane, 1982).

In cases where the adult parent has remarried, stepgrandparenting can create more problems than satisfaction. Because they have no biological ties to their "new" grandchildren, grandparents' role in the newly constituted family is often ambiguous and stressful, complicating the difficulties that blended families face (Novatney, 1990). Trygstad and Sanders (1989), however, found that stepgrandchildren maintained their relationship with, and derived satisfaction from interacting with a stepgrandparent. Many of these children felt quite positive about their relationship with a stepgrandparent even though their specific expectations from this person were low. Indeed, many stepgrandchildren wanted more contact than they had with this older individual. A somewhat less obvious implication of divorce is that it becomes more likely that the grandparents themselves will be divorced (Smith, 1989).

If one grandparent assumes child-care responsibilities in the event of the divorce or death of a parent, his or her dependence on friends or extended family is heightened when difficulties arise. Although grandparenthood as a normative experience of middle and later adulthood potentially offers psychological benefits to grandparents (Bengt-son & Robertson, 1985; Kivnick, 1982a,b; Thomas, 1988), the return to active parenting as a result of the divorce, death, or serious illness of a parent may disrupt rather than enhance the lives of grandparent and grandchild. At the least, custodial grandparenting requires read-justment to a new role and the (re)learning of parenting skills in caring for a loved grandchild.

Impact on Grandparental Well-Being

Parenting young children may help some older persons defend against the realities of aging-related losses (Kennedy & Keeney, 1987). Others, however, may not welcome the burdens of caregiving brought about by the divorce or death of their children, to the extent that their needs for autonomy and/or mutual relationships and lifestyles are threatened (Cherlin & Furstenberg, 1986a). These effects may be due to (1) the dramatic change involved in adding the parental role at a time when relinquishing the role is viewed more positively; (2) the huge responsibilities accompanying parenting at an age when persons have less energy and patience for the task; and (3) the family trauma precipitating the surrogate parenting role for many grandparents.

Many grandparents, particularly if they are middle-aged or older, are likely also to be experiencing their own unique life-cycle changes (e.g., menopause, a midlife career change, rekindling their marriages, or retirement) and do not expect nor want to resume parenting. Additionally, if the grandparents have to resume full-time parent-ing, it is most likely to occur in the context of family trauma. Since the late 1960s, the dramatic increase in divorce, teenage pregnancies, single-parent families, working mothers, abusing parents, separation, and the abandonment of children by their natural parents has created an increasing number of situations in which troubled children are left with their grandparents for all or a major part of their rearing.

CUSTODIAL GRANDPARENTING

The U.S. Bureau of the Census report of 1981 indicated that a total of 2,295,000 children, or 3.7% of all unmarried, noninstitutional-ized children under 18 years of age, were living apart from their parents (Montemayor & Leigh, 1982). By 1990, this figure had increased to 4.1%, with a 17.9% *decrease* in the number of children under 18 who were living with both parents (U.S. Bureau of the Census, 1990). Where do these children live? Who cares for them? What will be the impact of such changes in their lives?

Historically, most parent-absent children live with relatives, grandparents representing the largest percentage (38.9%) of such persons (Montemayor & Leigh, 1982). Cherlin and Furstenberg (1986b) reported that, in their sample of grandparents in families where adult children had divorced, 30% took grandchildren into their homes about the time of the breakup. Johnson (1988) estimated that up to 40% of grandparents may assume parental responsibility for their grandchildren.

It is interesting that *perceived* responsibility for incidental caregiving has been suggested as a *positive* influence on grandparenting satisfaction and possibly psychological well-being (Thomas, 1988). Yet, expectations of *non*interference in their lives by a divorced adult child may mitigate these benefits for the grandparent (Johnson, 1988), just as the unanticipated resumption of the parental role by a grandparent might also do.

Studying grandparents' reactions to the resumption of the parental role is important to the extent that the older person's well-being, as well as the meaning and style associated with grandparenting, may be affected. As noted above, these variables have been identified as influences on grandchildren's perceptions of their relationship with a grandparent (King & Thomas, 1989; Shore & Hayslip, 1988). Consequently, as intergenerational relationships and caregiving are reciprocal (Parke, 1988), the actual return to the role of a full-time parent for the grandparent is likely to have an impact on not only the middle-aged or older person, but also on that child for whom he or she is now responsible.

A Model of Grandparental Well-Being

Although numerous studies have attempted to determine the antecedents of grandparental satisfaction, no published study comprehensively addresses the impact on grandparents of resuming parental responsibility. In this light, we will discuss the development of a model for predicting grandparent well-being.

The divorce literature (Cherlin & Furstenberg, 1986a,b; Johnson, 1988; Thomas, 1986a) clearly shows that grandparental kinship status, age, and gender have direct effects on which group of grandparents will engage in the caregiving for their grandchildren. It may also be that how long an older person has parenting responsibility influences his or her psychological functioning (Johnson, 1988). Time in the parental role was assumed to negatively affect grandparental satisfaction and the meaning of grandparenthood; it may have the same effect on well-being. As many grandparents may have the responsibility for children with behavioral problems for which help may not have been sought, age and income were investigated as potential antecedents of help seeking.

For the parental grandparent, the relationship with the grandchild may be perceived as being more of a parent–child relationship. A parent's perceptions of the parent–child relationship (and their veridicality) affect the parent's sense of well-being and relationships (Lee & Bates, 1985; Sprunger, Boyce, & Gaines, 1985). In this light, we assumed that the grandparents' perceptions of the grandchildren they are raising would affect the grandparents' well-being and satisfaction with grandparenting. Thus, a tenuous role (Rosow, 1985) may be made even more so, and the result may be role confusion and isolation.

This study investigated four major aspects of the psychological functioning of grandparents who are raising their grandchildren: (1) general psychological well-being (WB); (2) satisfaction with grandparenting (GPSAT); (3) perceptions of the grandparent–grandchild relationship (PERCEP); and (4) the personal meaning of grandparenthood (MNG).

It was anticipated that having parental responsibility (PR) would decrease scores on measures of well-being (WB), satisfaction with grandparenting (GPSAT), the meaning of grandparenthood (MNG), and perceptions of the grandparent–grandchild relationship (PERCEPT). Similarly, it was expected that time in the parental role (be it full time or part time) (TIMEPR) would have a negative effect on the psychological well-being (WB) of the respondents (see Figure 1 for the hypothesized model).

Path analysis was used to assess the hypothesized relations among the variables of the model in Figure 1. Paths that did not have significant coefficients ($p < .05$), were eliminated, as were those not in networks linked to at least one measure of psychological functioning. These changes necessitated a redefinition of the model. In

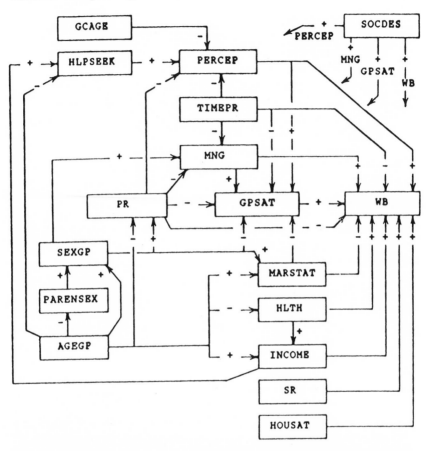

Key: Psychological well-being (WB), grandparenting satisfaction (GPSAT), perceptions of grandparent–grandchild relationship (PERCEP), meaning of grandparenthood (MNG), parental responsibility (PR), time with parental responsibility (TIMEPR), sex of grandparent (SEXGP), age of grandparent (AGEGP), sex of grandchild's parent (PARENSEX), grandparent's income (INCOME), grandparent's health (HLTH), grandparent's marital status (MARSTAT), grandparent's social resources (SR), housing satisfaction (HOUSAT), help seeking (HLPSEEK), grandchild's age (GCAGE), social desirability (SOCDES).

Figure 1. Hypothesized relations among variables predicting psychological functioning of grandparents.

order to evaluate the extent to which this restricted model was able to reproduce the original correlation matrix among the independent and dependent variables, a goodness-of-fit (GFI) index was used (Pedhazur, 1982).

Subjects and Procedure

The participants were 203 male and female grandparents solicited from the Dallas–Fort Worth area of Texas. Those who parented their grandchildren were considered the custodial (experimental) group (n = 103, M age = 54.6 years, SD = 8.2). They were defined as those who had assumed physical and financial responsibility for one grandchild who was age 18 or under and lived in the grandparent's home. In this case, minors were specified to help ensure that the participants would feel the full weight of parental responsibility (e.g., providing supervision and care). These grandparents parenting their grandchildren had legal custody in just over half the cases.

The control group participants (n = 100) were those whose grandchildren were in the care and custody of their parents (M = 58.4 years, SD = 6.7). These participants provided little or no care for their grandchildren and were referred to as *traditional grandparents*.

Fifty-two of the parents of the grandchildren being raised by the respondents were divorced and/or had abandoned the family. Almost 20% of the respondents reported physical abuse of their grandchildren by the parents, and between 28% and 38% indicated substance abuse as the reason for the family's breakup, necessitating their becoming surrogate parents. The average custodial respondent made between $20,000 and $30,000 a year, yet there were considerably more likely to be making less than $20,000 annually ($n$ = 34), relative to the traditional participants (n = 21).

The participants were recruited by a variety of methods to ensure a reasonably representative sample of both custodial and traditional grandparents. Both clinics and self-help groups were considered logical sources of custodial grandparents because of the high incidence of family trauma that required them to become surrogate parents. Additionally, senior centers, older adult organizations, and newspaper announcements were used to identify both custodial and traditional (control) grandparents.

In spite of the diverse sources and methods by which the participants were recruited, the final sample must be considered a somewhat biased one, especially because a portion of the custodial grandparents were seeking help for their grandchildren's personal or school difficulties, and because of the generally positive response bias associated with community samples of middle-aged and older adults. However, a chi-square analysis of custodial and traditional grandparents crossed by referral source (clinic versus nonclinic) was nonsignificant ($\chi_1^2 = 3.01$, $p > .05$), a result suggesting that both groups were equally likely to be recruited from each source.

The questionnaire designed for this study was composed of a number of sections corresponding to the variables of interest, as well as one section that sampled the respondents' inclinations toward giving socially desirable answers. When perceptions were rated (e.g., How important is this club or group to your life?) or internal constructs were assessed (e.g., Are you satisfied with your annual income?), a 5-point Likert scale was used (e.g., very unsatisfied to very satisfied).

The initial section of the questionnaire focused on demographic information such as age, gender, and marital status. Perceptions of social resources were evaluated in terms of visits and other contacts with the grandchildren's parents, other relatives, or friends (Havighurst, 1973), as well as the extent to which this social network provided physical resources (e.g., transportation, money, food, and clothing) and psychological help (e.g., "cheering me up") (Beyer & Woods, 1963). The respondent was also asked to recall the frequency with which he or she went to clubs and social groups, as well as the importance of these clubs or groups to the individual (Dorfman & Moffett, 1987; O'Brien, 1981).

Regarding the respondent's grandchildren, questions targeted the total number of grandchildren in the respondent's family, the ages of both the male and the female grandchildren, whether the respondents had legal custody, whether any of the respondent's children still lived at home, and whether these children were the parents of grandchildren whom the respondent was helping to raise.

Consistent with the procedure of Thomas (1988), the respondents also reported salient features of their relationship with only one grandchild below the age of 18. This procedure was used because different grandchildren affect grandparental feelings and perceptions in different ways (Cherlin & Furstenberg, 1986b), and such responses are likely to be confounded by different feelings toward one's various grandchildren.

The selection criteria specified that the grandparents report on a grandchild for whom they provided sole parenting and who might or might not be in their legal custody. If the respondents did not parent a grandchild, they were instructed to report on a grandchild for whom the primary responsibility of care lay with the child's parents, whom they saw the most frequently of all their grandchildren, and for whom they were most likely to provide only minimal or nominal care.

The respondents were also asked numerous questions regarding difficulties of a behavioral or emotional nature experienced by their grandchildren (e.g., school difficulties, drug abuse, or behavior problems), as well as about the nature of professional help that they had sought to cope with such difficulties (e.g., grandparent support groups, individual or family therapy).

Regarding custodial grandparenting, the participants were also asked about why the grandchild's parents were no longer available to raise the child and why the job of parenting had fallen to the respondents, their feelings toward the son or daughter who was the grandchild's parent, and their feelings about parenting the grandchild. The respondents were also asked to indicate the services they had had difficulty obtaining (e.g., medical treatment, insurance, or school registration) as a result of not having legal custody.

Satisfaction with grandparenting was assessed from 15 questions (coefficient alpha = .79) used in the Thomas (1988) study. Each question was answered on a 5-point Likert scale (strongly disagree to strongly agree), for a potential range of 0 to 75. Higher scores indicated greater satisfaction.

The meaning of grandparenthood was evaluated through items from the Thomas (1988) project "Grandparenting in the 1980s." These items were originally developed by Kivnick (1982a,b), who derived five dimensions of meaning pertaining to grandparenthood: centrality, valued elder, immortality through clan, reinvolvement with past, and indulgence. For the purposes of this study, the total score for the items was used in an initial data analysis. If the total score differentiated groups, subsequent analysis would be carried out to determine the relative contribution of each dimension to the differences found between the custodial and traditional groups. In light of the high correlation among the meaning subscales, using the total scores seems justifiable (see Miller & Cavanaugh, 1990). The responses were made on a 5-point Likert scale (strongly disagree to strongly agree). Low scores reflected a diminished meaning of grandparenthood for the respondent; high scores reflected an important and increased meaning of grandparenthood. In previous research (Kivnick, 1982a), coefficient alpha (an index of internal consistency) had ranged from

.685 (questions pertaining to indulgence) to .898 (questions pertaining to centrality).

The grandparents' perceptions of their relationships with a grandchild were measured by 22 questions, principally defined by the Positive Affect Index and Negative Affect Index (Bence & Thomas, 1988). The Positive Affect Index asked the grandparents to describe the extent of their mutual understanding with, trust in, respect for, and affection for the grandchild, and the Negative Affect Index measured the extent to which the grandparents felt negatively toward irritating behavior of the grandchild. Each Index had 10 questions measured across a 5-item Likert scale (none to a great amount). Two additional questions asked the participants to rate the quality of the relationship (5-item scale: very negative to very positive) and their satisfaction with the relationship (5-item scale: very unsatisfied to very satisfied). A Cronbach alpha for this measure, as reported by Thomas (1989a,b), is .79, and it has been demonstrated to predict measures of well-being in samples of grandparents (Thomas, 1988).

Psychological well-being was evaluated with Liang's 15-item self-report scale (1985), which integrates respondents' short- and long-term subjective and long-term cognitive feelings about their lives. It was assumed that including items covering a long-term time frame would reduce a possible distortion of results due to the effects of temporary situations. Positive and negative affect (transitory affective components), happiness (a long-term affective component), and congruence (a long-term cognitive component) were assessed by an integration of items from the Bradburn Affect Balance Scale (Bradburn, 1969) and the Life Satisfaction Index A (Neugarten, Havighurst, & Tobin, 1961). Each is a widely used measure of well-being with more than acceptable reliability and validity with older samples (see Liang, 1985). Again, a 5-point Likert scale (strongly disagree to strongly agree) was used. Liang (1985) reported that factor loadings reflecting aspects of overall subjective psychological well-being for the four dimensions ranged from −.642 to .890; this factor structure was replicated over four independent samples of adults.

In order to assess a potential social-desirability-response bias, the Marlowe-Crowne Social Desirability Scale (MCSDS; Crowne & Marlowe, 1960) was administered as part of the questionnaire (coefficient alpha = .88). The scores from this scale were included as independent variables in regression analyses that assessed the contribution of socially desirable response bias to the self-report measures of well-being, grandparental meaning and satisfaction, and relationship quality.

An initial version of the questionnaire was piloted with 10 elderly participants (M_{age} = 70.1) of a local senior-citizen center to determine any difficulties inherent in self-administration. On the basis of this pilot study, several changes were made to make the questionnaire more concise and clear.

Tables 1 and 2 present the comparisons of our custodial and

Table 1. Demographic Characteristics of Grandparents[a]

Characteristic	Custodial	Traditional	Total	Tests of significance
Number				
Female	82	81	163	$\chi^2 = 2.96$
Male	21	19	40	(df = 1)
Total	103	100	203	
Mean age in years	54.4	58.5	56.4	$t = -3.80**$
	(8.3)	(6.8)	(7.8)	(df = 201)
Race				
White	84	82	166	$\chi^2 = 2.09$
Black	14	12	26	(df = 2)
Hispanic	5	6	11	
Maternal/paternal[b]	1.59	1.66	1.63	$\chi^2 = -.72$ (df = 1)
Marital status				
Married	76	83	159	
Divorced	11	7	18	$\chi^2 = 61.99**$
Separated	3	2	5	(df = 3)
Widowed	13	8	21	
Mean education in years	12.2	13.4	12.8	$t = -3.27*$
	(2.7)	(2.8)	(2.8)	(df = 201)
Work status[c]				
Full time	47	50	97	$\chi^2 = 35.01**$
Part time	17	23	40	(df = 2)
Retired	14	8	22	
Income[d]	3.3	4.9	4.1	$t = -5.66*$
	(1.9)	(2.2)	(2.2)	(df = 201)
Help seeking[e]	2.46	.14	1.32	$t = .93$
	(2.45)	(.35)	(2.11)	(df = 201)

[a]Standard deviations are in parentheses except as noted.
[b]1 = paternal; 2 = maternal.
[c]Does not sum to total number of respondents in sample.
[d]3 = $20,001–$30,000; 4 = $30,001–$40,000.
[e]Assessed via a series of questions regarding whether help had been sought for oneself or a grandchild as well as the nature of the source of such help.
**p < .01   *p < .05

Table 2. Psychological Constructs: Observed Means

Construct[a]	Sex[b] × group	Observed means	Standard deviations
WB	Male		
	Traditional	66.11	4.58
	Custodial	44.10	14.10
	Female		
	Traditional	63.99	8.43
	Custodial	45.73	13.24
	Total	54.75	14.51
GPSAT	Male		
	Traditional	67.32	6.78
	Custodial	48.90	14.16
	Female		
	Traditional	63.11	8.41
	Custodial	51.36	11.65
	Total	57.32	12.26
PERCEP	Male		
	Traditional	104.32	6.80
	Custodial	77.24	23.98
	Female		
	Traditional	99.60	10.97
	Custodial	83.25	17.77
	Total	91.21	18.01
MNG	Male		
	Traditional	124.95	17.49
	Custodial	145.24	35.96
	Female		
	Traditional	140.23	30.27
	Custodial	136.51	39.51
	Total	138.18	34.44

[a]WB = Well-being; GPSAT = Satisfaction with grandparenting; PERCEP = Perceptions of the relationship with the grandchild; MNG = Meaning of grandparenting.
[b]n males = 40; n females = 163.

traditional grandparents in terms of sociodemographic and psychological characteristics (see Shore & Hayslip, 1990).

Results

DIRECT EFFECTS. Correlations among all the variables initially included in the path model are presented in Table 3. As a first step, the results of the regression analyses were compared with those hypothesized in Figure 1. Of 39 paths, 15 were retained in the final model; 24 paths (effects) were deleted. The variables that were dropped from

Table 3. Correlations among Variables in the Study[a]

	1	2	3	4	5	6	7	8	9	10	11	12	13	14	15	16	17	18	19
SEXGP[1,b]	—	-14*	23**	-13	-16*	04	03	-25**	-02	06	-08	03	03	03	-01	01	23**	01	-17*
AGEGP[2]		—	04	03	05	-44**	00	51**	-11	-10	18**	-04	10	-31**	04	19*	-13	-27**	06
MARSTAT[3,b]			—	-28**	-42**	-20**	-05	01	12	06	-14*	10	-08	-06	-16*	-25**	13*	10	08
EDUC[4]				—	61**	34**	15*	-07	-26**	-05	21**	-19*	17*	-11	16*	38**	-18*	-22**	12
INCOME[5]					—	-35**	23**	-01	-35**	-04	39**	-20**	22**	-06	26**	48**	-15*	-38**	13
HLTH[6]						—	-21**	-21**	-26**	07	17*	-14*	31**	31**	35**	36**	04	-12	-04
GCSEX[7,b]							—	-02	-33**	02	13	-29**	40**	14*	39**	35**	02	-33**	08
GCAGE[8]								—	06	-02	14*	08	-03	-30**	01	04	-10	-06	05
TIMEPR[9]									—	-09	-25**	-51**	-52**	00	-53**	-65**	-19**	86**	09
PARSEX[10,b]										—	-03	00	00	09	-02	-06	-02	04	-09
HOUSAT[11]											—	-26**	25**	00	29**	36**	01	-31**	09
HLPSEEK[12]												—	-49**	-19**	-50**	-56**	-11	54**	04
PERCEP[13]													—	37**	87**	74**	11	-49**	-02
MNG[14]														—	44**	24**	16*	04	-01
GPSAT[15]															—	74**	11	-52**	-04
WB[16]																—	15*	-65**	-04
SR[17]																	—	-17*	-02
PR[18,b]																		—	09
SOCDES[19]																			—

[a]Psychological well-being (WB), Grandparenting Satisfaction (GPSAT), Perceptions of the grandparent-grandchild relationship (PERCEP), Meaning of grandparenthood (MNG), Parental Responsibility (PR), Time with Parental Responsibility (TIMEPR), Sex of Grandparent (SEXGP), Age of the Grandparent (AGEGP), Sex of the Grandchild's Parent (PARENSEX), Grandparent's Income (INCOME), Grandparent's Health (HLTH), Grandparent's Marital Status (MARSTAT), Grandparent's Social Resources (SR), Housing Satisfaction (HOUSAT), Helpseeking (HLPSEEK), Grandchild's Age (GCAGE), Social Desirability (SOCDES), Sex of the Grandchild (GCSEX), Level of Education in Years (EDUC); decimals omitted.

[b]Point biserials or phi coefficients as appropriate.

*$p < .05$ **$p < .01$

the final model were duration of grandparent responsibility (TIMEPR), grandchild age (GCAGE), sex of the grandparent (SEXGP), marital status (MARSTAT), satisfaction with housing (HOUSAT), and social desirability (SOCDES) (see Figure 1). In this regard, the data did not fully support the hypothesized model. Fortunately, the lack of impact of SOCDES supported the conclusion that socially desirable response bias was not a factor in this study.

In order to statistically evaluate the adequacy of the hypothesized model, the proportion of variance accounted for in the four criteria of psychological functioning (i.e., well-being, grandparental satisfaction, perceptions of the grandparent–grandchild relationship, and meaning of grandparenthood) was calculated and found to be significant ($R^2 = .459$, $F = 9.86$, $p < .01$). The restricted model was then compared with the hypothesized one to determine if there was a significant difference between them in the variance accounted for. This comparison suggested that there was no substantive difference between the models in terms of the variance each accounted for in measures of psychological functioning ($GFI = 25.004$, $p < .30$), even after 7 variables and 24 paths had been deleted from the original model.

Beginning with well-being (WB), the model (see Figures 1 and 2) was supported by several paths. As predicted, when the respondents were surrogate parents to their grandchildren (parental responsibility: PR), their scores on well-being were reduced (negative path PR to WB). Having parental responsibility also reduced scores on satisfaction with grandparenting (GPSAT) and perceptions of the grandparent's relationship with the grandchild (PERCEP). These latter relations gave rise to the indirect effects of parental responsibility on well-being through perceptions of the relationship with the grandchild (PERCEP) and satisfaction with grandparenting (GPSAT). In other words, having parental responsibility produced reductions in scores on PERCEP and GPSAT, which in turn reduced the respondents' feelings of well-being (WB) (see below).

Also, as expected, were found the positive paths from perceptions of the grandchild relationship (PERCEP) and grandparenting satisfaction (GPSAT) to well-being (WB). This result supported the hypothesis that more positive perceptions of the grandparent–grandchild relationship and a higher degree of satisfaction with the grandparenting experience directly lead to greater well-being.

Respondents with higher levels of income (INCOME) and social resources (SR) also reported greater well-being (positive paths from

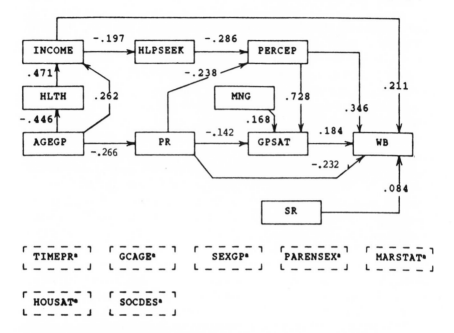

Key: Psychological well-being (WB), grandparenting satisfaction (GPSAT), perceptions of grandparent–grandchild relationship (PERCEP), meaning of grandparenthood (MNG), parental responsibility (PR), time with parental responsibility (TIMEPR), sex of grandparent (SEXGP), age of grandparent (AGEGP), sex of grandchild's parent (PARENSEX), grandparent's income (INCOME), grandparent's health (HLTH), grandparent's marital status (MARSTAT), grandparent's social resources (SR), housing satisfaction (HOUSAT), help seeking (HLPSEEK), grandchild's age (GCAGE), social desirability (SOCDES).
[a] = Variables deleted from the final model.

Figure 2. Final model of direct effects.

INCOME and SR to WB). In a separate investigation of these data, Shore and Hayslip (1990) found that such persons were typically found in the traditional group, as indicated by their higher mean scores on INCOME, SR, and WB (see Tables 1 and 2).

Expectations of the model pertaining to satisfaction with grandparenting (GPSAT) were met by three significant paths to this variable. As mentioned above, the fact of being a surrogate parent (PR) decreased scores on grandparenting satisfaction (GPSAT) (negative path from PR to GPSAT). On the other hand, having more positive perceptions of the grandparent–grandchild relationship (PERCEP) predicted higher scores in respondents' satisfaction with grandparenting (positive path from PERCEP to GPSAT). This same relationship held regarding the meaning of grandparenting (MNG) and satisfaction with the role (GPSAT), as higher scores on the MNG scale were associated with higher GPSAT scores. Unexpectedly, neither the amount of time a participant spent in the parenting role (TIMEPR) nor the gender of the grandparent (SEXGP) predicted satisfaction with grandparenting.

Perceptions of the grandparent–grandchild relationship (PERCEP) were found to be predicted by two of three hypothesized associations in the model. As with previous criteria, a surrogate parenting role (PR) detracted from PERCEP, consistent with the hypothesis. Help-seeking behaviors (HLPSEEK) (see above) were also significant predictors of PERCEP, but opposite the direction predicted (negative path from HLPSEEK to PERCEP), a result suggesting that respondents seeking *less* help for themselves or for their grandchildren had more positive perceptions of their relationships with their grandchildren.

Although the grandparent's sex (SEXGP) was hypothesized to be the only variable predicting the meaning of grandparenthood (MNG), SEXGP's effects were insignificant, and it was therefore, deleted from the final model.

The variable AGEGP (age of the grandparent) was a frequent contributor, three significant paths being retained in the final model. As expected, younger respondents were more likely to become surrogate parents (negative path from AGEGP to PR). A respondent's perception of his or her health (HLTH) also mediated the effects of AGEGP on INCOME. When health was a concern of the respondents (reflected in lower scores measuring self-reported health), lower levels of income were reported (positive path from HLTH to INCOME). If health was not a concern (higher scores on self-reported health), AGEGP had a significant direct effect on INCOME; that is, older participants reported more income (positive path from AGEGP to INCOME). In other words, a grandparent's age was a powerful predictor of income as long as the grandparent was in good health. When respondents reported relatively lower health scores, the effects of AGEGP on income were mediated through health.

Finally, older participants were expected to be more likely to seek professional help (HLPSEEK), but the results did not bear out this expectation; that is, the path from AGEGP to HLPSEEK was insignificant. Traditional grandparents, the older and higher income group in this study, did not seek professional help for parenting problems associated with their grandchildren. As discussed above, help seeking was a characteristic primarily of the custodial group. Hence, the path from INCOME to HLPSEEK was negative, a result indicating that the lower income respondents engaged in more help seeking, a relationship not anticipated by the model.

INDIRECT EFFECTS. Indirect effects were calculated from beta weights and are presented with other direct effects in Table 4. In most cases, indirect effects did not change the results of the regression analysis; that is, the strength of a direct effect primarily dictated the significance of the effect coefficient (i.e., the total effect and the sum of direct and indirect effects). In the case of the effects of parental

Table 4. Path-Analytic Findings[a]

Variables		Direct	+	Indirect	=	EC	+	Other[b]	=	Corr	Error e
DV	IV			Effects							
WB											.2813
	GPSAT	.184*	+	0	=	.184*	+	.570	=	.754	
	PERCEP	.346***	+	.134	=	.480***	+	.258	=	.738	
	MNG	.024	+	.031	=	.055	+	.189	=	.244	
	PR	−.232**	+	−.137*	=	−.369***	+	−.287	=	−.656	
	MARSTAT	−.075	+	−.012	=	−.087	+	−.168	=	−.255	
	HLTH	.036	+	.105	=	.141	+	.222	=	.363	
	INCOME	.211***	+	.027	=	.238***	+	.241	=	.479	
	TIMEPR	−.041	+	−.078	=	−.119	+	−.461	=	−.580	
	SR	.084*	+	0	=	.084*	+	.069	=	.153	
	HOUSAT	.038	+	0	=	.038	+	.325	=	.363	
	SOCDES	−.024	+	−.009	=	−.033	+	−.013	=	−.046	
GPSAT											.1986
	PERCEP	.728***	+	0	=	.728***	+	.149	=	.877	
	MNG	.168***	+	0	=	.168***	+	.270	=	.438	
	PR	−.142*	+	−.137**	=	−.279***	+	−.253	=	−.532	
	MARSTAT	−.075	+	−.012	=	−.087	+	−.074	=	−.161	
	SEXGP	−.031	+	−.008	=	−.039	+	.025	=	−.014	
	TIMEPR	−.022	+	−.118	=	−.140	+	−.330	=	−.470	
	SOCDES	−.005	+	−.015	=	−.020	+	−.023	=	−.043	

(Continued)

Table 4. (*Continued*)

Variables		Effects									Error e
DV	IV	Direct	+	Indirect	=	EC	+	Other[b]	=	Corr	
PERCEP											.6866
	PR	−.238*	+	0	=	−.238*	+	−.272	=	−.510	
	TIMEPR	−.153	+	0	=	−.153	+	−.308	=	−.461	
	HLPSEEK	−.286***	+	0	=	−.286***	+	−.200	=	−.486	
	GCAGE[c]	.000	+	0	=	.000	+	−.034	=	−.034	
	SOCDES	.023	+	0	=	.023	+	−.049	=	−.026	
MNG											.9972
	PR	.055	+	0	=	.055	+	.031	=	.024	
	TIMEPR	−.038	+	0	=	−.038	+	.040	=	.002	
	SEXGR	.035	+	.003	=	.032	+	.005	=	.037	
	SOCDES	−.013	+	0	=	−.013	+	−.003	=	−.016	
PR											.9397
	AGEGP	−.266***	+	.008	=	−.258***	+	0	=	−.258	
	SEXGP	−.056	+	0	=	−.056	+	.039	=	−.017	
MARSTAT											.9497
	AGEGP	.078	+	.035	=	.043	+	0	=	.043	
	SEXGP[d]	.243**	+	0	=	.243**	+	.011	=	.232	
HLTH											.8050
	AGEGP	−.446***	+	0	=	−.446***	+	0	=	−.446	
INCOME											.8277
	AGEGP	.262***	−	.210***	=	.052	+	.001	=	.051	
	HLTH	.471***	+	0	=	.471***	+	.117	=	.354	
SEXGP											.9876
	PARENSEX	.041	+	0	=	.041	+	.015	=	.056	
	AGEGP[d]	−.139*	+	.004	=	−.143*	+	0	=	−.143	
PARENSEX											.9940
	AGEGP	−.104	+	0	=	−.104	+	0	=	−.104	
HLPSEEK											.9692
	AGEGP	−.028	+	.010	=	−.038	+	0	=	−.038	
	INCOME	−.197**	+	0	=	−.197**	+	−.002	=	−.199	

[a] DV = dependent variable; IV = independent variable. Indir = indirect; EC = effect coefficient = direct + indirect effects; Corr = correlation of IV with DV; error (e) or unaccounted variance = $\sqrt{1 - R^2_{adj}}$

[b] "Other" effects include *spurious* effects from common causes and *unanalyzable* effects from correlated causes. Spurious effects are caused by variables "upstream" of the independent variable of interest and the criterion, yet these effects are part of the independent variable's correlation with the criterion. Unanalyzable effects arise when two variables influence one another and these influences cannot be distinguished; hence, the effect cannot be analyzed (Pedhazur, 1982).

[c] Beta weight was less than .0005.

[d] The path network, consisting of the two significant paths SEXGP to MARSTAT (.243**) and AGEGP to SEXGP (−.143*), was not connected with significant paths to the criteria WB, GPSAT, PERCEP, or MNG. As a consequence, this path network did not contribute to the prediction of the dependent variable and was dropped from the model.

*$p < .05$ **$p < .005$ ***p .0005

responsibility (PR) on both well-being (WB) and satisfaction with grandparenting (GPSAT), however, indirect effects added significantly to the total effects of PR (see Table 1).

One other change was found when we considered indirect effects. Adding indirect effects caused the total effects of a grandparent's age (AGEGP) on INCOME to become insignificant. As previously discussed, older grandparents tended to report larger income levels unless health was a problem; if it was, lower income levels were reported.

Though it was not included in the original model, the sex of the grandchild (GCSEX) was explored as a correlate of parental responsibility as well as of the meaning of grandparenthood, the relationship quality with the grandchild, and the grandparent's well-being and satisfaction with grandparenting. As indicated in Table 2, having a female grandchild was associated (all p's $\leq .01$, except as noted) with greater contact with that grandchild, greater satisfaction with grandparenting ($p < .05$), better health, more positive relationships with a grandchild, greater well-being, and less help seeking. With regard to parental responsibility, custodial grandparents were more likely to be raising boys.

Discussion

A model was hypothesized that predicted certain aspects of the psychological functioning of grandparents who were parenting their grandchildren. Of the 16 variables studied, 4 were the criteria of a grandparent's psychological functioning: psychological well-being (WB), satisfaction with grandparenting (GPSAT), perceptions of the grandparent–grandchild relationship (PERCEP), and the personal meaning of grandparenthood (MNG). It was expected that the respondents would have lower scores on all four measures of psychological functioning as a result of having parental responsibility (PR). Additionally, it was anticipated that the longer the participants had had parenting responsibility (TIMEPR), the lower their scores would be on the criteria of psychological functioning. These were the primary hypotheses of interest here.

The final model suggests that having parental responsibility (PR) significantly detracts from psychological functioning in grandparents' satisfaction with grandparenting (GPSAT), perceptions of the grandparent–grandchild relationship (PERCEP), and overall well-being (WB). A fourth criterion of such functioning, the meaning of grandparenthood (MNG), was unaffected by PR.

These results support findings in the divorce literature suggesting that most grandparents prefer a fun-loving, voluntary role with their grandchildren, without parental responsibility for them (Johnson, 1988). If grandparents do parent their grandchildren, their satisfaction with grandparenting (GPSAT) is undermined. Furthermore, these results extend Johnson's 1988 work by identifying two additional constructs—WB and PERCEP—that are negatively affected by parental responsibility.

The effects of parental responsibility on psychological functioning may be explained by several factors:

The first is the trauma in the parents' family that precipitates a surrogate parenting role for the grandparent. Recall that a significant number of grandchildren in this study had been abused by their parents or had lived with substance abuse by one parent that had contributed to divorce or to abandonment of the family.

Second, the expectations that many grandparents may have had for their children were very likely dashed by the divorces, addictions, and similar problems leading to parental failure. Shore and Hayslip's results (1990) showed that nearly two thirds of the grandparents raising grandchildren expressed disappointment in their children and that 31% felt guilty about their children's behavior. Over 30% felt that their children had taken advantage of them, and 28% expressed resentment toward their adult children, ostensibly because of having to assume these children's parenting responsibilities.

Third, the intrusion of parenting on the lives of older persons probably came at a time when they were facing and resolving developmental issues (e.g., reestablishing relationships with one's spouse after the children have left home). Such persons wanted to enjoy their grandchildren without having responsibility for them. This factor is especially important as many older adults replace parental responsibilities with an expanded social network of friends and activities when their children become more independent and/or leave home (Bengtson et al., 1990). Underlying this issue is the expectation that social resources would be a determinant of well-being in older adults. Wood and Robertson (1976), for example, observed in their sample that grandparents' activity level with their grandchildren was unrelated to life satisfaction, but that interactions with friends were important to maintaining morale as one aged.

Shore and Hayslip's results (1990) also showed that almost 40% of the custodial grandparents felt isolated from their friends because of their parenting responsibilities. Many grandparents expressed fears about the impact of diminished health on their ability to function in an active, involved manner regarding their grandchildren's lives. Although health by itself does not seem to be impaired by having primary responsibility for grandchildren (Geison & McCord, 1991), these conclusions are based on a secondary analysis of census data. It nevertheless may be that these fears are unfounded. Alternatively, such concerns may be warranted as grandparents age and become more susceptible to chronic illness.

As they grow older, adults typically give up parental responsibilities as their children are able to live independently and to care for themselves. However, for older adults raising their grandchildren, no compensatory role reduction or change is possible, and thus such adults become more vulnerable not only because their support networks are disrupted, but because their grandchildren can no longer rely on them should their grandparents' health fail. In this study, not only was there a real concern about the physical welfare of grandchildren, but losing their grandparents would represent yet another loss of caregivers, potentially causing serious emotional consequences.

Other role reductions appear to exacerbate the dilemma of grandparents raising grandchildren. Many grandparents also felt isolated from the grandchildren *not* being raised by them and indicated that they felt guilty because they were not able to give their noncustodial grandchildren attention equal to that given to the grandchildren in their care. In view of these restrictions, it was not surprising that the guardian group reported significantly fewer social resources than the traditional group (Shore & Hayslip, 1990) (see Tables 1 and 2).

In general, then, these findings indicate that, for many of our respondents raising grandchildren, there were restrictions in their role of grandparent as well as in their social roles. These restrictions no doubt helped to reduce social resources for the custodial grandparents, as they were seeing neither their other grandchildren nor their friends as much as they wanted. It is apparent that, for many grandparents, the social network or convoy is an important source of well-being (Antonucci, 1990). They regret not being able to rely on this convoy as much as they would have liked, because of their parenting responsibilities. In turn, this restriction of both grandparenting and social roles may contribute to reduced well-being.

In addition to the role restriction experienced by many grandparents resulting from their parental responsibilities, role confusion may also have contributed to their reduced scores on measures of psychological functioning. Thirty-five percent of the sample reported that, because of their parenting tasks, they were not free to be a grandparent to the grandchild they were raising in the way they would have desired (Shore & Hayslip, 1990). This response points to the difficulties of being a parent with all the attendant responsibilities and at the same time, playing a grandparental role, with its preferred *lack* of primary-care responsibility *vis-à-vis* the grandchild. No doubt, for many custodial respondents, the roles of parent and grandparent were in conflict.

The behavior of the grandchildren being raised by guardian grandparents may also have contributed to decreased well-being. In Shore and Hayslip's study (1990), over 40% of the guardian group had sought therapy for their grandchildren because of behavior problems. Another 25% indicated their intention to seek help for such problems. Thus, almost two thirds of the sample of guardian respondents were experiencing enough behavioral difficulties with the grandchildren in their care to seek outside help, a far larger proportion than in the traditional group. Even though the participants were approximately equally distributed between clinical and public sources, three times as many grandchildren of the custodial group were in treatment as were those of the controls (Shore & Hayslip, 1990).

Why were the guardian grandparents reporting increased rates of behavioral difficulties for the grandchildren they were raising in comparison to the traditional respondents? An interesting hypothesis involves the gender characteristics of the grandchildren of the respondents: Males were overrepresented in the custodial group in comparison to the control group (Shore & Hayslip, 1990). Moreover, the grandchild's gender was related to numerous indicators of both physical and psychological health (see above).

It is common that mental health professionals see more male than female children for behavior problems (Wells & Forehand, 1985). One possibility explaining the overrepresentation of boys in therapy involves their greater constitutional vulnerability to stress than girls' (Rutter, 1979). In addition, in times of family stress, boys are more likely than girls to be exposed to parental conflict. Parents fight more often and longer in the presence of sons (Hetherington, Cox, & Cox, 1982). Moreover, Hetherington (1989b) found that families with sons are less likely to divorce than those with daughters. Consequently, boys may be exposed to more family conflict than girls.

After the family breaks up, the typical reconstituted family consists of the custodial mother and her children. Past research suggests a correlation between distress in the child and the leaving of the same-sex parent (Herzog & Sudia, 1973). Moreover, the detrimental effects of marital discord, divorce, and life in a single-parent family in which the mother is the parent are more pervasive for boys than for girls (Hetherington, Cox & Cox, 1985; Porter & O'Leary, 1980; Rutter, 1987). Boys in such families show a higher rate of behavioral disorders and interpersonal conflicts at home and at school. In comparison to girls, boys are also more likely to be noncompliant for a longer period of time after divorce (Hetherington et al., 1985), tend to be more rigid in their views of relationships, and do not see the possibilities for reconciliation in conflictual situations. As a result, they interpret family disagreements more negatively than do girls (Epstein, Finnegan, & Gythell, 1979). Additionally, in times of family stress, boys are less able than girls to disclose their feelings and to negotiate for support from the significant persons in their lives (Hetherington, 1989a).

These findings help explain why parents may tend to give boys to grandparents during times of family conflict and breakup, while keeping female children. Consequently, the grandparents, faced with raising their acting-out grandsons, are the ones who take them to mental health facilities. However, although the higher rate of the custodial grandchildren in treatment was another suggestion of the trauma accompanying family breakup and reformation, it was not clear to what extent behavior problems were due to the trauma in the family of origin, or to the current caregiving relationship with the grandparents.

Contrary to expectations, parental responsibility (PR) did not affect the meaning of grandparenthood (MNG) for our respondents. Four explanations are considered here: (1) the items of the scale were not sensitive enough to discriminate between the two groups; (2) the role of surrogate parent may have obscured the grandparental role to a point where the latter had little or no meaning for many custodial respondents; (3) the meaning of grandparenthood was not a psychological construct defined in the same way that well-being or satisfaction with grandparenting was; and (4) the measure of MNG used here did not reflect its complexity (Kivnick, 1982a,b). MNG, unlike the other criteria, remained unaffected by changes in PR. However, in light of the fact that grandparental meaning and grandparents' mental health are independent (Thomas, 1989c), this finding is not particularly unexpected.

In light of the role confusion discussed above, the original dimensions of MNG developed by Kivnick nevertheless may not have applied to the sample of participants in this study, in that her sample was limited to traditional grandparents. In contrast, for many of our custodial respondents, the role of grandparent may have been subordinated to the role of parent, and therefore, the meaning of grandparenthood had been obscured for them. Limited by the constraints of the items, our custodial participants may have responded in an idealized fashion; that is, they may have responded to what they believed the meaning of grandparenting *should* be rather than to what they truly felt in their current situation.

MNG may also not be defined in the same way that the other three criteria (i.e., well-being, grandparental satisfaction, and perceptions of the relationship) are. Items on the MNG scale do not appear to be as affectively loaded as the items on the other three scales, instead asking for a more cognitive evaluation of grandparenthood (e.g., "I value being able to teach things to my grandchild"). In contrast, well-being, satisfaction, and perceptions of the grandchild relationship elicit primarily emotional responses (e.g., "I feel excited," "Being my grandchild's grandparent has made me as happy as anything ever has," and "How much affection do you have toward your grandchild?") (see Thomas, 1988). This suggests that parental responsibility for older adults involves emotional consequences rather than cognitive ones. The results of this study have shown that these consequences are negative for many older adults.

As MNG was globally defined here, a more powerful effect of PR on MNG might have been obtained if its subscales (i.e., centrality, valued elder, reinvolvement with personal past, immortality, and indulgence; see Kivnick, 1982a,b) had been utilized. Thomas's results (1988) suggest, however, that this result was unlikely, in that the dimensions of meaning did not predict mental health in grandparents. Moreover, Miller and Cavanaugh (1990) found these dimensions to be highly interrelated.

Johnson (1988) found that the longer grandmothers were compelled to be surrogate parents to their grandchildren, the more their satisfaction with their grandparental role was undermined. In the present study, this did not prove to be the case. One explanation for the deletion of TIMEPR from the final model may have been that many grandparents adjusted over time to either a full-time or a part-time caregiving role to a point where their psychological functioning ceased to change. Consequently, either floor or ceiling effects may account for this finding. Some support for this explanation was found in one respondent's note on a returned questionnaire: "I was very upset when we first took custody of our grandchild, but I'm resigned to do what I have to do now and just want to do the best for her." It is noteworthy that, in these data, there is, however, limited support for this process because, at a bivariate level (see Table 3), there does seem to be a negative relationship between TIMEPR and many variables in the model, though in concert with other factors TIMEPR did not ultimately prove to be predictive of psychological functioning in this sample (see Figure 2). To further explore this possibility, more intensive longitudinal investigations are necessary to explore the process by which grandparents come to terms (or do not come to terms) with their new role of parenting.

Grandparental satisfaction (GPSAT) was found, as expected, to be positively associated with well-being (WB), consistent with the findings of Thomas (1988). In this light, Kivnick's deprivation–compensation model of grandparenthood (1985) suggests that the role of grandparent compensates for the lower levels of well-being that many older adults suffer from because of the deprivation experienced in later life. For example, the grandparental role may compensate for the loss of a spouse, or it may allow for a reworking of earlier, inadequately resolved psychosocial conflicts, thereby enhancing current psychological well-being. If, for example, a grandmother feels guilty over her perceived failure as a parent, she may assuage this guilt by helping her child raise his or her children.

Erikson (1963) proposed that older adults experience personal growth and enhanced well-being through the ties they initiate with younger persons, and as has been pointed out earlier, grandparents often view themselves as free of the responsibility for parenting their grandchildren (Albrecht, 1954; Apple, 1956; Johnson, 1988). Indeed, the present findings show that enhanced well-being stems from ties that are free of parenting responsibility for grandchildren.

The positive relation found between perceptions of the grandparent–grandchild relationship (PERCEP) and well-being (WB) was expected. It is consistent with the findings of Kornhaber (1985), Kornhaber and Woodward (1981), and Thomas, Bence, and Meyer (1988). Shore and Hayslip's results (1990) show that the traditional group's perceptions of the relationship with the grandchild were more positive than those of the custodial group. Thus, there may be relationship problems with the grandchildren within this group, inferred from the fact that professional help was sought more often by these respondents. Whether these difficulties are primary or secondary to the resumption of the parental role is difficult to ascertain and are candidates for future research.

For the grandparent raising a grandchild, the relationship with the grandchild may be perceived as more of a parent–child relationship. Indeed, mothers who perceive their children as difficult in terms of temperament and behavior experience a sense of incompetence and unhappiness in their relationships with them (Buss & Plomin, 1984; Lee & Bates, 1985; Sprunger *et al.*, 1985). As, in the present study, many custodial grandchildren were being seen by professionals because of their behavior problems, it is certainly possible that their guardians were feeling incompetent and unhappy as "parents." This reaction may have contributed to the custodial group's negative perceptions of their relationships with these grandchildren.

The custodial respondents were of a lower socioeconomic status (SES) than the traditional group (Shore & Hayslip, 1990), in part because more traditional grandparents than custodial ones worked either part time or full time. Perhaps the burdens of parenting prevented many in the latter group from seeking employment. If this is true, then parenting grandchildren may represent a double-edged financial sword: reduced income potential plus the increased costs associated with raising grandchildren. This circumstance probably operated to reduce SES for many custodial participants and thus contributed to a reduction in their well-being.

The model predicted a positive relationship between perceptions of the grandparent–grandchild relationship (PERCEP) and grandparental satisfaction (GPSAT); this prediction was confirmed (see Figure 2). However, through PERCEP, parental responsibility (PR) also had a significant indirect effect on GPSAT. When our respondents became surrogate parents (PR), their perceptions of their relationships with the grandchildren they were raising (PERCEP) diminished, which similarly affected their satisfaction with the grandparental role (GPSAT). This finding represented an extension of Johnson's work (1988), though she did not account for the mediating role of a grandparent's perception of the relationship with a grandchild. As explained above, grandparents assuming a surrogate parent role may experience themselves more as parents than as grandparents, and the result is role confusion. Furthermore, as parents, our custodial respondents bore the full brunt of misbehaving grandchildren, a situation that very likely affected their perceptions of the relationship with their grandchildren in a negative way (see Lee & Bates, 1985). Because the custodial respondents were not free to be grandparents in the way they would have liked, their satisfaction with grandparenting was reduced.

In addition to PR, help seeking (HLPSEEK) also (and independently) predicted PERCEP (perceptions of the grandparent–grandchild relationship) in the final model (see Figure 2). For the custodial grandparents, seeking professional help was predicted to ameliorate the stresses stemming from reactivating the parental role. For the traditional grandparents, seeking help for their grandchildren might be seen as a way of helping the parents, who may have been, for example, financially strapped; these respondents were doing all they could as "good" grandparents. However, the respondents seeking *less* help had more positive perceptions of their relationship with a grandchild (see Figure 2), and thus, help seeking may have been perceived as disruptive rather than facilitating.

Several explanations are offered here for this negative relationship. First, traditional grandparents, who as older persons, would not normally seek help either for their grandchildren or for parenting problems (Lasoski, 1986), seeking help may interfere with an ongoing relationship with an adult child (see above). Alternatively, persons may simply deny the need for help to promote high PERCEP scores. Moreover, for the custodial grandparents, who were more likely to seek help than were the traditional ones (Shore & Hayslip, 1990), this help may not have been ameliorative to the extent that their relationships with their grandchildren were improved. Seeking help instead may simply have reflected the level of distress being experienced by many grandparents in this group. Consequently, more help sought by guardian grandparents might have been associated with more negative perceptions of the relationship with a grandchild.

Future research might specifically address the causal role that guardianship has on help-seeking activities and relationship perceptions among grandparents. Furthermore, questions addressing the timeliness and effectiveness of such help as well as the reasons why certain sources are more helpful, if so, than others would be fruitful questions to explore.

The negative relationship between grandparents' age (AGEGP) and PR was in accord with the model and supports the work of Johnson (1988). In her research, younger grandmothers were more likely to have younger grandchildren, who required more support after divorce, thereby drawing the grandmothers into child care. In the current study, the younger respondents were also more likely to become surrogate parents, consistent with the work of Neugarten and Weinstein (1964), as well as with the more recent findings of Cherlin and Furstenberg (1985), who concluded that the older grandparents' relationships with grandchildren were more distant and formal. In contrast, younger grandparents had a greater number of interactions with their grandchildren and were less rigid in their expressions of this relationship, because of better health and higher energy (Cherlin & Furstenberg, 1985).

IMPLICATIONS FOR GRANDPARENTS AND GRANDCHILDREN

Many questions have been raised by this study that should be addressed in further research. For example, why were there almost twice as many boys as girls being raised by grandparents in this study? Did distress in the family affect males to a point where their subsequent disruptive behavior was more extreme than that of the female children, making them less desirable in comparison to their sisters? It may be that parents who were left with children after divorce or abandonment, in trying to reduce the demands of parenting, may have decided that giving up their male children to surrogate parents was an easier choice than giving up their female children. It may also be that grandparents simply find boys more difficult to raise than girls, a factor contributing negatively to the psychological functioning of the grandparents raising them. Indeed, the associations between the grandchild's sex and the measures of psychological functioning found in this study suggest that this may be a real possibility. These questions have implications for custody deliberations as well as for parent-skills-training programs specifically designed for custodial grandparents.

In this study, it was not clear whether the grandchildren of the custodial respondents were experiencing behavior problems *because of* distress in their family of origin, or because of their present living situation with their grandparents. If, for example, the grandparents understood that their grandchildren's maladaptive behavior was caused by family-of-origin distress, they may not have felt as guilty as if they believed the behavior stemmed from the home life they were providing these grandchildren. On the other hand, the grandchildren's problem behavior may have been exacerbated by the use of poor parenting techniques by the grandparents. It should be clear that these assertions are purely speculative and remain questions for future research. Such work, for example, might compare the parenting skills of custodial grandparents who complain of the behavior of the grandchildren in their care with those of grandparents who express no such complaints. In this light, it may be beneficial to assess and train grandparents in parenting techniques as an adjunct to their assuming parental responsibility (see Strom & Strom, 1987, 1989, 1990). Alternatively, making grandparents aware of the community resources for respite or of day care may alleviate the stress they are experiencing.

A related research question would be whether, as younger parents, guardian grandparents have been ineffective parents. Consequently, reassuming the parental role later in life may activate a sense of failure they had as younger parents. In any event, if guardian grandparents do demonstrate a lack of knowledge of parenting skills, it may contribute to the distress they are experiencing.

On one hand, many of our custodial grandparents *had* aggressively sought help for their grandchildren's problems. Yet, raising these children did seem to interfere with their personal adjustment and relationship with age peers. Clearly, more research is needed to explore more specifically the difficulties, if any, that custodial grandparents face in parenting their grandchildren, as well as to suggest ways in which such difficulties may be overcome. Moreover, such problems, if they indeed exist, need to be viewed in the larger matrix of aging-related changes in health, marital quality, access to professional help, and interpersonal relationships.

Although almost two thirds of our custodial grandparents were experiencing enough behavior difficulties with their grandchildren to seek help for them, seeking help for themselves was a different matter. Only 8%–10% were in individual counseling or some form of group or family therapy, and only 24% were in support groups, usually church- or community-based and led by one of their own members (Shore & Hayslip, 1990). Considering these data, our custodial group appears to have been similar in some respects to other families in which parenting problems, relationship difficulties, or other conflicts exist (Anderson & Stewart, 1983). In this light, it is noteworthy that Ehrle (1987), who studied both guardian and nonguardian grandparents, found the former to express less marital satisfaction, to see themselves as less able to resolve difficulties between them, to com-

municate openly less often, and to reach consensus about important issues less frequently. Yet, the guardian grandparents expressed
a greater commitment to nurturing their relationship in spite of the
demands of parenting. Indeed, love was reported as the most important quality essential to helping them adjust to assuming the guardianship of their grandchildren. These findings underscore the dualistic
nature of custodial grandparenting, with its attendant stresses and joys.

Our respondents were asked to give reasons for not seeking help
for themselves. Over 30% indicated that they had no need, 18% did
not know where to go (perhaps an indirect indication of not feeling a
strong enough need), 14% endorsed an inability to pay for therapy,
and somewhat less than 10% expressed having no time (Shore &
Hayslip, 1990).

Although those who might have sought help for themselves may
not have done so because they perceived that such help was ineffective, the fact remains that, whereas two thirds of the custodial respondents had found the resources, money, and time to provide treatment
for their grandchildren (or were intending to do so), less than 20%
were seeking professional help for themselves, even though many
endorsed feelings of resentment, guilt, anger, and other negative sen-
timents toward their children and the experience of resuming parenting. Consequently, these data have implications for the design of
mental health services for this segment of older persons, particularly
at the tertiary level of prevention (Baltes & Danish, 1980). Such help
might involve individual or group therapy, parent-skills training, or
respite care.

Several limitations of this work are to be noted. As noted above,
it may be that the meanings embedded in the measure of MNG did
not adequately capture the experience of grandparenting for our custodial respondents. Additionally, MNG appeared to represent strictly
cognitive dimensions of the grandparenting experience, an aspect
undermining its utility in comparison to the other constructs (i.e.,
well-being, satisfaction with grandparenting, and perceptions of the
grandparent–grandchild relationship). Moreover, more revealing results might have been found had MNG been defined multidimen-
sionally (Kivnick, 1982a,b).

Another limitation of the study was the use of recursive path
analysis to analyze the data. Although path analysis may be used to
decompose relations among variables and to test causal models, it is
based on a set of restrictive assumptions, one of which is that the

causal flow is unidirectional. This assumption is rarely, if ever, met in applied settings. For example, perceptions of the grandparent–grandchild relationship (PERCEP) was used as a predictor variable affecting changes in well-being. It might be just as tenable to expect more positive well-being to affect PERCEP positively. Similarly, the relationship between health and well-being, as well as that between help seeking and perceived relationship quality with a grandchild, may also be bidirectional. It is suggested that future work include reciprocal causation among variables.

Last, it should be recognized that the sample was not a random or representative one. The volunteers were obviously self-selected, and generalizations to the underlying population of grandparents are limited. This may be particularly true in the case of our custodial participants, whose experiences and perceptions of grandparenthood were more negative. Perhaps more explicitly matching custodial and traditional grandparents on numerous sociodemographic variables, and incorporating a variety of grandchild characteristics into the pool of relevant influences in the context of a large longitudinal study, would be desirable.

Despite these limitations, this study demonstrates that many grandparents raising grandchildren experience lower well-being with respect to aspects of grandparenting, in comparison to traditional grandparents. It is possible that resuming parenting responsibilities interferes with well-being, creates isolation from others, and contributes to role confusion. Although the grandparental role may be a natural transition from the parental one, reactivating the parental role for many grandparents may be a stressful process that compromises their psychosocial health.

Though these data suggest that custodial grandparenting is a stressful role, it must be made clear that not all grandparents raising a grandchild experience difficulties. Indeed, many do adjust to their new role and enjoy their relationships with the grandchildren they are caring for. One might consider custodial grandparenting a potentially stressful role, one whose demands some individuals are more able to cope with than are others, in light of such other concurrent influences as health, social and economic resources, the specific demands of the grandchild, marital status, and access to full-time or part-time work or respite care. Indeed, the model we have presented suggests that a number of such influences, in concert with parental responsibility, did predict multiple indicators of psychological functioning in this sample of grandparents.

The love and dedication of many custodial grandparents to their family motivates them to raise their grandchildren, and foster care or giving the child up to the remaining parent may be neither possible nor acceptable to them. Given their desire to care for their grandchildren, such persons may benefit from at least temporary assistance in helping them adjust to their new role as well as in coping with the daily demands of parenting a grandchild. Indeed, these data underscore the difficulties that some custodial grandparents may face in reassuming parental responsibilities later in life and suggest that social and mental health services specifically targeting such older persons are sorely needed, especially if they are raising boys. Through such support and assistance, older persons' personal adjustment and the quality of their relationships with their grandchildren may be enhanced.

REFERENCES

Albrecht, R. (1954). *Kinship in an urban setting.* Chicago: Markham.

Anderson, C., & Stewart, S. (1983). *Mastering resistance: A practical guide to family therapy.* New York: Guilford Press.

Antonucci, T. (1990). Social supports and social relationships. In R. H. Binstock & L. K. George (Eds.), *Handbook of aging and the social sciences* (3rd ed., pp. 204–227). New York: Academic Press.

Apple, D. (1956). The social structure of grandparenthood. *American Anthropologist, 58,* 656–663.

Baltes, P. B., & Danish, S. F. (1980). Intervention in life-span development and aging. In R. R. Turner & H. W. Reese (Eds.), *Life-span developmental psychology: Intervention* (pp. 49–78). New York: Academic Press.

Barranti, C. (1985). The grandparent/grandchild relationship: Family resources in an era of voluntary bonds. *Family Relations, 34,* 343–352.

Bence, S. L., & Thomas, J. L. (1988, November). *Grandparent-parent relationships as predictors of grandparent-grandchild relationships.* Paper presented at the annual meeting of the Gerontological Society of America, San Francisco.

Bengtson, V. L., & Dannefer, D. (1987). Families, work, and aging: Implications of disordered cohort flow for the 21st century. In R. A. Ward & S. S. Tobin (Eds.), *Health in aging: Sociological issues and policy directions* (pp. 256–289). New York: Springer.

Bengtson, V. L., & Robertson, J. F. (Eds.). (1985). *Grandparenthood.* Beverly Hills, CA: Sage.

Bengtson, V., Rosenthal, C., & Burton, L. (1990). Families and Aging: Diversity and

Heterogeneity. In R. H. Binstock & L. K. George (Eds.), *Handbook of aging and the social sciences* (3rd ed., pp. 263–280). San Diego: Academic Press.

Beyer, G. H., & Woods, M. E. (1963). Living and activity patterns of the aged. *Research Report No. 6*. Ithaca, NY: Center for Housing and Environmental Studies, Cornell University.

Bradburn, N. M (1969). *The structure of psychological well-being*. Aldine: Chicago.

Burton, L. M., & Martin, P. (1987, June). Thematicken der Mehngenerationenfamilie: Ein Beispeil. *German Journal of Gerontology, 21*.

Buss, A. H., & Plomin, R. (1984). *Temperament: Early developing personality traits*. Hillsdale, NJ: Erlbaum.

Cherlin, A., & Furstenberg, F. F. (1985). Styles and strategies of grandparenting. In V. Bengtson & J. F. Robertson (Eds.), *Grandparenthood* (pp. 97–116). Beverly Hills, CA: Sage.

Cherlin, A., & Furstenberg, F. F. (1986a). Grandparents and family crisis. *Generations*, 26–28.

Cherlin, A., & Furstenberg, F. F. (1986b). A special case: Grandparents and divorce. In A. Cherlin & F. Furstenberg (Eds.), *The new American grandparent: A place in the family a life apart* (pp. 136–167). New York: Basic Books.

Connidis, J. (1989). *Family ties and aging*. Toronto: Butterworths.

Crowne, D. P., & Marlowe, D. (1960). A new scale of social desirability independent of psychopathology. *Journal of Consulting Psychology, 24*, 349–354.

Dorfman, L. T., & Moffett, M. M. (1987). Retirement satisfaction in married and widowed rural women. *Gerontologist, 27*, 215–221.

Ehrle, G. M. (May, 1987). *Dyadic adjustment and family functioning in guardian and nonguardian grandparent families*. Unpublished master's thesis, Texas Women's University, Denton.

Epstein, N., Finnegan, D., & Gythell, D. (1979). Irrational beliefs and perceptions of marital conflict. *Journal of Consulting and Clinical Psychology, 67*, 608–609.

Erikson, E. H. (1963). *Childhood and society* (2nd ed.). New York: Norton.

Gatz, M., Bengtson, V. L., & Blum, M. J. (1990). Caregiving families. In J. E. Birren & K. W. Schaie (Eds.), *Handbook of the psychology of aging* (3rd ed., pp. 395–426). New York: Academic Press.

Geison, L. W., & McCord, G. (1991, November). *Health behavior of grandparents raising grandchildren*. Paper presented at the Annual Scientific Meeting of the Gerontological Society, San Francisco.

Hagestad, G. (1978). *Patterns of communication and influence between grandparents and grandchildren*. Paper presented at World Conference of Sociology, Helsinki, Finland.

Hagestad, G. (1986). The aging society as a context for family life. *Daedalus, 115*, 119–139.

Hagestad, G. O. (1988b). Continuity and Connectedness. In V. L. Bengtson & J. F. Robertson (Eds.), *Grandparenthood* (pp. 31–48). Beverly Hills, London, New Delhi: Sage.

Hagestad, G. (1988a). Demographic change and the life course: Some emerging trends in the family realm. *Family Relations, 37*, 405–410.

Hagestad, G., & Burton, L. (1985). Grandparenthood, life context, and family development. *American Behavioral Scientist, 29*, 471–484.

Havighurst, R. J. (1973). Social roles, work, leisure, and education. In C. Eisdorfer & M.

P. Lawton (Eds.), *The psychology of adult development and aging* (pp. 598–618). Washington, DC: American Psychological Association.

Herzog, E., & Sudia, C. (1973). Children in fatherless families. In B. M. Caldwell & H. N. Ricuiti (Eds.), *Review of child development research: Vol. 3. Child development and child policy* (pp. 51–75). Chicago: University of Chicago Press.

Hetherington, E. M. (1989a). Coping with family transitions: Winners, losers, and survivors. *Child Development, 60,* 1–14.

Hetherington, E. M. (1989b). Marital transitions: A child's perspective. *American Psychologist, 44,* 303–312.

Hetherington, E. M., Cox, M., & Cox, R. (1982). Effects of divorce on parents and children. In M. Lamb (Ed.), *Nontraditional families* (pp. 233–288). Hillsdale, NJ: Erlbaum.

Hetherington, E. M., Cox, M., & Cox, R. (1985). Long-term effects of divorce and remarriage on the adjustment of children. *Journal of American Academy of Psychiatry, 24,* 518–830.

Hodgson, L. G. (1991, November). *Adult granddaughters and grandsons: Do they relate differently to their grandparents?* Paper presented at the Annual Scientific Meeting of the Gerontological Society, San Francisco.

Hodgson, L. G. (1992). Adult grandchildren and their grandparents: The enduring bond. *International Journal of Aging and Human Development, 34,* 209–225.

Hoffman, E. (1979–1980). Young adults' relations with their grandparents: An exploratory study. *International Journal of Aging and Human Development, 10,* 299–310.

Johnson, C. L. (1983). A cultural analysis of the grandmother. *Research on Aging, 5,* 547–567.

Johnson, C. L. (1985). Grandparenting options in divorcing families: An anthropological perspective. In V. L. Bengtson & J. F. Robertson (Eds.), *Grandparenthood* (pp. 81–96). Beverly Hills, CA: Sage.

Johnson, C. L. (1988). Active and latent functions of grandparenting during the divorce process. *The Gerontologist, 28,* 185–191.

Juster, S., & Vinorskis, M. (1987). Changing perspectives on the American family in the past. *Annual Review of Sociology, 13,* 193–216.

Kahana, E., & Kahana, B. (1970). Grandparenthood from the perspective of the developing grandchild. *Developmental Psychology, 3,* 98–105.

Kahn, R., & Antonucci, T. (1980). Convoys over the life course: Attachment, roles, and social support. In P. Baltes & O. Brim (Eds.), *Live-span development and behavior* (Vol. 2, pp. 254–286). New York: Academic Press.

Kennedy, G. E. (1990). College students' expectations of grandparent and grandchild role behaviors. *The Gerontologist, 30,* 43–48.

Kennedy, J. F., & Keeney, V. T. (1987). Group psychotherapy with grandparents rearing their emotionally disturbed grandchildren. *Group, 11,* 15–25.

King, C. M. & Thomas, J. L. (1989, August). *Adult grandchildren's views of grandparents.* Paper presented at the Annual Convention of the American Psychological Association, New Orleans.

Kivett, V. R. (1985). Consanguinity and the kin level: Their relative importance to the helping network of older adults. *Journal of Gerontology, 40,* 228–234.

Kivett, V. R. (1991). Centrality of the grandfather role among older rural black and white men. *Journal of Gerontology: Social Sciences, 46,* S250–S258.

Kivnick, H. Q. (1982a). Grandparenthood: An overview of meaning and mental health. *The Gerontologist, 22,* 59–66.

Kivnick, H. Q. (1982b). *The meaning of grandparenthood.* Ann Arbor: UMI Research Press.

Kivnick, H. Q. (1985). Grandparenthood and mental health: Meaning, behavior, and satisfaction. In V. L. Bengtson & J. F. Robertson (Eds.), *Grandparenthood* (pp. 151–158). Beverly Hills, CA: Sage.

Kornhaber, A. (1985). Grandparenthood and the "new social contract." In V. L. Bengtson & J. F. Robertson (Eds.), *Grandparenthood* (pp. 159–172). Beverly Hills, CA: Sage.

Kornhaber, A., & Woodward, K. L (1981). *Grandparents-grandchildren: The vital connection.* New York: Anchor Press.

Langer, N. (1990). Grandparents and adult grandchildren: What do they do for one another? *International Journal of Aging and Human Development, 31,* 101–110.

Lasoski, M. C. (1986). Reasons for low utility of mental health services by the elderly. *Clinical Gerontologist, 5,* 1–18.

Lee, C., & Bates, J. (1985). Mother-child interaction at age two years and perceived difficult temperament. *Child Development, 56,* 1314–1325.

Lerner, R. M., & Spanier, G. (1978). A dynamic interactional view of child and family development. In R. Lerner & G. Spanier (Eds.), *Child influences on marital and family interaction* (pp. 1–22). New York: Academic Press.

Liang, J. (1985). A structural integration of the Affect Balance Scale and the Life Satisfaction Index A. *Journal of Gerontology, 40,* 552–561.

Matthews, S. H., & Sprey, J. (1984). The impact of divorce on parenthood: An exploratory study. *The Gerontologist, 24,* 41–47.

Matthews, S. H., & Sprey, J. (1985). Adolescents' relationships with grandparents: An empirical contribution to conceptual clarification. *Journal of Gerontology, 40,* 621–626.

Mickus, M., & Hirsch, B. (1991, November). *Grandparental influence on adolescent development: Race, gender and family structure variations.* Paper presented at the Annual Scientific Meeting of the Gerontological Society, San Francisco.

Miller, S. S., & Cavanaugh, J. (1990). The meaning of grandparenthood and its relationship to demographic, relationship, and social participation variables. *Journal of Gerontology: Psychological Sciences, 45,* P244–P247.

Montemayor, R., & Leigh, G. K. (1982). Parent-absent children: A demographic analysis of children and adolescents living apart from their parents. *Family Relations, 31,* 567–573.

Neugarten, B. L., Havinghurst, R. J., & Tobin, S. S. (1961). The measurement of life satisfaction. *Journal of Gerontology, 36,* 134–143.

Neugarten, B. L., & Weinstein, K. K. (1964). The changing American grandparent. *Journal of Marriage and the Family, 26,* 199–204.

Newman, B., & Newman, P. (1990). *Development through life: A psychosocial approach* (4th ed.). Homewood, IL: Dorsey.

Novatney, J. P. (1990, November). *Grandparents' ties to step and biological grandchildren.* Paper presented at the Annual Scientific Meeting of the Gerontological Society, Boston.

O'Brien, G. E. (1981). Leisure attributes and retirement satisfaction. *Journal of Applied Psychology, 66,* 371–384.

Parke, R. (1988). Families in lifespan perspective: A multilevel, developmental approach. In M. Hetherington, R. M. Lerner, & M. Perlmutter (Eds.), *Child development in the lifespan perspective* (pp. 49–68). Hillsdale, NJ: Erlbaum.

Pedhazur, E. J. (1982). Path analysis. In E. J. Pedhazur (Ed.), *Multiple regression in behavioral research: Explanation and prediction* (2nd ed., pp. 577–635). New York: Holt, Rinehart & Winston.

Porter, B., & O'Leary, K. D. (1980). Marital discord and childhood behavior problems. *Journal of Abnormal Psychology, 8,* 287–295.

Preston, S. (1984). Children and the elderly: Divergent paths for America's dependents. *Demography, 21,* 435–457.

Roberto, K. A., & Stroes, J. (1992). Grandchildren and grandparents: Roles, influences, and relationships. *International Journal of Aging and Human Development, 34,* 227–239.

Robertson, J. F. (1976). Significance of grandparents: Perceptions of young adult grandchildren. *The Gerontologist, 16,* 137–140.

Robertson, J. F. (1977). Grandmotherhood: A study of role conceptions. *Journal of Marriage and the Family, 33,* 165–174.

Rosow, I. (1985). Status and role change through the life cycle. In R. Binstock & E. Shanas (Eds.), *Handbook of aging and the social sciences* (pp. 62–93). New York: Van Nostrand Reinhold.

Rutter, M. (1979). Sex differences in children's responses to family stress. In E. J. Anthony & C. Koupernik (Eds.), *The child in his family* (pp. 47–77). Huntington, NY: Krieger.

Rutter, M. (1987). Psychological resilience and protective mechanisms. *American Journal of Orthopsychiatry, 57,* 316–331.

Shore, R. J., & Hayslip, B. (1988, August). *Variables affecting children's perceptions of grandparents.* Paper presented at the Annual Convention of the American Psychological Association, Atlanta.

Shore, R. J., & Hayslip, B. (1990, November). *Comparisons of custodial and noncustodial grandparents.* Paper presented at the Annual Scientific Meeting of the Gerontological Society. Boston.

Smith, B. K. (1989). *Grandparenting in today's world.* Hogg Foundation for Mental Health, Austin, TX.

Sprey, J. S., & Matthews, S. H. (1982). Contemporary grandparenthood: A systematic tradition. *Annals of the American Academy of Political and Social Sciences, 464,* 91–103.

Sprunger, L., Boyce, W. T., & Gaines, J. A. (1985). Family-infant congruence: Routines and rhythmicity in family adaptations to a young infant. *Child Development, 56,* 564–572.

Strom, R., & Strom, S. (1987). Preparing grandparents for a new role. *Journal of Applied Gerontology, 6,* 476–486.

Strom, R., & Strom, S. (1989). Grandparents and learning. *International Journal of Aging and Human Development, 29,* 163–169.

Strom, R., & Strom, S. (1990). Raising expectations for grandparents: A three generational study. *International Journal of Aging and Human Development, 31,* 161–167.

Thomas, J. L. (1986a). Age and sex difference in perceptions of grandparenthood. *Journal of Gerontology, 41,* 417–423.

Thomas, J. L. (1986b). Gender differences in satisfaction with grandparenting. *Psychology and Aging, 1,* 215–219.

Thomas, J. L. (1988, November). *Relationships with grandchildren as predictors of grand-*

parents' psychological well-being. Paper presented at the annual scientific meeting of the Gerontological Society of America, San Francisco.

Thomas, J. L. (1989a, November). *Contact with grandchildren and views of grandparent-grandchild bonds*. Paper presented at the Annual Scientific Meeting of the Gerontological Society, Minneapolis.

Thomas, J. L. (1989b). Gender and perceptions of grandparenthood. *International Journal of Aging and Human Development, 29*, 269–282.

Thomas, J. L. (1989c, August). *Grandparent-parent solidarity, perceptions of grandparenthood, and grandparents' mental health*. Paper presented at the Annual Convention of the American Psychological Association, New Orleans.

Thomas, J. L. (1990). The grandparent role: A double bind. *International Journal of Aging and Human Development, 31*, 169–177.

Thomas, J. L., & King, C. M. (1990, August). *Adult grandchildren's views of grandchildren: Racial and gender effects*. Paper presented at the Annual Convention of the American Psychological Association, Boston.

Thomas, J. L., Bence, S. L., & Meyer, S. M. (1988, August). *Grandparenting satisfaction: The roles of relationship meaning and perceived responsibility*. Paper presented at the Annual Convention of the American Psychological Association, Atlanta.

Thompson, R. A., Tinsley, B. R., Scalora, M. J., & Parke, R. D. (1989). Grandparents' visitation rights: Legalizing the ties that bind. *American Psychologist, 44*, 1217–1222.

Tomlin, A. M., & Passman, R. H. (1989). Grandmothers' responsibility in raising two-year olds facilitates their grandchildren's adaptive behavior: A preliminary intrafamilial investigation of mothers' and maternal grandmother's effects. *Psychology and Aging, 4*, 119–121.

Tomlin, A. M., & Passman, R. H. (1991). Grandmothers' advice about disciplining grandchildren: Is it accepted by mothers, and does its rejection influence grandmothers' subsequent guidance? *Psychology and Aging, 6*, 182–189.

Troll, L. E. (1980). Grandparenting. In L. W. Poon (Ed.), *Aging in the 1980's: Psychological issues* (pp. 475–481). Washington, DC: American Psychological Association.

Troll, L., Miller, L., & Atchley, R. (1979). *Families in later life*. Belmont, CA: Wadsworth.

Trygstad, D. W., & Sanders, G. F. (1989). The significance of stepgrandparents. *International Journal of Aging and Human Development, 22*, 119–134.

U.S. Bureau of the Census (1990). *Statistical Abstract of the United States*. Washington, DC: U.S. Government Printing Office.

Wells, K. C., & Forehand, R. (1985). Conduct and oppositional disorders. In P. Bornstein & A. Kazdin (Eds.), *Handbook of clinical behavior therapy with children* (pp. 218–265). Homewood, IL: Dorsey.

Wilcoxon, S. A. (1987). Grandparents and grandchildren: An often neglected relationship between significant others. *Journal of Counseling and Development, 65*, 289–290.

Wilson, K. B., & DeShane, M. R. (1982). The legal rights of grandparents: A preliminary discussion. *The Gerontologist, 22*, 67–71.

Wilson, M. N. (1986). The black extended family: An analytical consideration. *Developmental Psychology, 22*, 246–256.

Wood, V., & Robertson, J. F. (1976). The significance of grandparenthood. In J. Gubrium (Ed.) *Time, roles, and self in old age* (pp. 278–304). New York: Behavioral Publications.

III
OVERVIEW

In this part, results are integrated across chapters. A. E. and A. W. Gottfried advance a new conceptual perspective regarding alternative families and child development, called the "developmental impingement perspective of family functioning." Implications for developmental theories of family functioning and legal and social policies are proposed.

8

Impact of Redefined Families on Children's Development

Conclusions, Conceptual Perspectives, and Social Implications

Adele Eskeles Gottfried and Allen W. Gottfried

The chapters contained in this book represent families whose structure is at variance with both historical and traditional views. The conventional perspective that families comprise a mother/housewife, a father/sole earner, and a child(ren) is demographically in the minority in U.S. contemporary society (Wetzel, 1990). Each chapter and its research findings reveal a reformulation and redefinition of the parental role. The implications for children extend far beyond the family unit and pervade all institutions and aspects of our society and culture.

The chapters present literature reviews that address the biases and negative presumptions regarding differing family arrangements.

Adele Eskeles Gottfried • Department of Educational Psychology and Counseling, California State University, Northridge, California 91330.   **Allen W. Gottfried** • Department of Psychology, California State University, Fullerton, California 92634.

Redefining Families: Implications for Children's Development, edited by Adele Eskeles Gottfried and Allen W. Gottfried. Plenum Press, New York, 1994.

It is noteworthy that we (i.e., the editors of this book) did not request the authors to address the literature in this manner. The contents of the chapters were left up to the authors' discretion. However, that the chapters emerged identifying and addressing these issues is illuminating. It indicates the preponderance of negative presumptions regarding alternative family forms and assumptions concerning the fabric of society within which families must exist. In this overview and integration of the chapters in this book we are not forming an opinion or a judgment about what arrangements are optimal for children; rather, we are approaching the issues and questions with neutrality. We do not put forth recommendations about what family arrangement is ultimately in children's best interests.

Alternative family structures are currently in a position to prove themselves as viable for children's development in comparison to the traditional family arrangements. The reason is that the traditional family has provided the foundation of child development knowledge. This approach may ultimately prove to be inadequate, however, as the traditional family is now the minority family. Further, if so many families are no longer "traditional," how can it be considered "optimal" for children's development? It is our contention that the traditional family structure (single-earner male and two heterosexual parents) should no longer be the yardstick by which all other families are measured. We are at a fascinating crossroad in the definition, conceptualization, and scientific study of family structure as it pertains to children's development. Various perspectives, which have served as heuristics, can be extracted from the existing literature.

PERSPECTIVES

Maternal Deprivation Perspective

The main issue pertinent to the maternal-deprivation perspective is that, when the mother is no longer the primary caretaker, deprivation occurs and children's development suffers as a consequence. In our view, this perspective has its roots in the psychoanalytic view of family functioning, in which the mother–child relationship is regarded as being of unparalleled significance in the child's psychological development (Bretherton, 1993). In our reading of the literature, we conclude that the concept of maternal deprivation is the most pervasive one that underlies the assumptions of modern research into alternative family forms. Theories of attachment and early experience in which the mother is typically and normally the primary caretaker have abounded. Developmental psychology and psychiatry, as well as allied fields, have promoted a view that, when the mother is not the primary caretaker, there is inevitable detriment to the children. This view has had social and legal implications in that it may have served as the impetus for the "tender years doctrine" (or for a "primary-caretaker presumption"), which in the past provided a basis for child custody determinations (Folberg, 1991; Marafiote, 1985).

Father-Absence Perspective

Complementary to the maternal-deprivation perspective is the father-absence perspective, in which the lack of a father is viewed as detrimental to children's development (e.g., see review by Shinn, 1978), or as not conducive to optimal child development (Hanson & Bozett, 1985; Lamb & Sagi, 1983). In our view, it is related to the maternal deprivation perspective in that the absence of the parent is viewed as an inherently damaging condition that produces adverse and long-term consequences in and of itself. It is based on the traditional view of the father's masculine role in the family setting.

Compensation Perspective

Emerging from the literature on nontraditional families is the compensation perspective. An example is the maternal-employment literature, in which the father's increased involvement in dual-earner families may be viewed as compensating for the mother's absence due to her employment. Certainly, the data indicate a pattern of increased paternal involvement in dual-earner families (e.g., Chapter 3 of this book; A. E. Gottfried, A. W. Gottfried, & Bathurst, 1988; Hoffman, 1989) and in father-primary-caretaker families (Chapter 2). However, the compensation perspective continues to operate under the presumption of deficit. That is, the absence of the mother requires a special family effort to overcome the assumed deficit. The data showing greater father involvement in mother-employed families do not necessarily imply compensation. Instead, increased father involvement when the mother is employed may represent societal and/or family values with regard to parental roles. Hence, mothers and fathers may not view increased father involvement as a compensatory mechanism; rather, they may perceive, or strive toward, more egalitarian family roles.

Developmental Impingement Perspective

We propose a new approach, which we term the *developmental impingement perspective* of family functioning. In this perspective, there is no assumption of deficit, because the body of accumulating evidence across various types of nontraditional families shows *no* clear, consistent, or convincing evidence that alterations in family structure *per se* are detrimental to children's development. Certainly, stresses, undue burdens, and complicated societal factors operate when families are at variance with the expected norm. For example, it seems obvious that single-parenting places a great burden on a parent. However, this does not mean that the children inevitably suffer because of being raised by one parent. Confounding factors, such as limited resources due to low socioeconomic status, may impinge on the child in single-parent families. As the Depner model suggests (Chapter 4), one must account for a variety of factors that may be associated with one another and that affect children's development. Hence, future research must be directed at addressing how these factors interplay or impinge on each other in affecting children's development. Moreover, this interplay must be seen in a context of neutrality rather than negatively, as in the preceding perspectives. It is the interplay of a multiplicity of factors over time that we conceptualize as the core of the developmental impingement perspective.

Specifically, our perspective comprises four basic tenets:

1. There is no presumption of deficit, detriment, or benefit to children being raised in families with alternative structures. Outcomes rest on the empirical data base.
2. The developmental level of the child must be taken into account. For example, in Chapter 3 of this book, fathers' patterns of increased time involvement with their children as a function of the mothers' employment were established during the preschool period. As Radin pointed out (Chapter 2), the impact of high father participation is different at various ages and appears to be related to the cognitive ability of the child to interpret the maternal and paternal roles she or he experiences. In conjunction with developmental level, parent–child relationship factors must be reexamined. Other characteristics

of children, such as gender, in relationship to parental characteristics may moderate certain outcomes.

3. The multivariate nature of children's development across a broad array of developmental domains must be taken into account. Many published articles on alternate family types use a single outcome measure of limited significance at one point in time. Such articles often contain explicit statements regarding the negative or favorable outcome of the family based on restricted evidence. Only multivariate, longitudinal studies can address the breadth and cross-time/developmental aspects of effects.

4. A multiplicity of factors must be investigated at various ecological levels, and these effects must be examined with regard to the spectrum of possible outcomes, including positive, negative, or no differences. For example, children in lesbian and gay families may experience negative reactions (teasing and exclusion from play) from individuals outside the family. Negative consequences may emanate from extrafamilial individuals within society, and not from the family itself. As indicated in their respective chapters, positive parental outcomes may be more sensitive parenting in lesbian families (Falk, Chapter 5) or simply the nurturance and love provided to a child (Barret & Robinson, Chapter 6). One speculation may be that the children in these families develop greater tolerance of a diversity of human qualities.

With regard to grandparenting, children generally enter grandparental families because of significant and often devastating parental problems, such as drug abuse, mental incompetence, incarceration, and the inability of a teenage parent to care for a child. It seems obvious that a typical grandparent would be placed under a considerable burden. However, within the social and legal constraints, this arrangement may be the best alternative for the child and may be a prophylaxis and/or retardant of additional or potential adverse developmental consequences. On one hand, the adverse conditions that result in the child's being raised by a grandparent may be detrimental; on the other hand, the grandparent may provide ameliorative or facilitative parenting. Both the antecedent conditions and the grandparenting circumstances interface and impinge on each other and the child in determining the developmental outcome (Chapter 7).

In the case of maternal employment in dual-earner families,

the *developmental impingement perspective* appears to be a balance-of-factors model in which there are no net differences between the developmental outcomes of children in families in which mothers are employed or nonemployed. One outcome of dual-earner families is the increased availability of the fathers as the mothers' work hours increase (Chapter 3), which we consider an effort in coordinated parenting.

When fathers are primary caretakers, their motivation for this role often focuses on the desire to provide their children with a warm relationship that they had not experienced with their own fathers (Chapter 2). Radin found that, in other countries, the outcome depended on the context of the culture. Hence, cultural factors need to be included as an aspect of impingement, as they modify the meaning of the family type within a broader society. Again, there was no evidence of detriment across cultures.

With regard to custodial arrangements, many complicating factors may be operating or may impinge on the various outcomes (Chapter 4). The predisposing, contemporaneous, and subsequent variables are likely to be interwoven. Hence, to assign detriment or advantage to any one type of custodial arrangement ignores the complexity of the conditions surrounding a divorce, the antecedent factors, and its aftermath.

In sum, the essence of the *developmental impingement perspective* is to examine if and how children are affected by the interplay of the multiplicity of factors that exist within families of alternate structure and to consider the developmental status or age of the child and the manner in which society interfaces with the child and the family. This perspective must account for the longitudinal aspects of children's development across a spectrum of domains (e.g., emotional, social, behavioral, attitudinal, cognitive, and academic). In this regard, the range and net effect of children's developmental outcome can be appraised more thoroughly.

FUTURE RESEARCH

The complexity of the research poses an enormous task for further elucidation of these issues. This is not clean and neat experimental research in which causes and effects can be readily identified. Children are not randomly assigned to family conditions. Hence, the selective nature of the families requires multivariate statistical techniques to disentangle the contributions of different variables to various outcomes. The availability of subject samples has also been a problem. Whereas maternal employment and divorce have provided large samples, there is a relatively low frequency of families with primary-caretaking fathers, gay and lesbian parents, and custodial grandparents. Future researchers in these areas will need to make concerted efforts to find more representative samples. On a related issue, most of the research in this book concerns white middle-class families, although Chapter 2 highlights the need for considering cultural differences. Hence, the inclusion of varying cultural and socioeconomic groups is needed. Longitudinal research following up families over time is also essential to distinguishing between short- and long-term outcomes.

CONCLUSIONS

1. It is our preliminary conclusion that living in redefined family structures is not inherently disadvantageous to children's development. As data become increasingly available, we will be able to define more precisely the specific family situations and conditions that are optimal for children.
2. We have considered several explanations of the absence of detriment to children. First, there is a great deal of evidence regarding the resilience of children (e.g., Masten, Best, & Garmezy, 1990). Hence, resilience may be a general property of children's development that provides a capability to cope with stressful situations or atypical conditions. Second, it may be that children do not perceive their families as different or stressful, and there is no need for resilience. If a family is characterized by a nurturant, stimulating environment, the basic foundation for positive development is present (A. E. Gottfried & A. W. Gottfried, 1988), regardless of family structure. Third, parents who take on the challenge of an alternative role have the resources and personal qualities to "make it work" despite being at odds with tradition and portions of society. This possibility is well articulated in Chapters 5 and 6.
3. Developmental psychologists and psychiatrists must abandon the view that the traditional family is the cornerstone by which

comparisons are made. By no means should the traditional nuclear family serve as the control group.

4. The legal and social-policy ramifications of redefined families in children's development are great. They concern child custody determinations, adoptions, legislation regarding health-care and dependent-care leave, media presentations of child development research, and work place policies. As the current body of research indicates no detriment to the children growing up in redefined families, there is no foundation for discrimination against or partiality in favor of one family form as it pertains to children's development or needs. Because of the social relevance of this research, we strongly urge these findings to be disseminated accurately to the public, students of developmental psychology, mental health professionals, professionals in related fields (e.g., attorneys, judges, and pediatricians), and as legislators.

In conclusion, these findings of no detriment to children raise critical issues about the essence of good parenting across diverse family arrangements. Perhaps, very simply, love, nurturing, encouragement, respect, empathy, and the like are the ingredients that are basic to positive developmental outcomes in any family configuration.

REFERENCES

Bretherton, I. (1993). Theoretical contributions from developmental psychology. In P. G. Boss, W. J. Doherty, R. LaRossa, W. R. Schumm, & S. K. Stenmetz (Eds.), *Sourcebook of family theories and methods: A contextual approach* (pp. 275–297). New York: Plenum Press.

Folberg, J. (Ed.). (1991). *Joint custody and shared parenting* (2nd ed. New York: Guilford Press.

Gottfried, A. E. & Gottfried, A. W. (Eds.). (1988). *Maternal employment and children's development: Longitudinal research.* New York: Plenum Press.

Gottfried, A. E., Gottfried, A. W., & Bathurst, K. (1988). Maternal employment, family environment, and children's development: Infancy through the school years. In A. E. Gottfried & A. W. Gottfried (Eds.), *Maternal employment and children's development: Longitudinal research* (pp. 11–58). New York: Plenum Press.

Hanson, S. M. H., & Bozett, F. W. (Eds.). (1985). *Dimensions of fatherhood.* Newberry Park, CA: Sage.

Hoffman, L. W. (1989). Effects of maternal employment in the two-parent family. *American Psychologist, 44,* 283–292.

Lamb, M. E., & Sagi, A. (Eds.). (1983). *Fatherhood and family policy.* Hillsdale, NJ: Erlbaum.

Marafiote, R. A. (1985). *The custody of children: A behavioral assessment model.* New York: Plenum Press.

Masten, A. S., Best, K. M., & Garmezy, N. (1990). Resilience and development: Contributions from the study of children who overcome adversity. *Development and Psychopathology, 2,* 425–444.

Wetzel, J. R. (1990). American families: 75 years of change. *Monthly Labor Review, 113,* 4–13.

Index